Competitive Government: Public Private Partnerships

Series Editors

Simon Hakim, Center for Competitive Government, Temple University, Philadelphia, PA, USA

Adrian Moore, School of Computing and Information Engineering, University of Ulster (Coleraine), Coleraine, UK

Robert M. Clark, University of Cincinnati, Cincinnati, OH, USA

A shift from monopolistic government to a competitive setting is expected to improve efficient production and stimulate innovation. That shift has typically been in the form of Public-Private Partnerships (PPP), where each partner contributes its share of comparatively advantaged resources towards the production and delivery of the services. The shift to PPP, the types of services, and the methods used in the shift are increasing and becoming ever more sophisticated. This book series intends to capture a state of the art of such PPPs and present a guide for the implementation of such ventures. The book series will present, evaluate, and suggest policy implications based upon PPP experiences in fields like: police, prisons, courts, water and wastewater, telecommunications, air and water ports, rail, highways, schools, garbage collection, postal services, cyber security, foster care and child adoption, and homeland security management. The audience of this book series are students in courses on privatization and public finance, consultants and researchers in both government and the private sector, and members of think tanks that promote the ideas of more-focused government, competitive government, and privatization.

More information about this series at http://www.springer.com/series/16085

Carlos Oliveira Cruz • Joaquim Miranda Sarmento

The Renegotiations of Public Private Partnerships in Transportation

Theory and Practice

Springer

Carlos Oliveira Cruz
CERIS, Instituto Superior Técnico
Universidade de Lisboa
Lisbon, Portugal

Joaquim Miranda Sarmento
Advance/CSG, ISEG - Lisbon School of Economics and Management
Universidade de Lisboa
Lisbon, Portugal

ISSN 2524-4183 ISSN 2524-4191 (electronic)
Competitive Government: Public Private Partnerships
ISBN 978-3-030-61257-3 ISBN 978-3-030-61258-0 (eBook)
https://doi.org/10.1007/978-3-030-61258-0

This Springer imprint is published by the registered company Springer Nature Switzerland AG.
The registered company address is: Gewerbestrasse 11, 6330 Cham, Switzerland

To Filipa, Carmo, and Vicente
Carlos Oliveira Cruz

To Madalena, Catarina, and Alexandra, to my Father, and to the memory of my Mother
Joaquim Miranda Sarmento

Acknowledgments

Carlos Oliveira Cruz gratefully acknowledges financial support from CERIS—Civil Engineering Research and Innovation for Sustainability.

Joaquim Miranda Sarmento gratefully acknowledges financial support from FCT—Fundação para a Ciencia e Tecnologia (Portugal), national funding through research grant UIDB/04521/2020.

Contents

1 Introduction 1
References 6

2 Defining PPP Renegotiations 9
References 16

3 Theory on PPP Renegotiations 19
3.1 Overview 19
3.2 Contract Theory 19
3.3 Transaction Costs Theory 20
3.3.1 Procurement Stage 21
3.3.2 Operational Stage 23
3.3.3 Contract Termination Phase and Rebidding 24
3.4 Institutional Theory 25
References 26

4 Renegotiation Analysis 29
4.1 Research Methods 29
4.2 Literature Overview 35
4.3 Analysis of Main Patterns 35
4.3.1 Frequency 35
4.3.2 Timing 46
4.3.3 Motives 48
4.3.4 Outcomes 50
4.4 Determinants of PPP Renegotiations 51
4.5 Analysis of the Results 54
4.6 Discussion of Results 57
4.6.1 How Frequent Are Renegotiations in PPPs? 58
4.6.2 Who Initiates the Renegotiation Process? 58
4.6.3 When Do Renegotiations Happen? 58

4.6.4 What Are the Main Motives for the Occurrence of Renegotiations? . . . 58
4.6.5 What Are the Main Results of Renegotiations? . . . 59
4.6.6 What Are the Main Determinants of Renegotiation Processes? . . . 59
4.7 Main Literature Gaps . . . 60
4.8 Policy Implications . . . 60
References . . . 61

5 Country Analysis . . . 65
5.1 USA . . . 65
5.1.1 Framework . . . 65
5.1.2 Overall Legal and Regulatory Framework . . . 66
5.1.3 PPP Governance and Management . . . 66
5.1.4 Projects Overview . . . 68
5.2 UK . . . 69
5.2.1 Framework . . . 69
5.2.2 Overall Legal and Regulatory Framework . . . 70
5.2.3 PPP Governance and Management . . . 72
5.2.4 Projects Overview . . . 74
5.3 Brazil . . . 76
5.3.1 Framework . . . 76
5.3.2 Overall Legal and Regulatory Framework . . . 76
5.3.3 PPP Governance and Management . . . 80
5.3.4 Projects Overview . . . 81
5.4 Chile . . . 82
5.4.1 Framework . . . 82
5.4.2 Overall Legal and Regulatory Framework . . . 83
5.4.3 PPP Governance and Management . . . 85
5.4.4 Projects Overview . . . 87
5.5 Portugal . . . 87
5.5.1 Framework . . . 87
5.5.2 Overall Legal and Regulatory Framework . . . 89
5.5.3 PPP Governance and Management . . . 91
5.5.4 Projects Overview . . . 93
5.6 Spain . . . 93
5.6.1 Framework . . . 93
5.6.2 Overall Legal and Regulatory Framework . . . 96
5.6.3 PPP Governance and Management . . . 97
5.6.4 Projects Overview . . . 97
Appendix . . . 100
References . . . 132

6 Renegotiation Case Studies 137
6.1 Methodology Framework 137
6.2 Case Study: The Indiana Toll Road in the US 139
6.2.1 Introduction 139
6.2.2 The PPP Process 140
6.2.3 The Financial Structure of the PPP 140
6.2.4 The Risk Allocation Matrix 141
6.2.5 The Motives for the Renegotiation 142
6.2.6 The Renegotiation Case 143
6.2.7 Main Findings from the Case-Study 143
6.3 Case Study: The A1(M) Highway in the UK 144
6.3.1 Introduction 144
6.3.2 The PPP Process 145
6.3.3 The Financial Structure of the PPP 145
6.3.4 The Risk Allocation Matrix 146
6.3.5 The Motives for the Renegotiation 147
6.3.6 The Renegotiation Case 147
6.3.7 Main Findings from the Case-Study 148
6.4 Case Study: MG50, Brazil 148
6.4.1 Introduction 148
6.4.2 The PPP Process 148
6.4.3 The Financial Structure of the PPP 149
6.4.4 The Risk Allocation Matrix 149
6.4.5 The Motives for the Renegotiation 149
6.4.6 The Renegotiation Case 150
6.4.7 The Main Findings from the Case-Study 151
6.5 Case Study: TranSantiago, Chile 153
6.5.1 Introduction 153
6.5.2 The PPP Process 154
6.5.3 The Financial Structure of the PPP 155
6.5.4 The Risk Allocation 155
6.5.5 The Motives for the Renegotiation 156
6.5.6 The Renegotiation Case 156
6.5.7 The Main Findings from the Case-Study 158
6.6 Case Study: Fertagus, Portugal 158
6.6.1 Introduction 158
6.6.2 The PPP Process 159
6.6.3 The Financial Structure of the PPP 159
6.6.4 The Risk Allocation Matrix 160
6.6.5 The Motives for the Renegotiation 160
6.6.6 The Renegotiation Case 160
6.6.7 The Main Findings from the Case Study 162

6.7 Case Study: The AP7 Highway, Spain 163
6.7.1 Introduction 163
6.7.2 The PPP Process 163
6.7.3 The Financial Structure of the PPP 164
6.7.4 The Risk Allocation 164
6.7.5 The Motives for the Renegotiation 164
6.7.6 The Renegotiation Case 166
6.7.7 The Main Findings from the Case-Study 167
6.8 Comparative Analysis and Policy Implications 168
References 171

7 Conclusions 177
7.1 Renegotiations 179
References 180

About the Authors

Carlos Oliveira Cruz is Associate Professor of Construction and Infrastructure Management and Economics at Instituto Superior Técnico (University of Lisbon). Carlos is also Invited Professor of Economics of Infrastructure at Fundação Getúlio Vargas (Rio de Janeiro, Brazil). He served as an advisor in the Portuguese Ministry of Public Works and was a visiting scholar at the Harvard Kennedy School of Government. He has been a consultant to international organizations such as the OECD and EBRD, among several other public and private institutions.

Joaquim Miranda Sarmento is Assistant Professor of Finance at the ISEG—Lisbon School of Economics and Management, Universidade de Lisboa, Portugal. He graduated from the ISEG with a degree in management and completed an MSc in Finance at the ISCTE; in addition, he holds a PhD in Finance from Tilburg University, the Netherlands. He was Chief Economic Advisor to the President of the Portuguese Republic (Professor Cavaco Silva) from 2012 to 2016, and he has previously worked at UTAO (the Technical Budget Support Unit at Parliament) and served for more than 10 years at the Portuguese Ministry of Finance.

List of Figures

Fig. 1.1 Different procurement models. Source: Sarmento and Renneboog (2016a) 2
Fig. 1.2 Typical PPP structure. Source: Sarmento and Renneboog (2016a) 4
Fig. 4.1 Workflow of the methodological approach 31
Fig. 5.1 States which have enacted legislation for PPPs (Source: FHWA, 2018) 67
Fig. 5.2 Six basic functions for the management of complex capital investment programmes (Source: H.M. Treasury, 2010) 74
Fig. 5.3 Portfolio of current PFI and PF2 projects (number and capital value; Source: H.M. Treasury and Infrastructure and Projects Authority, 2019) 75
Fig. 5.4 Portfolio of current PFI and PF2 projects (number and capital value by Department; Source: H.M. Treasury and Infrastructure and Projects Authority, 2019) 75
Fig. 5.5 PPP Gross payments (left axis—Euros; right axis—% of GDP) ... 94
Fig. 6.1 Mechanism payment for the A1 Darrington–Dishforth PFI. Source: Highways Agency 146
Fig. 6.2 Traffic bands and real traffic. Note: Pk1 stands for the upper limit, and Pk4 for the lower limit. PKreal stands for the real demand. Source: the Authors 161

List of Tables

Table 1.1 The Government's perspective for traditional procurement, PPP, and privatisation 3
Table 4.1 Search expressions and results 31
Table 4.2 Theoretical papers on PPP renegotiations 32
Table 4.3 Empirical papers on PPP renegotiations 36
Table 4.4 Description of PPP renegotiation studies 47
Table 4.5 Initiator of PPP renegotiations 49
Table 4.6 Timing of PPP renegotiations 49
Table 4.7 Motives for PPP renegotiations 50
Table 4.8 Outcomes of PPP renegotiations 51
Table 4.9 Determinants of PPP renegotiations 52
Table 4.10 Determinants of PPP renegotiations 55
Table 5.1 FHWA P3 toolkit core components 68
Table 5.2 Profile of the analysed Brazilian states´ PPP units 81
Table 5.3 Largest PPP Projects in Brazil 82
Table 5.4 Most recent PPP Projects in Brazil 82
Table 5.5 Public investment in concessions by type of infrastructure per year (Source: adapted from Seopan) € million 98
Table 5.6 Priority investment (Source: adapted from Seopan) 99
Table A1 PPP status in the US by State 100
Table 6.1 Main features of A1 PFI 144
Table 6.2 Financial structure of A1 PFI 145
Table 6.3 Risk matrix for the MG-050 concession 150
Table 6.4 Renegotiations of the MG-050 concession 151
Table 6.5 Main features of the AP7 highway 164
Table 6.6 Comparative analysis 169

Chapter 1
Introduction

There has been a worldwide growing demand for infrastructure and construction assets, both greenfield and brownfield projects, across different sectors—such as housing, commercial buildings, bridges, roads, water supply and sanitation, and hospitals, among others (Estache et al. 2007; Engel and Galetovic 2014). On the one hand, emerging economies need to overcome their infrastructure gap and unlock their full economic growth potential, (e.g., India and Brazil) (Tortajada 2016; Neto et al. 2017, 2019). On the other hand, mature economies are also suffering from outdated and under-performing infrastructures, (e.g., the U.S. or Germany) (Ortega 2016). In the US alone, ASCE estimates a 10-year infrastructure gap of 2.0 Trillion Dollars, which correspond to the need to raise 2.5–3.5% of GDP in both public and private investment (ASCE 2017).

These trends have pressured governments (federal, regional, and local) to raise the necessary resources, select the projects, and then put into place the necessary procurement models and processes to deliver the required infrastructure and to provide the proper maintenance for the built environment (Andrade et al. 2018). This is a gigantic task, which requires capital and expertise (Sarmento and Renneboog 2016a). Public-private partnerships (PPPs) have emerged as one of the solutions which can provide both these resources (capital and expertise), and which can additionally propose a life cycle approach that enhances the optimisation and efficiency of construction projects (Sarmento 2010).

The International Monetary Fund defines PPPs as being:

> Arrangements whereby the private sector provides infrastructure assets and services that traditionally have been provided by the government, such as hospitals, schools, prisons, roads, bridges, tunnels, railways, and water and sanitation plants. (IMF 2008).

OECD (2008) defines PPP as

> long term agreements between the government and a private partner, where the private partner delivers and funds public services using a capital asset, sharing the associated services.

C. Oliveira Cruz, J. Miranda Sarmento, *The Renegotiations of Public Private Partnerships in Transportation*, Competitive Government: Public Private Partnerships, https://doi.org/10.1007/978-3-030-61258-0_1

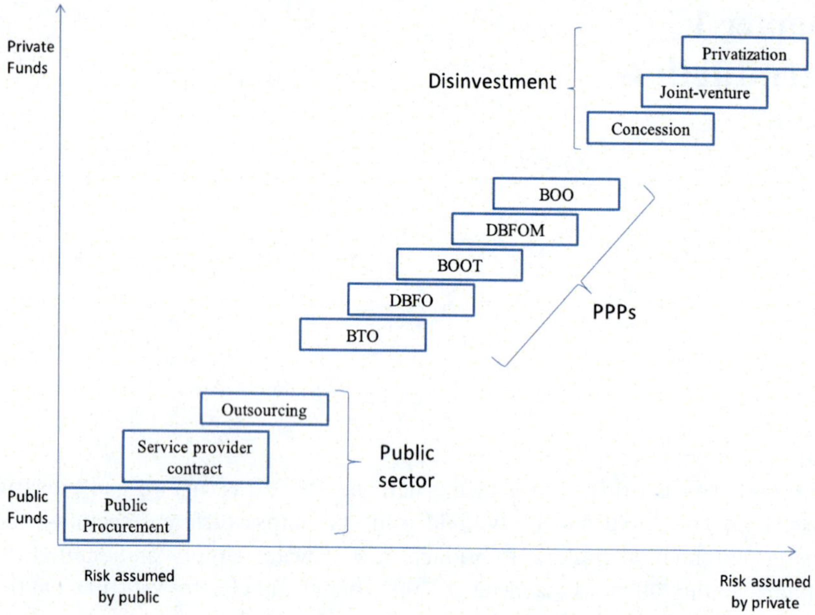

Fig. 1.1 Different procurement models. Source: Sarmento and Renneboog (2016a)

PPP are a procurement option which lies midway between traditional public procurement and full privatisation (Fig. 1.1). Table 1.1 presents the main differences between traditional procurement, PPP/Concessions, and privatisations. Figure 1.1 presents the main procurement models and Fig. 1.2 shows the typical structure of a PPP project. For each PPP project, a Special Purpose Vehicle (SPV) is created, which is a legal entity that only operates and owns one specific project/concession during the total contract period. This company is the government's counterpart in the PPP contract (see Fig. 1.2). This company will be responsible for all the stages of the project which fall under the private sector (for instance: design, construction, financing, operations, and maintenance). The reason for the creation of an SPV is the use of a project finance scheme (Yescombe 2013). This scheme has several advantages, namely: first, the lenders can evaluate the fluctuations of cash flows which cannot be diverted to other businesses and hence enables the monitoring of the debt service of the project; second, the shareholders are protected by limited liability should financial difficulties lead to insolvency; and third, it ensures that the business of the project company is not affected by problems arising from any unrelated businesses.

The relevance of PPPs is mainly due to the phenomenon of the growing demand for infrastructures (Cruz and Sarmento 2019), as well as the fact that governments are becoming increasingly subject to fiscal pressure (Sarmento and Renneboog 2016b). Emerging economies need to overcome their infrastructure gap and unlock their full economic growth potential, (e.g., India or Brazil) (see more in Kumar et al. 2018; Tortajada 2016; Neto et al. 2017). However, mature economies also suffer from outdated and underperforming infrastructures (e.g., the U.S. or Germany)

Table 1.1 The Government's perspective for traditional procurement, PPP, and privatisation

Characteristics	Traditional procurement	PPPs	Privatisation
Project responsibility	The government is responsible for all stages of the project.	The government is responsible for planning the output and outcomes of the project and usually also for payments. The other issues are the responsibility of the private sector.	The private sector is responsible for all stages of the project.
Risk	The risk is entirely (or almost entirely) assumed by the public sector.	The risk is shared between the public and the private sector. The private sector assumes several risks, (usually: design, construction, financing, operations and, in some cases, demand).	The risk is completely assumed by the private sector.
Costs	The private sector is only responsible for the construction costs of the asset.	The private sector is responsible for the 'whole life costing' (capex and opex) of the project.	The private sector is responsible for all of the project costs.
Budget treatment	Capital and operational expenditures (capex; opex) are public expenditures, which affect the both the Government's budget and the national debt.	No impact on the budget during the investment stage (PPPs are off the Balance Sheet). Only payments, during the operational stage are public expenditures.	No public funds. The private sector pays a price for buying the business.
Financing	The investment is financed through the public budget (i.e., taxes or public debt).	The investment is financed by the private sector, equity, and debt (usually through a syndicated bank).	The investment is completely private.
Contract	Only a construction contract exists between the government and a private firm.	A concession contract is granted for a number of years (usually 30 years or more), which specifies the conditions of the design, construction, financing, operation, payments, and the residual value/transfer.	A selling contract exists for the provision of the asset/service to the private firm, without a time limitation.
Ownership	The asset is owned by the public sector.	The asset is public, or it reverts to public ownership at the end of the contract.	The asset is completely private.

Source: Adapted from Sarmento and Renneboog (2016a)

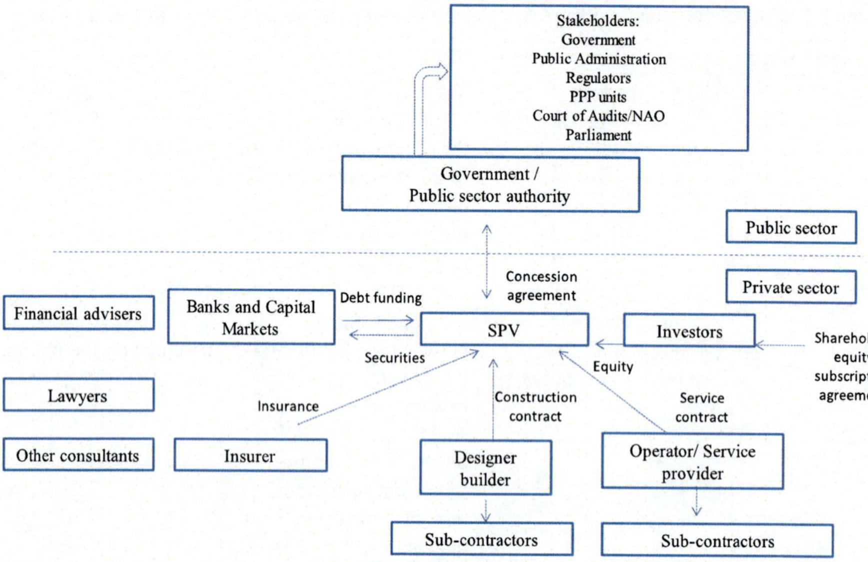

Fig. 1.2 Typical PPP structure. Source: Sarmento and Renneboog (2016a)

(Ortega 2016) and consequently they need to embark on large programmes for upgrading infrastructures. These trends have forced governments to raise the necessary finance and to effectively select the projects and implement the necessary business models and procurement processes which are required to construct the required infrastructures. This is a gigantic task, which requires both capital and expertise (Cruz and Marques 2013a).

A fundamental principle of PPPs is the integration of several stages of the life cycle of a typical construction project, particularly the design, construction, and operation/maintenance stages (Grimsey and Lewis 2002, 2005). Each infrastructure is a unique project, which requires a specific design, as well as specific construction activities and a "tailor-made" maintenance and operation programme. This does not happen in many other industrial sectors, such as IT hardware, or the automotive and manufacturing sectors, for example (Argyres and Liebeskind 1999). Construction projects therefore have significant frontier risks between each stage, particularly between design—construction—maintenance (Sarmento et al. 2017). These risks can be mitigated when bundled under the same contract, instead of being subject to separate contracts. This bundling reduces the likelihood of disconformities between technical drawings and execution and/or maintenance contracts (Athias and Saussier 2018; Cruz and Sarmento 2018b). Bundling enables the possibility to anticipate the risk associated with construction and maintenance, and also ensures that engineers are aware of any future faulty design or inefficiency during the design stage which would inevitably impact the company. It is important to notice that the maintenance and operation costs of infrastructures can represent between 30% and 50% of the initial investment, depending on the complexity of the project (Cruz and Marques 2013c). Significant savings, in terms of life-cycle costs, can be achieved by contractually enforcing long-term technical planning (Cruz and Marques 2013c). The private sector focusses on the whole-life costs of the project, rather than just on the construction costs, as tends to happen in the case of traditional public procurement (Domingues et al. 2014; Catalão et al. 2019).

The advent of PPPs promised both the existance of capital to leverage investments, as well as the efficiency and expertise of the private sector for delivering projects on-time and on-budget (Cruz and Sarmento 2018a). The theoretical rationale of PPPs is that governments can choose to transfer the responsibility for building, managing, and operating infrastructures, and, in return, brings an increase in projects' Value for Money (VfM) (Yescombe 2011). This equates to obtaining infrastructures at a lower cost and/or with a higher quality than those achieved through public management. Achieving value for money is directly related with the ability to effectively transfer risk. In fact, as discussed by Kumar et al. (2018), risk allocation is a central cornerstone in PPP, which can affect both the likelihood and the results of renegotiation, as is discussed later.

Many critics have pointed out that in most countries PPPs were not used for VfM, but rather for avoiding fiscal constraints (Engel et al. 2009, 2013). The motivations for the use of PPPs is far more complex than the implied technical opportunities. Experience has shown that, irrespective of the potential benefits of this procurement model for project delivery, renegotiations are a significant potential pitfall—which in turn represents a substantial risk for a project's success (Guasch 2004; Guasch et al. 2006; Cruz and Marques 2013b, c; Domingues and Sarmento 2016; Estache et al. 2003, 2009; Sarmento and Renneboog 2017). Renegotiation occurs whenever the existing contractual relationship is no longer able to cope with the emergence of new circumstances. The need to renegotiate can be a consequence of the effects of uncertainty regarding long term investment-specific relationships, although renegotiation can also be triggered and aggravated by the strategic and opportunistic behaviour of both/either parties.

This book re-examines the theoretical justification underlying the phenomenon of renegotiations, and also analyses the empirical contributions from around the world that have tried to identify the main determinants for the likelihood of renegotiations, as well as their motives and the outcomes. The book also provides a project-based analysis of selected case studies from different countries, to help understand why and how renegotiations come about. To the best of our knowledge, this book is the first attempt to provide a comprehensive and holistic review of the theory and empirical evidence of PPP renegotiations.

This book is structured in seven chapters, as briefly summarised below:

- Chapter 1 contains the introduction (current chapter).
- Chapter 2 provide the definition of renegotiations, and an explanation of the types of potential renegotiation.
- Chapter 3 presents the theoretical background of renegotiations, explaining the main theories and contributions.

- Chapter 4 focusses on the contributions in the literature which provide empirical evidence of the main patterns, outcomes, motives, and determinants of renegotiations, through the means of an extensive literature review.
- Chapter 5 presents a country analysis, for all of the countries where case studies were selected.
- Chapter 6 presents the case studies (six in total), explaining the methodology for the analysis, context, PPP structure, risk matrix, motives for renegotiation, and the renegotiation case.
- Chapter 7 presents the conclusions.

References

Andrade, I., Cruz, C. O., & Sarmento, J. M. (2018). Renegotiations of water concessions: Empirical analysis of main determinants. *Journal of Water Resources Planning and Management, 144* (11), 04018073. (IF2018: 3,404) (Scopus: Q1 Civil and Structural Engineering).

Argyres, N. S., & Liebeskind, J. P. (1999). Contractual commitments, bargaining power, and governance inseparability: Incorporating history into transaction cost theory. *Academy of Management Review, 24*(1), 49–63.

ASCE. (2017). *Infrastructure report card*. Technical Report, USA

Athias, L., & Saussier, S. (2018). Are public private partnerships that rigid? And why? Evidence from price provisions in French toll road concession contracts. *Transportation Research Part A: Policy and Practice, 111*, 174–186.

Catalão, F., Cruz, C. O., & Miranda Sarmento, J. (2019). Exogenous determinants of cost deviations and overruns in local infrastructure projects. *Construction Management and Economics, 37*(12), 697–711.

Cruz, C. O., & Marques, R. C. (2013a). Endogenous determinants for renegotiating concessions: Evidence from local infrastructure. *Local Government Studies, 39*(3), 352–374. https://doi.org/10.1080/03003930.2013.783476.

Cruz, C. O., & Marques, R. C. (2013b). Exogenous determinants for renegotiating public infrastructure concessions: Evidence from Portugal. *Journal of Construction Engineering and Management, 139*(9), 1082–1090. https://doi.org/10.1061/(ASCE)CO.1943-7862.0000710.

Cruz, C. O., & Marques, R. C. (2013c). Flexible contracts to cope with uncertainty in public–private partnerships. *International Journal of Project Management, 31*(3), 473–483.

Cruz, C. O., & Sarmento, J. M. (2018a). The price of project finance loans for highways. Research in Transportation Economics, 70, 161–172.

Cruz, C. O., & Sarmento, J. M. (2018b). Maximizing the value for money of road projects through digitalization. Competition and Regulation in Network Industries, 19(1–2), 69–92.

Cruz, C. O., & Sarmento, J. M. (2019). Traffic forecast inaccuracy in transportation: A literature review of roads and railways projects. *Transportation*, 1–36.

Domingues, S., & Sarmento, J. M. (2016). Critical renegotiation triggers of European transport concessions. *Transport Policy, 48*, 82–91.

Domingues, S., Zlatkovic, D., & Roumboutsos, A. (2014). Contractual flexibility in transport infrastructure PPP. In *European transport conference* (Vol. 29).

Engel, E., Fischer, R., & Galetovic, A. (2009). *Soft budgets and renegotiations in public-private partnerships*. National Bureau of Economic research working paper series (Vol. No. 15300). https://doi.org/10.2139/ssrn.1460688

Engel, E., Fischer, R., & Galetovic, A. (2013). The basic public finance of public–private partnerships. *Journal of the European Economic Association, 11*(1), 83–111.

Engel, E., & Galetovic, A. (2014). *Urban transport: Can public-private partnerships work?* Policy research working paper series 6873, The World Bank.

Estache, A., Guasch, J. L., Iimi, A., & Trujillo, L. (2009). Multidimensionality and renegotiation: Evidence from transport-sector public-private-partnership transactions in Latin America. *Review of Industrial Organization, 35*. https://doi.org/10.1007/s11151-009-9225-0

Estache, A., Guasch, J.-L., & Trujillo, L. (2003). *Price caps, efficiency payoffs and infrastructure contract renegotiation in Latin America*. World Bank policy research working paper 3129. https://doi.org/10.1596/1813-9450-3129

Estache, A., Juan, E., & Trujillo, L. (2007). *Public-private partnerships in transport*. Policy research working paper 4436. The World Bank, Washington, DC.

Grimsey, D., & Lewis, M. K. (2002). Evaluating the risks of public private partnerships for infrastructure projects. *International Journal of Project Management, 20*(2), 107–118.

Grimsey, D., & Lewis, M. K. (2005). Are public private partnerships value for money?: Evaluating alternative approaches and comparing academic and practitioner views. *In Accounting forum, 29* (4), 345–378. No longer published by Elsevier.

Guasch, J. L. (2004). *Granting and renegotiating infrastructure concessions: Doing it right*. The World Bank.

Guasch, J. L., Laffont, J. J., & Straub, S. (2006). Renegotiation of concession contracts: A theoretical approach. *Review of Industrial Organization, 29*(1–2), 55–73. https://doi.org/10.1007/s11151-006-9109-5.

IMF. (2008). *Manual on fiscal transparency*. IMF, Washington DC, Glossary.

Kumar, L., Jindal, A., & Velaga, N. R. (2018). Financial risk assessment and modelling of PPP based Indian highway infrastructure projects. *Transport Policy, 62*, 2–11.

Neto, D. D. C. E. S., Cruz, C. O., & Sarmento, J. M. (2017). Understanding the patterns of PPP renegotiations for infrastructure projects in Latin America: The case of Brazil. *Competition and Regulation in Network Industries, 18*(3–4), 271–296.

Neto, D. D. C. S., Cruz, C. O., & Sarmento, J. M. (2019). Renegotiation of transport public private partnerships: Policy implications of the Brazilian experience in the Latin American context. *Case Studies on Transport Policy, 7*(3), 554–561.

OECD (2008) Public-private partnerships: In Pursuit of Risk Sharing and Value for Money. ISBN Number: 9789264042797.

Ortega, I. (2016). Review of the road taken: The history and future of America's infrastructure by Henry Petroski. *Journal of Performance of Constructed Facilities, 30*(5). https://doi.org/10.1061/(ASCE)CF.1943-5509.0000923.

Sarmento, J. M. (2010). Do public-private partnerships create value for money for the public sector? The Portuguese experience. *OECD Journal on Budgeting, 10*(1), 1–27.

Sarmento, J. M., & Renneboog, L. (2016a). Anatomy of public-private partnerships: Their creation, financing and renegotiations. *International Journal of Managing Projects in Business, 9*, 94–122.

Sarmento, J. M., & Renneboog, L. (2016b). *Renegotiating public-private partnerships*. European Corporate Governance Institute (ECGI)-finance working paper (416).

Sarmento, J. M., & Renneboog, L. (2017). Cost overruns in public sector investment projects. Public Works Management & Policy, 22(2), 140–164.

Sarmento, J. M., Renneboog, L., & Matos, P. V. (2017). Measuring highway efficiency by a DEA approach and the Malmquist index. *European Journal of Transport and Infrastructure Research, 17*(4), 530–551.

Tortajada, C. (2016). Policy dimensions of development and financing of water infrastructure: The cases of China and India. *Environmental Science & Policy, 64*, 177–187.

Yescombe, E. (2011). *Public-private partnerships: Principles of policy and finance*. Oxford: Butterworth-Heinemann.

Yescombe, E. R. (2013). *Principles of project finance*. Academic Press.

Chapter 2
Defining PPP Renegotiations

There is a growing interest in the literature on Public-Private Partnerships (PPPs) with regards the topic of renegotiations. A renegotiation occurs when there is a need to change/readapt the PPP contract. Guasch et al. (2014) provide the following definition of renegotiation:

> A renegotiation of PPP contracts involves a change in the original contractual terms and conditions, as opposed to an adjustment in the payments (or tariffs) that takes place under a mechanism defined in the contract.

The concept of renegotiation assumes that the contract has failed, which means that an event or a change in existing circumstances is not properly addressed in the contract. The economic literature analyses the phenomenon of renegotiations from three different perspectives: (1) the contract theory; (2) the transaction cost theory (which can also be related with the contract theory), and; (3) the institutional & governance theory (as discussed by de Brux (2010)).

The increasing number of papers on PPP renegotiations has led to similar conclusions across different regions and sectors, whereby PPP renegotiations appear to follow consistent patterns, even though some of them are country-specific differences. However, there is a gap in the literature in terms of presenting the overall perspective. This chapter documents the results of an up-to-date and structured overview of the literature on PPPs renegotiations. Over the next chapters of this book this research not only provides a synthesis of the methods used and describes what is already known, but it also presents the conceptual framework of the literature, as well as the explicit structure which explains how dependent and independent variables are related. The following chapters also provide a novel perspective on the empirical research, by explicitly analysing the dependent and independent variables (the main determinants of renegotiations), under alternative theoretical frameworks.

PPPs often tend to have renegotiations over the life of the contracts as a response to various types of changes which prevent the original terms of the contract from

C. Oliveira Cruz, J. Miranda Sarmento, *The Renegotiations of Public Private Partnerships in Transportation*, Competitive Government: Public Private Partnerships, https://doi.org/10.1007/978-3-030-61258-0_2

being maintained (Reis and Sarmento 2019; Andrade et al. 2018). Financial renegotiation or rebalancing occurs when events, either foreseen or not in the concession agreement, change the financial conditions, and above all, the remuneration of the private shareholders (Sarmento and Renneboog 2016a, b). Renegotiations (also known as financial rebalances, or financial rebalance agreements (FRAs) are usually triggered by a specific event and they affect the financial conditions of the concession (Neto et al. 2017, 2019; Yescombe 2011).

There are three main events which trigger renegotiations:

(i) SPV bankruptcy, forcing the public sector to rescue the project;
(ii) Failure, due to incorrect contractual assumptions which affect the profitability of the private partner; or
(iii) A unilateral proposal to amend the terms of the concession by the government.

Renegotiations can thus be divided into the following types:

- A unilateral modification or renegotiation on the initiative of the State, which implies a change of the objectives and priorities of government policy in response to the need to restore the economic and financial balance of the contract.
- A financial balance of the original concession agreement, due to the failure to verify a risk which has not been transferred to the private partner, which negatively affects the minimum return of the shareholder.
- The "opportunistic" renegotiation by the private partner, taking advantage of both the information asymmetry and the fact that a competitive contest is no longer required, but rather a two-way negotiation. This is often a regulatory capture problem (Estache et al. 2003, 2009).

Estache et al. (2007) identified a set of problems which a project may suffer, resulting in negative implications for its financing and profitability:

- The projections for the project base scenario prove to be very optimistic;
- A significantly lower debt maturity than project maturity, without the project subsequently being able to roll-over this debt, at least under similar conditions;
- Interest rate risk;
- Exchange rate risk;
- Unbearable levels of debt for the project size and/or level of cash flows available to service the debt;
- Misallocation of risk and a public sector which is unwilling to renegotiate contracts.

In order for private sector participation in a PPP/concession to be successful and achieve both parties' objectives, the contracts and regulations need to be well designed and properly implemented (Cruz and Sarmento 2019a, b). However, not all changes result in a financial rebalance. For example, tariff updates, inflation adjustments, or other changes provided for in the contract do not fit into this type of renegotiation, as they are automatic, because they are contractually provided for, whether they occur, or not (Guasch 2004; Sarmento 2010; Guasch et al. 2003, 2006). These adjustments are typically subject to a formula which is defined in the contract.

Financial rebalances are also referred to in the academic literature as "bad refinance", as opposed to refinancing, which occurs a few years after the start of the project and when favourable circumstances and lower project risk is conducive for the refinancing of the remaining debt, with more favourable conditions (which is referred to in the literature as "good refinance"—Sarmento and Renneboog 2016b). It is important to mention that PPP contracts often have an adaptation mechanism embedded in the agreement (Cruz and Marques 2012, 2013a), with one of the most common examples being a price revision formula which, in function of the consumer price index, energy, or labour variations, has the effect of updating the value of the periodical payments from the government or the users' fees (Guasch et al. 2014). Whenever an annual based price revision occurs, rather than a regular adaptation, this should not be considered to be a renegotiation, as, in effect, it is merely a revision based on a pre-established contractual provision. Another basic principle should be that small uncontrollable events, as long as they have minor impacts on shareholder profitability, should not lead to financial rebalances, neither adjustments. Such rebalances and adjustments should only occur in the case of events which have a significant impact on private profitability, i.e., when the initial conditions change significantly and negatively, examples being demand, prices, costs, or other market conditions. PPP renegotiations can be an opportunity to adjust and address new conditions and terms of a project and can thus increase the value of a project, be it public or private (de Brux 2010).

Some authors perceive PPP renegotiations to be a pitfall, or a failure of the project (Froud and Shaoul 2001; Jamali 2004; Cruz and Marques 2013b, c; Domingues and Sarmento 2016), assuming that if the contract were to function appropriately, then renegotiations would not even be necessary. However, PPPs have characteristics which justify a certain level of renegotiations, as they are long-term and incomplete contracts, which involve high levels of investment, in highly-regulated and politically-sensitive markets (Engel et al. 2006). Renegotiations can well represent a natural development of the evolution of the contract (as no contract is capable of contemplating solutions for all circumstances that can arise in the future) and often enable a better adaptation of the obligations of the parties to new conditions. The objective of this type of renegotiation is to increase the PPP VfM, and it can either lead to an increase in well-being, or to the strategic or opportunistic behaviour of the parties in their attempt to maximise their situation, taking advantage of, or surpassing the legal mechanisms and contracts required for renegotiation (Spiller 2008). If this was the case, then one would expect a quasi-normal distribution of the benefits between the parties. The empirical evidence suggests that this is hardly ever the case. Renegotiations are considered to be one of the pitfalls of PPPs for two reasons: the abnormal frequency of renegotiation (especially shortly after contracts have been signed) (Guasch et al. 2003, 2006; Estache et al. 2009; Sarmento 2019) and the fact that renegotiations are perceived to be a source of minimizing potential efficiency of PPPs (Guasch et al. 2006). A large number of renegotiations undermine the credibility of the initial proposals, and accordingly impose an additional burden on the public budget and often reduce project performance and the quality of service. Furthermore, PPP renegotiations have been criticised on account of the fact that the initial bids tendered to win a concession may not be credible and can distort competition if anticipated losses at (*ex-ante*) the time of the original competition can be easily compensated for (*ex-post*) in posterior renegotiations.

Therefore, in effect, renegotiation should be the exception, rather than the rule, as it usually has an adverse effect on the public interest and reduce the initially-expected efficiency (Engel et al. 2009). As such, at the start of the concession partnership, the public sector should anticipate the possibility of renegotiation over the life of the concession and accordingly should clearly indicate in the concession agreement which conditions and events can trigger renegotiation. While some authors consider a renegotiation event to be a PPP failure (Estache et al. 2003), others consider it to be a natural and typical part of the PPP process (Engel et al. 2009).

The European Union legal framework specifically provides for the revision of contracts—provided that certain conditions and limits are met. Because these are public procurement contracts designed to pursue public purposes, the grantor can unilaterally determine that the content of the contract should be amended to better adjust it to the needs of the public interest (in particular in the event of changed circumstances). However, this should not jeopardise the principles of transparency and fairness, even though renegotiations are agreed upon in a bilateral discussion, and are not subject to the benefits of further competitions after that of the procurement phase. Renegotiation of the contract, by agreement between the parties, can also result from the terms of the contract itself (Sarmento 2015).

As PPP contracts are based on risk sharing, in theory, the rule is that only the verification of those events associated with the risks retained by the public entity should lead to renegotiation (in principle the private partner will have to bear the impact of the events associated with the risks which it has taken, without any change to the original contract) (Guasch 2004).

The category of risks assumed by the public partner includes specific legislative changes (directed in particular at the concession sector), administrative or regulatory decisions (such as the unilateral modification of the contract for public interest reasons), or cases of force majeure which alter the operating conditions of the service (including acts of God) (Grimsey and Lewis 2002, 2005). The impacts of such risks need to be neutralised, so as not to affect the originally-forecast economic and financial conditions of the PPP. The regularisation of these impacts corresponds to what has traditionally been called the 'restoration of the economic and financial balance of the contract'. Nevertheless, the impacts of those events that constitute a risk which is transferred to the private partner should be assimilated by the private partner, that is to say, these impacts should not give rise to any change in the assumptions of the contract. These impacts can translate into losses, as well as gains when compared with the initial projections. If the private partner is able to minimise the costs of debt financing, then the savings obtained translate into their (and their shareholders') gains. For example, should interest rates increase, then this additional cost is borne exclusively by the private partner (Cruz and Sarmento 2018).

Risks allocated to the private sector are usually related with the economic incentive for the private partner to be more efficient in the management of the project. The risk allocation theory supports that risks should be allocated to the private partner only when the correct incentives are provided for the private sector to be more efficient than the public sector. These risks are usually the following (Andrade et al. 2018): construction risk, operation and maintenance risk, and financial risk (i.e., financing and interest rate risk). Construction risk is the most relevant of these three risks, as most infrastructure projects are perceived to be projects with high levels of capex and low levels of opex. Accordingly, cost and time deviations (see Sarmento and Renneboog 2017; Catalão et al. 2019a, b) become the responsibility of the private partner, which usually passes on these risks to a third party—usually a construction consortium.

Furthermore, in the case of certain operations, demand risk should be transferred to the private sector (Cruz and Sarmento 2019b), as demand risk is the most critical risk, as it is the only risk which cannot be transferred by the SPV to a third party. Demand risk is associated with the need to carry out a forecast exercise to project demand and revenues (Cruz and Sarmento 2019b).

On the other hand, while concession contracts are a more comprehensive form of regulation than other models for the allocation of public services, such as the licensing of a service, the fact that these contracts are long term makes it difficult, if not impossible, to predict or anticipate all the potential future scenarios during the lifetime of the contract (Spiller 2008). Cruz and Marques (2013a, b) highlight some features of PPPs which make them especially vulnerable to the inherent long-term uncertainty which characterises this type of contract:

(i) The high value of investments that represent sunk costs;
(ii) A high sensitivity to changes, when compared to other types of contract, especially in the case of greenfield projects;
(iii) A high exposure to financial markets (due to the high value of debt), and;
(iv) Vulnerability to political instability.

However, it can also be the case that renegotiations are a response to the natural development of the contract (in cases when it fails to provide the answer to all potential circumstances) and enables the partners' obligations to be better adapted to new conditions (Estache et al. 2009). Such renegotiations, which aim to increase PPP's VfM, can thus lead to increased welfare, and/or can also result from the strategic or opportunistic behaviour of partners who sole objective is to attempt to maximise their own welfare by taking advantage of, or by means of bypassing legal mechanisms and contractual clauses for renegotiation (Spiller 2008).

Although concession contracts are always "incomplete contracts", this does not necessarily mean that they do not provide, as clearly as possible, clauses for delimiting situations which justify renegotiation with a view to neutralising or at least minimising its impact and restoring the initial financial balance (Sarmento and Renneboog 2016a, b). These rebalancing clauses, although they often set some limits or benchmarks for renegotiation, they nevertheless leave the definition of the exact terms for negotiating the amendment among the partners, which can include changing the term of the contract, altering the prices charged by the concessionaire and the value of the financial compensation paid by the State (in the form of a lump-sum or time-phased compensation, such as annual payments), the review of the conditions of service, and/or the reduction of the investment, etc. (Guasch 2004).

While some risks associated with potential scenarios can be allocated to the private partner, the above-mentioned principle of efficient risk sharing constitutes an alert with regards the full transfer of all risks, either because some are better managed by the public sector (such as political risk), or because the risk premium required by the private partner becomes so high that it outweighs the efficiency gains.

In addition to the difficulties in predicting long-term demand, several authors identify a tendency towards overestimation, which they attribute to the strategic behaviour of public authorities with the objective to demonstrate the viability of the concessions or PPPs that they intend to contract out (Domingues et al. 2014). This optimism bias increases the uncertainty of contract assumptions.

Thus, as it is difficult or too costly to draft contracts which foresee all the possible circumstances that could occur and their consequences, PPP contracts are incomplete, as already discussed above. There is thus a trade-off between the extent of the anticipated contingencies and the cost of the contract. In such cases, the transaction costs of a complete contract are so exorbitant, that they are simply not feasible. Additionally, unforeseen contingencies always occur at the time of celebrating the contract. Nevertheless, the question arises as to whether the way in which incomplete contracts are drafted can prevent, limit, or condition the way that renegotiations can come to pass.

Athias and Saussier (2018) discuss the trade-offs between greater contract rigidity or flexibility, however they argue that in either case, renegotiation is inevitable. Rigid contracts (whose rules, particularly in terms of price, are designed to apply to the whole contract) entail higher enforcement costs (to ensure compliance with its rules) and they risk being inadequate in real life, which makes it impracticable to carry out their execution and they therefore require renegotiating. In the case of rigid contracts, private operators can be persuaded to underinvest, for fear that contracts can prove inappropriate.

Flexible contracts, as discussed by Martins et al. (2017) (which assume the willingness of the parties to renegotiate when uncertain situations arise, while setting certain limits to such renegotiation) address the issue of inadequacy, however they introduce the issue of renegotiation costs and also the risk of renegotiation. The competitive behaviours of bidders at the time of tendering can result in companies submitting lower bids in order to guarantee selection, even though they have no real intention to respect the value of their bid, as they regard the possibility to improve their position through future renegotiation (thus frustrating the purpose of the tender).

Athias and Saussier (2018) argue that the choice for greater rigidity or flexibility is associated with various circumstances and that there is no ideal contractual model. Based on an empirical assessment of 71 road project concessions from different countries, these authors show that flexible contracts are best used when uncertainty is highest (notably with regards demand), which makes the future rigidity of a rigid contract more likely. Confirming the hypothesis that the reputation and mutual knowledge of the parties reduces the likelihood of renegotiation costs, the study reveals that increasing the number of interactions between parties reduces the rigidity of pricing clauses.

Ho (2006), states that the grantor should, right from the outset, provide for this possibility of renegotiations, by considering that the concessionaire is likely to demonstrate opportunistic behaviour (enhanced by asymmetries of information, experience, and knowledge), especially in situations where the service may no longer be provided. The author also argues that the public sector should aim to prepare negotiation processes well, establish preventive measures (for when the base case fails to materialise), seek access to credible and diverse information (in order to avoid/minimise information asymmetry problems), and also ensure that enforcement costs remain low.

Generally, the result of a renegotiation which is aimed at restoring a PPP's financial rebalance is an increase in user tariffs, or financial compensation from the government. Renegotiations initiated by governments are usually related to political decisions which affect the concession contract or the financial conditions. These policy decisions can affect the various stages of the attribution of the concession. For example, during the design and construction phase, governments can make design changes (designed to reduce or increase additional investments and construction works), can change environmental requirements, or can bring about new administrative delays. Other changes can occur during the operational stage, such as specific legal changes or changes to the contract, such as tariffs, service requirements, or payments.

Public finances can be an important determinant of PPP renegotiations. Economic recessions and budget deficits increase the likelihood of contract renegotiations. Most European countries have had to implement a budget constraint which is due (in part) to the intensive use of PPPs (Kappeler and Nemoz 2010). However, most of the literature focussing on Public Finance in PPP renegotiations highlights the issue that often government-initiated renegotiations are a consequence of the need to overcome a budget constraint problem (Engel et al. 2013). Governments use renegotiation to increase spending and to pass on the burden of payments to future governments (Engel et al. 2009).

Accordingly, Ping Ho (2009) identifies a set of principles for good governance in negotiating financial rebalances, namely:

(i) Principle 1: be prepared for concession renegotiation issues, as no contract can forecast all the potential situations which could be in conflict or which need to be rebalanced.
(ii) Principle 2: although renegotiation is always possible, the concession contract should always seek to minimise this hypothesis. In addition, strategies should be put into practice that reduce over-subsidisation by the State, yet which also reduce the promoter's replacement costs.
(iii) Principle 3: during the negotiation process, the government's main effort should be to determine as objectively as possible the correct compensatory

allowance to be paid out to the private partner, rather than to negotiate the minimum possible value.

(iv) Principle 4: compensatory compensation shall compensate the private party for their responsibilities and risk allocation.

Renegotiation is a powerful tool, yet simultaneously they represent significant risks. Renegotiation is also a powerful tool because it enables the ability to adapt and readjust the contract to new and revealing circumstances, which is essential when taking into account the long term perspective of most concession contracts. However, renegotiation can also be used strategically, by both public and private partners, to maximise its utility at the expenses of the other partner. Renegotiation mechanisms are complex, and can often be rooted in the economic and organisational theory, which will be presented and discussed in the next chapter.

References

Andrade, I., Cruz, C. O., & Sarmento, J. M. (2018). Renegotiations of water concessions: Empirical analysis of main determinants. *Journal of Water Resources Planning and Management, 144* (11), 04018073. (IF2018: 3,404) (Scopus: Q1 Civil and Structural Engineering).

Athias, L., & Saussier, S. (2018). Are public private partnerships that rigid? And why? Evidence from price provisions in French toll road concession contracts. *Transportation research part a: policy and practice, 111*, 174–186.

Catalão, F., Cruz, C. O., & Sarmento, J. M. (2019a). Exogenous determinants of cost deviations and overruns in local infrastructure projects. *Construction Management and Economics, 37*(12), 697–711.

Catalão, F. P., Cruz, C. O., & Sarmento, J. M. (2019b). The determinants of cost deviations and overruns in transport projects, an endogenous models approach. *Transport Policy, 74*, 224–238.

Cruz, C. O., & Marques, R. C. (2012). Using probabilistic methods to estimate the public sector comparator. *Computer-Aided Civil and Infrastructure Engineering, 27*(10), 782–800.

Cruz, C. O., & Marques, R. C. (2013a). Endogenous determinants for renegotiating concessions: Evidence from local infrastructure. *Local Government Studies, 39*(3), 352–374. https://doi.org/10.1080/03003930.2013.783476.

Cruz, C. O., & Marques, R. C. (2013b). Exogenous determinants for renegotiating public infrastructure concessions: Evidence from Portugal. *Journal of Construction Engineering and Management, 139*(9), 1082–1090. https://doi.org/10.1061/(ASCE)CO.1943-7862.0000710.

Cruz, C. O., & Marques, R. C. (2013c). Flexible contracts to cope with uncertainty in public–private partnerships. *International Journal of Project Management, 31*(3), 473–483.

Cruz, C. O., & Sarmento, J. M. (2018). The price of project finance loans for highways. *Research in Transportation Economics, 70*, 161–172.

Cruz, C. O., & Sarmento, J. M. (2019a). Institutional "tetris" in infrastructure regulation: Harmonizing governance, regulation and policy-making in the transport sector. *Case Studies on Transport Policy, 7*(1), 22–27.

Cruz, C. O., & Sarmento, J. M. (2019b). Traffic forecast inaccuracy in transportation: A literature review of roads and railways projects. *Transportation*, 1–36

De Brux, J. (2010). The dark and bright sides of renegotiation: An application to transport concession contracts. *Utilities Policy, 18*(2), 77–85.

Domingues, S., & Sarmento, J. M. (2016). Critical renegotiation triggers of European transport concessions. *Transport Policy, 48*, 82–91.

Domingues, S., Zlatkovic, D., & Roumboutsos, A. (2014). Contractual flexibility in transport infrastructure PPP. In *European transport conference*.

Engel, E., Fischer, R., & Galetovic, A. (2006). Renegotiation without holdup: Anticipating spending and infrastructure concessions (No. w12399). National Bureau of Economic Research.

Engel, E., Fischer, R., & Galetovic, A. (2009). *Soft budgets and renegotiations in public-private partnerships*. National Bureau of economic research working paper series (vol. no. 15300). https://doi.org/10.2139/ssrn.1460688

Engel, E., Fischer, R., & Galetovic, A. (2013). The basic public finance of public–private partnerships. *Journal of the European Economic Association, 11*(1), 83–111.

Estache, A., Guasch, J. L., Iimi, A., & Trujillo, L. (2009). Multidimensionality and renegotiation: Evidence from transport-sector public-private-partnership transactions in Latin America. *Review of Industrial Organization*, 35. https://doi.org/10.1007/s11151-009-9225-0

Estache, A., Guasch, J.-L., & Trujillo, L. (2003). *Price caps, efficiency payoffs and infrastructure contract renegotiation in Latin America*. World bank policy research working paper 3129. https://doi.org/10.1596/1813-9450-3129

Estache, A., Juan, E., & Trujillo, L. (2007). *Public-private partnerships in transport*. Policy research working paper 4436. The World Bank, Washington, DC.

Froud, J., & Shaoul, J. (2001). Appraising and evaluating PFI for NHS hospitals. *Financial Accountability & Management, 17*(3), 247–270.

Grimsey, D., & Lewis, M. L. (2002). Evaluating the risks of public private partnerships for infrastructure projects. *International Journal of Project Management, 20*(2), 107–118.

Grimsey, D., & Lewis, M. K. (2005, December). Are public private partnerships value for money? Evaluating alternative approaches and comparing academic and practitioner views. In *Accounting forum* (vol. 29, no. 4, pp. 345–378). Elsevier.

Guasch, J. L. (2004). *Granting and renegotiating infrastructure concessions: Doing it right. World Bank*. Washington, D.C.: The World Bank. Retrieved from www.worldbank.org.

Guasch, J. L., Laffont, J. J., & Straub, S. (2003). *Renegotiation of concessions contracts in Latin America. Policy Research Working Paper 3011*. The World Bank.

Guasch, J. L., Benitez, D., Portables, I., & Flor, L. (2014). The renegotiation of PPP contracts: An overview of its recent evolution in Latin America. International transport forum discussion paper.

Guasch, J. L., Laffont, J. J., & Straub, S. (2006). Renegotiation of concession contracts: A theoretical approach. *Review of Industrial Organization, 29*(1–2), 55–73. https://doi.org/10.1007/s11151-006-9109-5.

Ho, S. P. (2006). Model for financial renegotiation in public-private partnership projects and its policy implications: Game theoretic view. *Journal of Construction Engineering and Management, 132*(7), 678–688.

Jamali, D. (2004). Success and failure mechanisms of public private partnerships (PPP) in developing countries: Insights from the Lebanese context. *International Journal of Public Sector Management, 17*(5), 414–430.

Kappeler, A., & Nemoz, M. (2010). *Public-private partnerships in Europe-before and during the recent financial crisis*. Economic and financial reports. European Investment Bank.

Martins, J., Marques, R. C., Cruz, C. O., & Fonseca, Á. (2017). Flexibility in planning and development of a container terminal: An application of an American-style call option. *Transportation Planning and Technology, 40*(7), 828–840.

Neto, D. D. C. E. S., Cruz, C. O., & Sarmento, J. M. (2017). Understanding the patterns of PPP renegotiations for infrastructure projects in Latin America: The case of Brazil. *Competition and Regulation in Network Industries, 18*(3–4), 271–296.

Neto, D. D. C. S., Cruz, C. O., & Sarmento, J. M. (2019). Renegotiation of transport public private partnerships: Policy implications of the Brazilian experience in the Latin American context. *Case Studies on Transport Policy, 7*(3), 554–561.

Ping Ho, S. (2009). Government policy on PPP financial issues: Bid compensation and financial renegotiation, in policy, finance & management for public-private partnerships. Edited by

Akintola Akintoye and Matthias Beck © 2009 Blackwell Publishing. ISBN: 978-1-405-17791-7.

Reis, R. F., & Sarmento, J. M. (2019). "Cutting costs to the bone": The Portuguese experience in renegotiating public private partnerships highways during the financial crisis. *Transportation, 46*(1), 285–302.

Sarmento, J. M. (2010). Do public-private partnerships create value for money for the public sector? The Portuguese experience. *OECD Journal on Budgeting, 10*(1), 1–27.

Sarmento, J. M. (2015). Auditoria nas parcerias público-privadas: O caso do Tribunal de Contas de Portugal. *Revista TCEMG*| jan fev mar, 20.

Sarmento, J. M. (2019). Contractual incompleteness and renegotiations of public private partnerships: A mixed-methods analysis. *European Journal of Management Studies, 24*(1), 3–19.

Sarmento, J. M., & Renneboog, L. (2016a). Anatomy of public-private partnerships: Their creation, financing and renegotiations. *International Journal of Managing Projects in Business, 9*, 94–122.

Sarmento, J. M., & Renneboog, L. (2016b). *Renegotiating public-private partnerships*. European Corporate Governance Institute (ECGI)-finance working paper (416).

Sarmento, J. M., & Renneboog, L. (2017). Cost overruns in public sector investment projects. *Public Works Management and Policy, 22*(2), 140–164.

Spiller, P. T. (2008). *An institutional theory of public contracts: Regulatory implications*. NBER working paper no. 14152.

Yescombe, E. R. (2011). *Public-private partnerships: Principles of policy and finance*. Oxford: Butterworth-Heinemann.

Chapter 3
Theory on PPP Renegotiations

3.1 Overview

The phenomenon of renegotiations can be grounded in the economic and organisational theories. Some theoretical perspectives include the contract theory, transaction cost theory, and institutional theory. This chapter provides an analysis of these theories and also of the theoretical background for understanding the phenomenon and its main results.

3.2 Contract Theory

The contributions of the contract theory to the understanding of renegotiations arise from the simple fact that contracts are necessarily incomplete (Tirole 1999; Blanc-Brude et al. 2006). The consequences of such incompleteness, the behaviour of each agent, and also the (as)symmetrical distribution of the benefits are more complex and will be discussed later on this chapter. First, it is essential to understand why contracts are necessarily incomplete.

Natural monopolies need to be regulated (Demsetz 1968). However, the belief that contractual regulation, i.e., the establishment of a contract to ensure that the behaviour of the concessionaire is in the public interest, was able to replace a more discretionary approach of regulation (see more in Gomez-Ibanez 2003) has not been supported either by the empirical evidence, nor by theoretic models (Marques 2017). For example, market and technologies uncertainties exist which can undermine the potential benefits of contractual devolution[1] (Williamson 1976). As discussed by

[1]Devolution in this context means to transfer to the private sector the responsibility for the provision of a service under government control.

C. Oliveira Cruz, J. Miranda Sarmento, *The Renegotiations of Public Private Partnerships in Transportation*, Competitive Government: Public Private Partnerships, https://doi.org/10.1007/978-3-030-61258-0_3

Tirole (1999), these uncertainties can give rise to information asymmetry problems, or at least aggravate them, thus tilting the level playing field for both parties, which inevitably leads to the need for renegotiation and an uneven distribution of the ensuing benefits/costs (whereby the first mover holds the advantage, as mentioned by Williamson (1985)).

Contracts are deemed to be incomplete because it is impossible to foresee all the potential contingencies and events that could have an impact on the contract (Hart and Moore 1988; Hart 2003). Abundant examples of events and contingencies that can affect PPP exist, considering the unique nature of these contracts. In general, PPP contracts are applied to long-term natural monopolies, which are asset-specific and investment-specific relationships operating in a complex network of stakeholders, with different objectives and motivations and in highly politically-sensitive sectors. In turn, PPP contracts are extremely susceptible to economic, financial, social, institutional, and political uncertainties.

PPPs usually involve significant construction works, which intrinsically implies a large degree of risk and uncertainty, particularly regarding potential cost overruns (for more on construction cost overruns, see, for example, Catalão et al. 2019a, b) and delays (Sweis et al. 2008). Furthermore, as discussed by Crocker and Reynolds (1993), the more complex and uncertain the environment is, the more costly will be contract incompleteness. The impact of a contract failure, or the inability of the contract to solve a specific situation, is much higher when the object of the contract is the construction and operation of an infrastructure asset which is worth hundreds of millions of Euros.

3.3 Transaction Costs Theory

The problem of contract incompleteness can also be analysed from the perspective of the transaction costs theory, which considers contract incompleteness to be a rational choice of the parties involved. This problem was raised several decades ago by Williamson (1976), who argued that difficulties exist in defining the right trade-off between transactional costs and the level of detail of the contract, by studying the example of the CATV in Oakland. The author fails to provide a definitive answer, but rather claims that:

> The level of detail that I have found useful in studying related transactional phenomena is what might be called a semimicroanalytic level of detail. Given the infeasibility of complex contingent claims contracting for the services in question, the properties of incomplete long-term and sequential spot contracts need to be assessed. (Williamson 1976).

Complete contracts are contingent to the possibility of having complete and verifiable data, to ensure that each party's obligations are comprehensively specified (Hart 2003; Holmstrom and Tirole 1989; Saussier 2000).

Acknowledging the incomplete nature of contracts, as defended in the transactional costs theory, agents tend to carry out rent-seeking strategies and demonstrate opportunistic behaviour during three critical moments, as discussed by Williamson (1976), namely: (i) the "*initial award*" (or procurement stage); (ii) "*execution difficulties*" (or the operation period), and; (iii) "*frictionless takeover or transfer*" (or contract termination). The motivations, strategies, and results of each party's behaviour during each stage are distinct, and should be analysed separately.

Common to all infrastructure construction project, is the fact that the design and procurement stage is critical. Indeed it is often reported that 90% of a project's success is defined before the contract is even awarded (Khalil 2002). In this context, project success is measured by "on time" and/or "on budget" delivery, with the specified level of quality of the infrastructure and/or associated operation services (Catalão et al. 2019a, b). According to the transactional costs theory, it is both challenging and expensive to draft and structure comprehensive, holistic, and exhaustive tender documents which ensure that potential bidders are provided with all the information that they require to put together their business case, taking into account the period under analysis, which is usually more than 30 years.

This can lead to two distinct and undesirable behaviours by bidders—one of which is known as *winner's curse* and the other as *strategic underbidding*. The *winner's curse* phenomenon occurs when the contract is awarded to the company that quotes the most optimistic forecasts for revenues and costs (which is not necessarily the most efficient one), even though the sustainability of the project may be at risk (de Brux 2010; Thaler 1988). *Strategic underbidding* corresponds to the intentional lowballing of the offer in order to secure the contract and lock-in by the grantor, with the undeclared intention that break-even (and thus profitability) will only be achieved during *ex-post* renegotiations (Guasch et al. 2007).

3.3.1 Procurement Stage

Winner's Curse

Winner's curse is an expression which is often used to describe situations when a winning bidder, after the start of the project, realises that its revenue and/or cost forecasts were excessively optimistic.

This usually occurs during the first 3 to 5 years of the contract—as will be discussed later on in Chap. 4. This renegotiation usually has an adverse effect on users' and taxpayers' benefits—for two distinct reasons (Guasch 2004): first, the selected firm is not necessarily the most efficient one, which thus diminishes the value for money, and, second; the concessionaire engages in rent-seeking strategies during renegotiation which also negatively affect the benefit for the users and taxpayers (Guasch 2004).

As the concessionaire which wins the tender may not necessarily be the most efficient one, the renegotiation strategy often focusses on the transfer of benefits from the users or taxpayers to the concessionaire, instead of increasing the overall monetary value of the project—as was initially promised when the PPP was first adopted as the preferred procurement model (Engel et al. 2006, 2009).

However, as discussed by Athias and Nuñez (2006, 2008), institutional strength plays a crucial role in the acceptance of future *ex-post* renegotiation and the subsequent outcomes.

Strategic Underbidding

The main difference of strategic underbidding compared to the winner's curse phenomenon is that in the cases of strategic underbidding, intentional and strategically-motivated underbidding takes place, i.e., the bidder is fully aware that the project is not financially viable under the terms of its bidding offer. Strategic underbidding occurs when two underlying assumptions are made. The first of these assumptions is that it is possible to reopen the contract and renegotiate the terms. As will be discussed later on, the empirical evidence supports this first assumption, which means that there is a very high likelihood that, at some point, contracts will be renegotiated (see more in Guasch 2004; Sarmento and Renneboog 2016a; Cruz and Marques 2013a). The second assumption is that, once the contract is reopened, it is possible to achieve better terms for the concessionaire (Sarmento and Renneboog 2016b). It should be noted that an increase in the benefits to the concessionaire[2] can only be achieved by: (i) a decrease in the surplus of the users, and/or; (ii) a decrease in the benefits for the Government—which in this case means the taxpayer. Very rarely does a situation occurs when renegotiation leads to a real increase in the value of a project, although theoretically this can happen (see, for example, de Brux 2010). An example is if the renegotiation involves the adoption of a new state-of-the-art operating and technological system, which ends up being more efficient than that which was initially planned for the contract, which thus increases the overall efficiency of the project. In theory, such a renegotiation can bring about an overall increase in the benefits for both parties. Naturally, this requires a quasi-symmetric skill and power of negotiation—in order to ensure a fair distribution of benefits.[3] Valéro (2015) claims that the governments' commitment to the long-term contract is essential to enable achieving the expected efficiency benefits of PPPs.

---

[2]For this discussion, we assume that the concessionaire is a unique and homogeneous entity, with a specific objective. Although it is a single entity—a Special Purpose Vehicle, in effect it is the result of several shareholders getting together with often conflicting goals and strategies, e.g., construction firms, engineering services firms, financiers (some with long-term strategies, others with short to medium-term strategies). This heterogeneity has implications at two levels: first, it adds complexity to any renegotiation process, as the private sector, or concessionaire, are in fact several entities which have to agree on the terms and proposals of the public sector, and; second, it can create conflicts and bring about another round of private-to-private renegotiations within the SPV. These issues are beyond the scope of this discussion.

[3]In fact, one can also argue that these efficiency gains are not part of the operational risk transfer to the concessionaire.

When a bidder presents an offer with a negative NPV for the company, this can be perceived to be a high-risk gamble, although, in fact, it is just a calculated risk, as the bidder assumes that it will soon be able to renegotiate the contract to its benefit (as discussed by Engel et al. 2009).

3.3.2 *Operational Stage*

The operational stage is the more extended phase of a project's life cycle. Some authors frequently claim that a significant proportion of risk fade away after construction, but that several risks can occur during the operation stage, namely: technological, market, legal, regulatory, economic and political risks, just to mention a few examples (Cruz and Marques 2012, 2013a, b, c). One evidence of the changing nature of the risk profile of the project is the frequent modification of the shareholder structure and the debt composition (Cruz and Sarmento 2018).

Using the contract theory, we can argue that in the case of a PPP, a significant investment is made (in infrastructure) which is specific and unique to the relationship established with the grantor—the concession contract. This is a non-tradeable investment or asset, which is only of value for that specific relationship. These relationship-specific investments can be used to leverage potential strategies for rent-appropriation. The private sector can use the negotiation power of owning the infrastructure and its know-how to try and achieve better contractual terms, as the transactional cost (financial, political, temporal, and social) of replacing the concessionaire can be prohibitive. Project complexity and negotiation power operate hand-in-hand—for the more complex a project is, the higher is the negotiation leverage. For example, the concessionaire can carry on negotiating until the transactional cost of replacing the concessionaire is equivalent to the value of the new terms of the contract (de Brux 2010). However, the problem is that too often there is a social and political cost resulting from the process of replacing a concessionaire, which, besides being costly, can take a long time. Contracts typically include mechanisms for calculating compensation to paid to the incumbent concessionaire in the case of their substitution due to the unilateral decision of the government, although these usually only penalise the grantor (Cruz 2011).

In theory, relationship-specific investments can also be used by the public sector to exert pressure on the concessionaire to accept new terms which are unilaterally imposed by the government, although this type of strategy can be disputed in the case of complex projects and it is potentially expensive for governments, as international arbitration is involved. Engel et al. (2006) argue that in the proximity of elections, governments tend to engage in renegotiations with the aim of anticipating investment with a minimum, or zero impact on public spending. Guasch and Straub (2009) claim that in the Latin American experience, most renegotiations were government-led.

A bilateral dependency occurs during the operation stage, which is known as "fundamental transformation" (Williamson 1985; Fehr 2009), during the transition from a competitive market (pre-award) to a bilateral relationship (post-award).

3.3.3 Contract Termination Phase and Rebidding

The contract termination phase and rebidding correspond to the period which runs from the termination of a contract to the celebration of a new contract, either with the incumbent concessionaire, or with a new bidder.

By the end of the contract, the grantor might choose to regain control of the management and operation of a public infrastructure (e.g., the re-municipalisation of water services in France—see more in Hall et al. 2013), or it can put the concession out to tender again. The first situation relates to a case of public management, while the latter corresponds to the instigation of a second PPP for the same project. The granting of a second contract does not involve the construction phase—although it can include some rehabilitation and repair, with the bulk of a second contract corresponding to the maintenance and operation of the original project. The incumbent of the original contract has a 'first-mover' advantage, as defined by Williamson (1976), in the sense of possessing a unique level of in-depth knowledge about the project with regards its critical success factors, and it also of retaining a better understanding of the main risks in comparison to new bidders. One can argue that the incumbent concessionaire possesses more experience and information than the grantor in preparing the tender for the second PPP, which provides a significant advantage. The problem of information asymmetry, as discussed by Williamson (1985), is critical—not just to improve the outcome of renegotiations, but also to help design better tender documents for the re-award of a contract. On the other hand, Estache et al. (2009) found that new bidders tend to bid more aggressively when challenging a "strong incumbent."

A common strategy practised by incumbent concessionaires—especially in the case of PPP projects which require periodical investments as the capacity increases, such as ports or airports, is to carry out significant investments during the last years of the concession, or to request that such expenditure be approved, and then claim an extension of the contract afterwards to recover such investments. Cruz and Marques (2012) carried out a case study on seaport concessions, which illustrates how a concessionaire can engage in rent-seeking contracts as the contract comes to an end, in order to obtain a longer duration of the partnership.

Bajari and Tadelis (2001) analysed price cap and cost-plus contracts and developed a theoretical model which supports the hypothesis that, in the case of complex projects, the best approach is to adopt cost-plus contracts, as not only are these the ones most likely to be renegotiated, but also because the cost-plus model reduces the likelihood of opportunistic renegotiations.

3.4 Institutional Theory

PPP projects and particularly renegotiations can both be affected by project governance. As discussed earlier, whether the renegotiation arises from the opportunistic and strategic behaviour of the agents, or whether it is due to the inherent uncertainty of the project, the regulatory, economic, legal, political and institutional environment also plays a role in the process (Guasch et al. (2003). Therefore, this phenomenon can be analysed through the Institutional Theory, whereby most authors who have analysed the empirical evidence of renegotiations have addressed what Cruz and Marques (2013a) and Sarmento and Renneboog (2016a) classify as "exogenous determinants".

The institutional theory builds upon the hypothesis that the environment (economic, political, legal, regulatory, etc.) affects an organisation and that it provides a layer of social constructions which affect both the organisations' behaviours and outcomes (Clegg 1981; North 1991). Significant research has been carried out which focusses on the importance of institutional factors within projects and which have a material impact on their performance (e.g., Engwall 2003; Miller and Hobbs 2005; Morris and Geraldi 2011; Scott et al. 2011). Many of the authors researching the relationship between institutional context and project performance have focused their studies on megaprojects—usually defined as being large scale projects costing more than 500 million US dollars (Biesenthal et al. 2018). Although these projects are both developed under public work contracts and more complex contractual arrangements such as PPP, the literature provides robust support for the fact that exogenous factors highly influence the projects' success.

Agents, both public and private, are influenced and act according to the institutional contexts, as discussed by Morris and Geraldi (2011) and also Lundin et al. (2015). The perception regarding the "rules of the game" are determinant in defining both the action and strategies of the parties, particularly in sectors which are influenced by political and regulatory uncertainties. Indeed, Miller et al. (2000) claim that institutional arrangements are the most critical factor in project performance.

Seen through the lens of the institutional theory, renegotiations are seen to be an institutional conflict between the two parties involved during the projects' life cycle. After taking into consideration that the scope of such contracts typically comprises large scale construction projects, or mega projects, as defined by the project management institutional theory, the process of overcoming this institutional conflict is affected by the ability to enforce contracts and influence political decisions, as well as the perception regarding levels of corruption and the quality of the government institutions and judicial systems, among other factors. Both the variables used to understand this context and the empirical evidence available regarding the influence of such variables will be discussed in the next chapter.

References

Athias, L., & Nuñez, A. (2006). Number of bidders and the winner's curse in toll road concessions: An empirical analysis (No. halshs-00331823).

Athias, L., & Nuñez, A. (2008). Winner's curse in toll road concessions. *Economics Letters, 101*(3), 172–174.

Bajari, P., & Tadelis, S. (2001). Incentives versus transaction costs: A theory of procurement contracts. *Rand journal of Economics*, 387–407.

Biesenthal, C., Clegg, S., Mahalingam, A., & Sankaran, S. (2018). Applying institutional theories to managing megaprojects. *International Journal of Project Management, 36*(1), 43–54.

Blanc-Brude, F., Goldsmith, H., & Valila, T. (2006). Ex-ante construction costs in the European Road Sector: A comparison of public-private partnerships and traditional public procurement. In Bank E. I. (Ed.), *European and financial report* (vol. 2006).

de Brux, J. (2010). The dark and bright sides of renegotiation: An application to transport concession contracts. *Utilities Policy, 18*(2), 77–85. https://doi.org/10.1016/j.jup.2009.07.003.

Catalão, F. P., Cruz, C. O., & Sarmento, J. M. (2019a). Exogenous determinants of cost deviations and overruns in local infrastructure projects. *Construction Management and Economics, 37*(12), 697–711.

Catalão, F. P., Cruz, C. O., & Sarmento, J. M. (2019b). The determinants of cost deviations and overruns in transport projects, an endogenous models approach. *Transport Policy, 74*, 224–238.

Clegg, S. (1981). Organization and control. *Administrative Science Quarterly, 26*, 545–562.

Crocker, K. J., & Reynolds, K. J. (1993). The efficiency of incomplete contracts: An empirical analysis of air force engine procurement. *The Rand Journal of Economics, 24*, 126–146.

Cruz. (2011). Essays in infrastructure public-private partnerships. In *PhD Thesis in Civil Engineering*. Instituto Superior Técnico: University of Lisbon (Portugal).

Cruz, C. O., & Marques, R. C. (2012). Using the economic and financial reequilibrium model to decrease infrastructure contract incompleteness. *Journal of Infrastructure Systems, 19*(1), 58–66.

Cruz, C. O., & Marques, R. C. (2013a). Endogenous determinants for renegotiating concessions: Evidence from local infrastructure. *Local Government Studies, 39*(3), 352–374. https://doi.org/10.1080/03003930.2013.783476.

Cruz, C. O., & Marques, R. C. (2013b). Exogenous determinants for renegotiating public infrastructure concessions: Evidence from Portugal. *Journal of Construction Engineering and Management, 139*(9), 1082–1090. https://doi.org/10.1061/(ASCE)CO.1943-7862.0000710.

Cruz, C. O., & Marques, R. C. (2013c). Integrating infrastructure and clinical management in PPPs for health care. *Journal of Management in Engineering, 29*(4), 471–481.

Cruz, C. O., & Sarmento, J. M. (2018). The price of project finance loans for highways. *Research in Transportation Economics, 70*, 161–172.

Demsetz, H. (1968). Why regulate utilities? *Journal of Law and Economics, 11*(1), 55–65.

Engel, E., Fischer, R., & Galetovic, A. (2006). *Renegotiation without Holdup: Anticipating spending and infrastructure concessions*. National Bureau of economic research working paper series (vol. no. 12399). https://doi.org/10.3386/w12399

Engel, E., Fischer, R., & Galetovic, A. (2009). *Soft budgets and renegotiations in public-private partnerships*. National Bureau of economic research working paper series (vol. no. 15300). https://doi.org/10.2139/ssrn.1460688

Engwall, M. (2003). No project is an island: linking projects to history and context. *Research Policy, 32*(5), 789–808.

Estache, A., Guasch, J. L., Iimi, A., & Trujillo, L. (2009). Multidimensionality and renegotiation: Evidence from transport-sector public-private-partnership transactions in Latin America. *Review of Industrial Organization, 35*, 41–71. https://doi.org/10.1007/s11151-009-9225-0.

Fehr, E. (2009). On the economics and biology of trust. *Journal of the european economic association, 7*(2–3), 235–266.

Gomez-Ibanez, J. (2003). *Regulating infrastructure: monopoly, contracts, and discretion* (3rd ed.). Cambridge, MA: Harvard University Press.

Guasch, J. L. (2004). *Granting and renegotiating infrastructure concessions: Doing it right*. Washington, DC: The World Bank. Retrieved from www.worldbank.org

Guasch, J. L., Laffont, J. J., & Straub, S. (2003). *Renegotiation of concessions contracts in Latin America*. Policy research working paper 3011. The World Bank

Guasch, J. L., Laffont, J. J., & Straub, S. (2007). Concessions of infrastructure in Latin America: Government-led renegotiation. *Journal of Applied Econometrics, 22*, 1267–1294. https://doi.org/10.1002/jae.

Guasch, J. L., & Straub, S. (2009). Corruption and concession renegotiations. Evidence from the water and transport sectors in Latin America. *Utilities Policy, 17*(2), 185–190. https://doi.org/10.1016/j.jup.2008.07.003.

Hall, D., Lobina, E., & Terhorst, P. (2013). Re-municipalisation in the early twenty-first century: water in France and energy in Germany. *International review of applied economics, 27*(2), 193–214.

Hart, O. (2003). Incomplete contracts and public ownership: Remarks, and an application to public-private partnerships. *The Econometrics Journal, 113*(486), C69–C76.

Hart, O., & Moore, J. (1988). Incomplete contracts and renegotiation. *Econometrica, 56*, 755–785.

Holmstrom, B. R., & Tirole, J. (1989). The theory of the firm. *Handbook of Industrial Organization, 1*, 61–133.

Khalil, M. I. A. (2002). Selecting the appropriate project delivery method using AHP. *International Journal of Project Management, 20*(6), 469–474.

Lundin, R. A., Arvidsson, N., & Brady, T. (2015). *Managing and working in project society*. Cambridge: Cambridge University Press.

Marques, R. C. (2017). Why not regulate PPPs? *Utilities Policy, 48*, 141–146.

Miller, R., & Hobbs, B. (2005). Governance regimes for large complex projects. *Project Management Journal, 36*(3), 42–50.

Miller, R., Lessar, D., & Floricel, S. (2000). *The strategic management of large engineering projects: shaping institutions, risks and governance*. Massachusetts: Imec Research Group.

Morris, P. W., & Geraldi, J. (2011). Managing the institutional context for projects. *Project Management Journal, 42*(6), 20–32.

North, D. C. (1991). Institutions. *The Journal of Economic Perspectives, 5*(1), 97–112.

Sarmento, J. M., & Renneboog, L. (2016a). Anatomy of public-private partnerships: Their creation, financing and renegotiations. *International Journal of Managing Projects in Business, 9*(1), 94–122.

Sarmento, J. M., & Renneboog, L. (2016b). *Renegotiating public-private partnerships*. European corporate governance institute (ECGI)-finance working paper (461).

Saussier, S. (2000). Transaction costs and contractual incompleteness: the case of Électricité de France. *Journal of Economic Behavior & Organization, 42*(2), 189–206.

Scott, W. R., Levitt, R. E., & Orr, R. J. (Eds.). (2011). *Global projects: Institutional and political challenges*. Cambridge: Cambridge University Press.

Sweis, G., Sweis, R., Hammad, A. A., & Shboul, A. (2008). Delays in construction projects: The case of Jordan. *International Journal of Project Management, 26*(6), 665–674.

Thaler, R. H. (1988). Anomalies: The winner's curse. *The Journal of Economic Perspectives, 2*(1), 191–202.

Tirole, J. (1999). Incomplete contracts: Where do we stand? *Econometrica, 67*(4), 741–781.

Valéro, V. (2015). Government opportunism in public-private partnerships. *Journal of Public Economics Theory, 17*(1), 111–135.

Williamson, O. E. (1976). Franchise bidding for natural monopolies – in general and with respect to CATV. *Bell Journal of Economics, 7*(1), 73–104.

Williamson, O. E. (1985). *The economic institution of capitalism*. New York: The Free Press.

Chapter 4
Renegotiation Analysis

4.1 Research Methods

The previous chapter provides a theoretical basis for understanding renegotiations. In this chapter we focus on those contributions in the literature which provide empirical evidence of the main patterns, outcomes, motives, and determinants of renegotiations. Our literature review presented in this chapter does not intend to provide an extensive analysis of contract and institutional & governance theories, but rather focusses on the contributions to the understanding of renegotiations and the occurrence of PPP contract failures, in an attempt to discover explanations for these theories. The objective is to move the discussion to the practical field.

This chapter of the book focusses on a set of research questions with the aim to provide a comprehensive and systematic overview of the empirical research on PPP renegotiations and it contributes to relevant empirical insights (by identifying the state of knowledge in the field), as well as an overview of the theories used and a conceptual model (providing evidence of the structure of the dependent and independent variables used in the previous studies).

Based on the existing literature, our key research questions can be posed as follows:

- How frequent are renegotiations in PPPs?
- Who initiates the renegotiation process?
- When do renegotiations happen?
- What are the main motives for the occurrence of renegotiations?
- What are the main results of renegotiations?
- What are the main determinants of renegotiation processes?

To answer these questions, we have focussed on a set of dimensions to analyse the empirical research on PPP renegotiations, namely: frequency, timing, motives, and outcomes. The main conclusions are that there is a consensus in the literature

C. Oliveira Cruz, J. Miranda Sarmento, *The Renegotiations of Public Private Partnerships in Transportation*, Competitive Government: Public Private Partnerships, https://doi.org/10.1007/978-3-030-61258-0_4

that renegotiations tend to be very frequent, occur early on during the contract, generally transfer costs to taxpayers and/users, involve a set of determinants that involve both project and institutional characteristics, and derive the necessary and relevant policy implications from a project management perspective.

There is a substantial amount of literature in the field of PPP renegotiations and it was necessary to establish a proper scientific approach to identify and select these contributions.

Over 25 papers were selected and analysed. These papers were selected using the databases from Web of Science and SCOPUS, applying the key words of "renegotiation", "PPP", "PFI", "contracts", and "empirical studies". Each of the results was then carefully analysed, and only those papers with direct relevance for the topic were selected, given the multiple entries obtained with these keywords. These papers are summarised in Table 4.2. The scope of the studies is diverse. For example: some studies only focussed on one sector, while others are multi-sectoral: some focus on one specific country, while others use international databases, and; some only focus on particular case studies. The objective of our literature review is not so much to analyse specific case studies, but rather to examine those studies that analysed multiple projects, which thus enables one to extract overall trends, although, we will mention a couple of case study-based papers.

Adopting the classification of types of literature review papers (LRPs) proposed by Wee and Banister (2016), the analysis provides the following added value:

- *Empirical insights*: summarises the existing body of knowledge, identifying the state of the art and also the main gaps and weaknesses;
- *Theories*: presents and discusses the existing theories and how they are reflected, implicitly or explicitly, in the empirical research, providing a basis for understanding the empirical results;
- *Conceptual model*: the research provides a view on the dependent variables which are used in the literature, and also how they are supported (or not) by the theoretical basis.

The methodology used is summarised in Fig. 4.1.

The methodology developed started with Phase 1—the paper search—using two public scientific databases—ISI Web of Science and Scopus, where a set of keywords was applied in the search. Table 4.1 summarises the keywords and results. As expected, a search using the simple expressions "contract theory", "public-private partnerships", or "renegotiations", resulted in several hundred papers, the vast majority of which have no connection with the study. On the other hand, the combined search using the following combinations—"renegotiations" and "public-private partnerships"; "renegotiation" and "determinants"; "renegotiation" and "infrastructure"—enabled us to obtain a greater number of focussed papers.

Phase 2 involved a paper analysis to ensure that all "false positives" were adequately disregarded meaning—in other words, all those papers that were captured in the search but which do not relate to the subject under discussion. This phase also involved an analysis of the type of paper, i.e., whether the paper is theoretical or empirical. Those papers that fall into the first category were analysed and included in

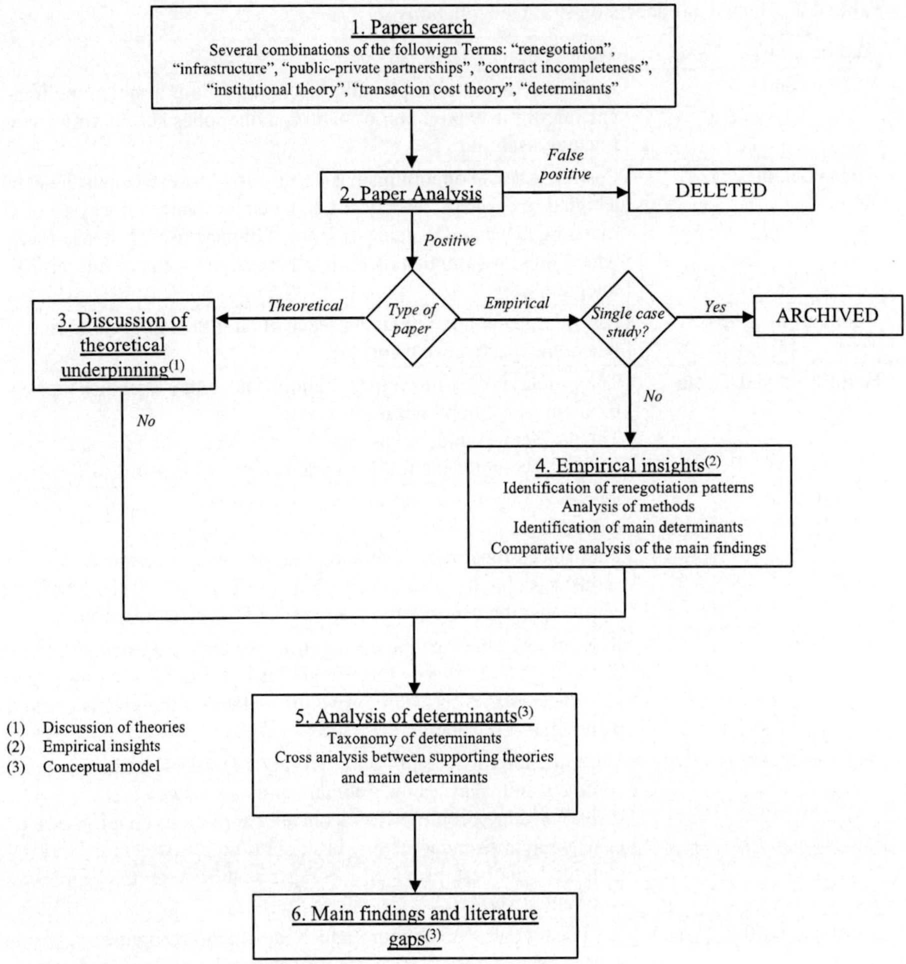

Fig. 4.1 Workflow of the methodological approach

Table 4.1 Search expressions and results

Query	WoS	Scopus
"Contract theory"	951	1468
"Transaction cost theory"	665	1017
"Institutional theory"	3849	5348
"Public-private partnerships"	3559	14,166
"Contract incompleteness"	29	37
"Renegotiation"	2131	2464
"Renegotiation" AND "public-private partnerships"	33	82
"Renegotiation" AND "determinants"	6	46
"Renegotiation" AND "infrastructure"	79	112
"Public-private partnerships" AND "infrastructure"	948	2418

Table 4.2 Theoretical papers on PPP renegotiations

Author (year)	Main findings
Williamson (1976)	Discusses (against the prevailing economic thinking) that the franchising of the exploration of natural monopolies suffers from "contractual disabilities".
Klein et al. (1978)	Post-contractual opportunism is particularly "bad" when the asset has a high degree of specialisation, i.e., when the "value for a given use is much higher than the value of its next highest use". In those cases where these assumptions are true, there is an incentive for vertical integration.
Williamson (1976)	Risk of renegotiation in the presence of "transaction-specific capital" when unexpected events occur.
Holmstrom and Tirole (1989)	The problem of *ex-post* renegotiation. The author specifies the problem as a "moral hazard in teams". The problem of underinvestment is explained by the fact that only one party captures the full marginal benefits of investment increases.
Tirole (1999)	Parties engaged in an incomplete contract have an incentive to renegotiate as soon as they acquire new information. The concessionaire discovers the true production costs and the sponsor is able to calculate the value of the project. The author also claims that the cancellation fees can lead to under-investment.
Dewatripont (1988)	Regardless of the fact that information asymmetries usually decrease the welfare (considering that the goal is optimal risk sharing), these asymmetries may in fact improve the welfare, if the goal is commitment against outsiders.
Hart and Moore (1988)	States the impracticability of specifying all possible contingencies in contracts and analyses the optimal contracts in two cases. If relationship-specific investments are carried out, then it is not possible to implement the first best, but if no investment is involved, then the "first-best, provided messages sent between the agents can be publicly verified".
Green and Laffont (1992)	"Efficient contracts" as those which are able to recognise unforecastable events. If such contracts can be renegotiated voluntarily, they can be better off doing so. When designing the contract, this renegotiation phase should be anticipated. No matter who has the bargaining power, it is always better to have a contract than not to have one.
Aghion and Tirole (1994)	"Efficient investments and optimal risk sharing can typically be achieved provided the initial contract is able to monitor the *ex-post* renegotiation process." "The analysis focusses on two features of renegotiation design, namely: default options and the allocation of all bargaining power to either of the contracting parties". These two features can be obtained in standard Rubinstein bargaining games through contractual provisions, such as specific-performance clauses and penalties for delay (or, the equivalent, namely financial "hostages" which are refundable without interest).

(continued)

Table 4.2 (continued)

Author (year)	Main findings
Edlin and Hermalin (1997)	"The ability of an agent and a principal to achieve the first-best outcome when the agent invests in an asset that has greater value if owned by the principal, rather than by the agent." "Investment by the agent can increase his value for the asset, thus improving his bargaining position in renegotiation." "Achieving the first best is difficult (or impossible) and if parties have an appropriate signal available, then the first is still attainable for a wide class of bargaining procedures."
Hart and Moore (1988)	Calculates a theoretical model to support the hypothesis that contracts are always incomplete.
Maskin and Moore (1999)	"The choice rules that can be implemented when agents are unable to commit themselves not to renegotiate the mechanism."
Tirole (1999)	Presents methodological insights regarding the standard approach to modeling incomplete contracts, namely the existence of transaction costs and rationality; The complete contract methodology does not account for standard institutions, such as authority and ownership; it concludes with a discussion of the research agenda."
Valéro (2015)	Discusses a government's commitment not to engage in opportunistic behavior is the key factor for determining the cost efficiency of a PPP. Specifies the economic determinants of government's choice between PPP and TP under government opportunism.
Ho (2006)	Provides a theoretic foundation for policy makers for prescribing effective PPP procurement and management policies and for examining the quality of PPP policies.
Nikolaidis and Roumboutsos (2013)	Presents a case study of renegotiation due to the financial crisis. Highlight the importance of the contextual environment and the limitations of solutions which appear to be "satisfying" for all the stakeholders involved.
Menezes and Ryan (2015)	Presents a theoretical model to identify the causes and consequences of financial distress in *ex-post* auction. Discuss firms' bid toll charges for a fixed-term highway concession, with the lowest bid winning the auction.
Soliño and Gago de Santos (2016)	Develops a theoretical model, based primarily on transaction costs, with which to compare the various tendering mechanisms for public-private partnership (PPP) projects.
Klijn and Koppenjan	The authors' findings cast doubt on earlier research into managing PPP performance and suggest that researchers, governments, and the private sector need to look beyond contract terms to properly understand and manage PPP performance.
Wu and Yang (2016)	Review and analysis the risk upon renegotiation and propose several risk-aversion strategies by exploring the key influencing factors of renegotiation based on several typical PPP renegotiation cases.
Khallaf et al. (2016)	Proposes a registry framework for risks associated with PPP renegotiation. This framework is based on the International Construction Risk Assessment Model (ICRAM-1)—which groups risks of international construction into three levels: macro level, consisting of general risks associated with work in a specific country; market level, consisting of risks emerging from the global construction market, and finally; the project level.

(continued)

Table 4.2 (continued)

Author (year)	Main findings
Xiong et al. (2017)	Proposes an ex-post risk management model, under which renegotiations and early terminations are introduced. The application of this model begins with risk impact evaluation, and then appraises the assessment, selection, and enforcement of *ex-post* risk response measures.
Li and Hao (2017)	Analyses two PPP projects renegotiation bargaining game models for the private and public sector respectively, through the analysis of the PPP projects renegotiation process, concluding with an estimation of the proportion of risks shared by each party, in accordance with the corresponding sub-game, by refining the Nash Equilibrium.
Sun and Yin (2017)	Highlights the necessity and positivity of renegotiations in some cases, describe the evolution routine and determinants of renegotiation. A notion of positive renegotiation is proposed, as well as the conditions which could lead to these positive renegotiations occurring.
Xiong et al. (2018)	Proposes a theoretical model game to study the influence of information asymmetry on the decision making of renegotiations in PPP projects. It is shown that a renegotiation decision resulting from information asymmetry is a Bayesian game, and thus the Bayesian Nash equilibrium is applied for solutions.
Sharafi et al. (2018)	Investigates some sharing mechanisms, based on cooperative game concepts, including the core, nucleolus, and Shapley value theories.
Shi et al. (2018)	Analyses the contractual efficiency of public-private partnership (PPP) infrastructure projects, with a focus on two financial aspects: the nonrecourse principal and the incompleteness of debt contracts. Proposes an optimal combination of a performance guarantee, the government's termination right, and a service fee to improve the contractual efficiency of PPP infrastructure projects.

This table presents the main findings of the theoretical papers on PPP renegotiations

the discussion of the theoretical background (Phase 3), and the second analysis of the empirical papers classified them into papers with a single case study, or papers which analyse a database of renegotiations. Although single case study papers were also included in the literature summary, as discussed later, the research on the empirical analysis focussed on papers which analyse more than one renegotiation. Phase 4 involved a detailed analysis of the empirical insights, including the identification of renegotiation patterns, the analysis of methods, the identification of the main determinants, and a comparative analysis of the main findings of the papers. The analysis of the patterns of renegotiations is organised in function of the following variables: frequency, timing, motives, and outcomes. One of the most relevant subjects of the empirical literature is the determinants of renegotiations—which were analysed in Phase 5, based on the results of the empirical insights (Phase 4) and the theoretical underpinning (Phase 3). Finally, Phase 6 presented the main findings, as well as the identification and discussion of the main gaps in the literature.

4.2 Literature Overview

As seen in Tables 4.1 and 4.2, the first empirical studies on PPP renegotiation appeared in 2003, in the form of two seminal studies (Guasch et al. 2003; Estache et al. 2003). Both of these studies analysed a sample of PPP projects in Latin American countries over a period from 1989 to 2000. The first study to be undertaken on European renegotiations is from De Brux (2010), which focusses on France, followed by that of Cruz and Marques (2012, 2013a, b), which analyses the situation in Portugal (a topic which is also addressed by Sarmento and Renneboog (2016a), Macário et al. (2015), and Andrade et al. (2018)).

Although different authors have analysed different regions, different sectors, and various types of PPPs, more similarities have emerged than differences among the patterns for each country and for each sector. Our analysis below provides an overview of the empirical literature on PPP renegotiation, followed by a more detailed analysis of each of the research questions cited above. As not all the papers provide comparable information with the same level of detail, for consistency purposes, the comparison often does not include the entire sample of papers, but only those which have comparable data (Table 4.3).

Table 4.4 summarises the number of PPPs analysed in each study and the number of PPPs that have been renegotiated. Different studies have used different sizes for their databases, with some studies using as few as 16 cases (Engel et al. 2006), while others use as many as 954 (Guasch et al. 2003). The geographical coverage is diverse, although there is a considerable concentration in Latin American countries, which can be explained by the effort carried out by the World Bank in the past to collect and organise large and powerful databases, such as that used by Guasch (2004).

4.3 Analysis of Main Patterns

4.3.1 Frequency

Based on the theoretical basis provided by the contract incompleteness theory, it was expected that the occurrence of renegotiation would be frequent, even though the frequency varies for different sectors. In most studies, the proportion of PPPs that have been renegotiated is above 50%, e.g., Engel et al. (2006), Cruz and Marques (2013b), Bitran et al. (2013), Sarmento and Renneboog (2016b), Neto et al. (2017), and Andrade et al. (2018). Guasch et al. (2003, 2006, 2008) found lower renegotiation rates of 32%.

With regards the initiator of the renegotiation, i.e., who was responsible for triggering the process, the results are more distinct (Table 4.5). Some authors, such as Guasch (2004) or Cruz and Marques (2013b), claim that the initiator was the private sector in most cases, while other studies, such as that of Bitran et al.

Table 4.3 Empirical papers on PPP renegotiations

Author (year)	Region/Country	Sectors	Period	Main findings
Crocker and Reynolds (1993)	n.a.	n.a.	n.a.	Discusses the costs of contract incompleteness, stating that the greater the complexity of the sector in which the contract develops, the greater these costs will be.
Artana et al. (1998)	n.a.	n.a.	n.a.	Evaluates contractual adjustments, renegotiations, and disputes which occurred in Argentina regarding various public utility industries 12 cases). Deficient design leads to both renegotiations and poor competition during the award process.
Bajari and Tadelis (2001)	n.a.	n.a.	n.a.	For complex contracts, the cost and the schemes decrease the likelihood of opportunistic behaviour, due to the fact that more adaptations are required.
Guasch et al. (2003)	Argentina, Brazil, Chile, Colombia and Mexico	Transport and water	1989–2000	Analyses a data set of nearly 1000 concessions awarded in Latin America and the Caribbean countries from 1989 to 2000; The probability of renegotiation is influenced by the existence of a regulatory body at the time that the concession was awarded, a price cap regulation model, the volume of investment, and political cycles.
Estache et al. (2003)	Latin American and Caribbean Countries	Telecommunications, energy, transport and water	1989–2000	Price caps imply higher costs of capital, and consequently high tariffs reduce levels of investment.

(continued)

Table 4.3 (continued)

Author (year)	Region/Country	Sectors	Period	Main findings
Guasch et al. (2006)	Latin American and Caribbean Countries	Telecommunications, energy, transport and water	1982–2000	A good regulatory framework is especially important in contexts of weak governance and political opportunism, especially when these phenomena are present at early stages of concessions' lifespans.
Engel et al. (2006)	Chile	Transport	1998–2002	Contract renegotiations enable organisations to replicate the effects of issuing debt; Renegotiations enable incumbents to spend more without being subject to parliamentary oversight.
Guasch et al. (2007, 2008, 2014)	Argentina, Brazil, Chile, Colombia and Mexico	Transport and water	1989–2000	Analyses the impact of regulatory institutions (whereby more powerful institutions lower the probability of renegotiation), economic shocks, and project characteristics on the probability of renegotiation.
Guasch and Straub (2009)	Argentina, Brazil, Chile, Colombia and Mexico	Transport and water	1989–2000	The effect of corruption varies depending to the type of renegotiations under consideration; A more corrupt environment clearly leads to more firm-led renegotiations and significantly reduces the incidence of government-led renegotiations.
Estache et al. (2009)	Latin American	Transport	1989–2000	Good governance practices are the best tool to mitigate potential renegotiation problems. Analyse the effect of

(continued)

Table 4.3 (continued)

Author (year)	Region/Country	Sectors	Period	Main findings
				different award criteria on the probability of renegotiations.
Engel et al. (2009)	Chile	Transport, security, environment and others	1993–2006	In a competitive market, firms tend to lowball their offers, expecting to break even through renegotiation to compensate the lowball effect. Renegotiations are used by governments to increase expenditure, which thus postpones payments and reduces the fiscal constraints at the current moment. Significant renegotiations occur during the early stages of a contract: e.g., during the construction phase.
De Brux (2010)	France	Transport	–	Presents two case studies of renegotiations: (1) When parties place an important value on their present and future bilateral relationships, they are prone to finding solutions that are sustainable and profitable for both parties; (2) Even when acting in their own self-interest, parties try to maximise joint utility during the renegotiation stage and in this way they reinforce the durability of their relationship.
Cruz and Marques (2013a)	Portugal	Transport	2005	Renegotiations for the public transport system normally involve direct payments from the government

(continued)

Table 4.3 (continued)

Author (year)	Region/Country	Sectors	Period	Main findings
				(without increasing users' tariffs). Contractual regulation is insufficient for infrastructure PPPs.
Cruz and Marques (2013b)	Portugal	Transportation, roads, rails, ports, health, water and energy	1984–2008	Analyses 87 concessions in Portugal. Renegotiations involve significant costs for the government. The duration, investment, and existence of a regulator, all represent key factors for decreasing the likelihood of renegotiations.
Cruz and Marques (2013c)	N.A.	N.A.	N.A.	Presents the effects of the economic and financial reequilibrium model through the provision of actual data and the case study of a concession. Provide several alternatives which are capable of improving the performance and management of infrastructure contracts with regards the renegotiation phenomenon.
Bitran et al. (2013)	Chile. Colombia and Peru	Road	1993–2010	Weak State institutions, unclear legislation, and deficient contract design have all encouraged frequent and costly renegotiation of road concessions. State-led renegotiations, which are more common than firm-led renegotiations, are often associated with

(continued)

Table 4.3 (continued)

Author (year)	Region/Country	Sectors	Period	Main findings
				the political cycle. Most of the renegotiations were not the unavoidable result of incomplete contracts, neither of firms seeking larger rents, nor compensation for low levels of traffic.
Lohmann and Rötzel (2014)	Germany	Security	N.A.	Opportunistic behaviour does not concern fiscal issues, as the government entity can control the fiscal objectives of PPPs where it is a majority shareholder; Certain exogenous factors which influence the level of opportunistic behaviour exhibited by the PPPs under study provide evidence of the causes and effects of such behaviour and indicate how this behaviour can be limited by the governmental entity.
Zhang and Xiong (2015)	The United Kingdom, The USA, Argentina, Mexico, Cambodia and China	Highways, airports, power plants, and water supply and drainage facilities	N.A.	Presents a case study of renegotiations. If a renegotiation-allowed contract is used, then contractor-led renegotiation is very likely to occur, especially during the early stage of a concession. Government-led renegotiation is less likely to occur, and when it does, this usually occurs during the middle stage of the concession. One party can use opportunistic

(continued)

Table 4.3 (continued)

Author (year)	Region/Country	Sectors	Period	Main findings
				renegotiation to delay the other party and can then consequently demand excessive compensation. Renegotiations must be regulated. Renegotiation of a PPP project can lead to a high real option value. The higher the uncertainty, the higher the renegotiation value.
Cruz et al. (2015)	Brazil	Transport	N.A.	Discusses the use of PPP contracts in the road sector, focussing on the Brazilian MG-050 case study.
Cruz et al. (2015)	Portugal	Transport	N.A.	Examines the main causes of renegotiation for the road sector in Portugal. The main causes of renegotiations are related to unilateral changes made by the government, changes in design due to environmental reasons, delays in expropriation, and levels of traffic below the forecast level.
Domingues and Zlatkovic (2015)	Portugal (04), Spain (02), Greece, Cyprus and Netherlands	Transport		Presents nine case studies of renegotiations. Renegotiation, per se, is not a solution for the successful implementation of PPP projects. Contractual flexibility is a tool which enables adaptation to uncertainty. Effective

(continued)

Table 4.3 (continued)

Author (year)	Region/Country	Sectors	Period	Main findings
				communication mechanisms enable a better response to unforeseen events, which thus reinforces the partners' commitment to deliver a win–win project.
Macário et al. (2015)	Portugal (04), Spain (02), Greece, Cyprus and Netherlands	Transport		Examines the transferability of success factors in renegotiations. There is a need for transferability to account for modal and national specificities.
Sarmento and Renneboog (2016a)	Portugal	Transport		Present two case studies. Renegotiation outcomes tend to rely on the position of the government, although joint decision-making can be difficult, due to the positions assumed by the different parties involved. Incomplete contracts and the long duration of concessions can lead to uncertainty and change in PPPs.
Domingues and Sarmento (2016)	13 European countries	Road and railway		Corroborates the literature, confirming that a country's economic and legal environment has an important impact on the likelihood of renegotiation. The occurrence of elections is shown to have an indirect impact on increasing renegotiations. Uncertainty when developing new PPP projects caused by budgetary motivations plays a critical role in contractual

(continued)

Table 4.3 (continued)

Author (year)	Region/Country	Sectors	Period	Main findings
				renegotiation, as does the performance during the operational stage of long-term contracts.
Sarmento and Renneboog (2016b)	Portugal	Roads, railway, ports, health, security	1995–2015	Renegotiations can undermine the efficiency of the initial bidding process. Analyse the private sector's bidding rank, bargaining extraction rate (the percentage of the claim realised during renegotiations), political connections, and, for the public sector, whether contract design and regulation affects the intensity of renegotiation.
Neto et al. (2017)	Brazil	Transports, Environment, Sports, Health, Security, Housing	2004–2017	Finds that a high number of renegotiations occur within a short period. The motives for renegotiations are largely failures in planning, concept, and bidding. Electoral periods and the political connections of shareholders also have an impact on renegotiations.
Owusu-Manu et al. (2018)	Ghana	N.A.	N.A.	Provides guidance to construction stakeholders in the PPP sector regarding the different causes and effects of adverse selection and moral hazard.
Khallaf et al. (2018)	USA	Transport	N.A.	Proposes a risk identification and framework with modelling and simulation and expand the analysis of interactions from the current focus on two

(continued)

Table 4.3 (continued)

Author (year)	Region/Country	Sectors	Period	Main findings
				parties to three parties. A case study of the Indiana Toll Road was carried out as a showcase for the application of the proposed approach
Andrade et al. (2018)	Portugal	Water	1995–2015	Shows that lower consumption and additional investments rank among the main motives for renegotiation, which can occur at any point during the lifetime of a concession. The analysis confirms some of the initial hypotheses, such as that larger concessions and longer contracts are more likely to be renegotiated. Indirectly, the occurrence of elections tends to increase renegotiations.
Howell and Sadowski (2018)	New Zealand	Telecom	N.A.	Through the use of the concept of regulatory commitment, compares the experiences gained in a hold-up situation in PPPs in other infrastructures (e.g., road construction) within the UFB context. A case study of New Zealand's Ultrafast Fibre Broadband Initiative is used to provide new insights for government purchasers and regulatory agencies.
Dolla and Laishram (2018)	India	Solid waste management	N.A.	Provides guidelines for governments on how to create and

(continued)

Table 4.3 (continued)

Author (year)	Region/Country	Sectors	Period	Main findings
				improve LC MSW PPP infrastructure projects to facilitate simultaneous achievement of both climate change mitigation and infrastructure delivery goals.
Lohmann and Rötzel (2018)	Germany	Defense	N.A.	Analyses the renegotiations that take place between institutionalised public-private partnerships (PPPs) and their public clients, drawing on survey data regarding the PPPs of the German Federal Armed Forces.
Fernandes et al. (2019)	Portugal	Transport	2012	Distinguishes between structural renegotiations (with changes in the risk-sharing agreement) and non-structural renegotiations (without shifting risk) and analyses the implications of structural renegotiations in a road concession, by comparing the *ex-ante* and *ex-post* financial implications for the government, the concessionaire, and the users. The selected project started as a shadow toll and was later

(continued)

Table 4.3 (continued)

Author (year)	Region/Country	Sectors	Period	Main findings
				changed to a real toll. The analysis shows that the renegotiation essentially transferred costs to the users.
Bae et al. (2019)	South Korea	Transport	N.A.	Presents a case study of a renegotiation framework based on the equivalent NPV constraint condition.

This table presents the literature on PPP renegotiations based on the empirical papers. It presents the region/country, the sectors of PPP, the period of analysis, and the main findings

(2013), provide evidence that the main initiator was the government. The analysis of the initiator provides some clue as to the identification of the strategies, potential motives, and behaviour of the parties. The theories that support that concessionaires tend to carry out rent-seeking strategies and demonstrate *ex-post* opportunism, help to explain why a high proportion of renegotiations are initiated by the concessionaire. However, relationship-specific investments can also be used, in theory, by the public sector to pressure the concessionaire to accept new terms which are unilaterally imposed by the Government, although these types of strategies can be alleged to be complex and potentially costly (for governments), and they often involve international arbitration. Engel et al. (2006) argue that governments tend to carry out renegotiations close to the time of elections, as a means of anticipating investment, with a minimum, or null impact on public spending. According to the author, in such cases, renegotiations give rise to an increase in public spending, without being subject to parliamentary control. Guasch and Straub (2009) claimed that government-led renegotiations were the most frequent type in Latin America.

4.3.2 Timing

Table 4.6 presents the timing of renegotiations, which is calculated as being the average duration of the time-lapse from the start of the contract up until the first renegotiation occurs. In most cases, the first renegotiation occurs within the first 3–4 years of a concession, with many even taking place within the first year. This pattern contradicts the argument that renegotiations are inevitable, given the long-term nature of these projects and the inherent uncertainty for long-term planning.

Table 4.4 Description of PPP renegotiation studies

Author (year)	Sector	Region/Country	N° of PPPs	N° of PPPs renegotiated	Percentage of PPPs renegotiated
Guasch et al. (2003)	Transport and water	Argentina, Brazil, Chile, Colombia and Mexico	954[b]	307	32%
Estache et al. (2003)	Telecommunications, energy, transport and water	Latin American and Caribbean Countries	954[a, b]	–	
Guasch et al. (2006)	Telecommunications, energy, transport and water	Latin American and Caribbean Countries	954[b, e]	307	32%
Engel et al. (2006)	Transport	Chile	16	12	75%
Guasch et al. (2008)	Transport and water	Argentina, Brazil, Chile, Colombia and Mexico	954[b]	307	32%
Guasch and Straub (2009)	Transport and water	Argentina, Brazil, Chile, Colombia and Mexico	954[b]	307	32%
Estache et al. (2009)	Transport	Latin American	96	–	
Engel et al. (2009)	Transport, security, environment and others	Chile	–	50	
Cruz and Marques (2013a)	Transport	Portugal	1	1	
Cruz and Marques (2013b)	Transportation, roads, rails, ports, health, water and energy	Portugal	87	58	67%
Bitran et al. (2013)	Roads	Chile, Colombia, Peru	61	50	82%
Lohmann and Rötzel (2014)	Security	Germany	–	108	
Zhang and Xiong (2015)	Highways, airports, power plants, and water supply and drainage facilities	United Kingdom, the USA, Argentina, Mexico, Cambodia and China	–	8[c]	
Domingues and Zlatkovic (2015)	Transport	Portugal (04), Spain (02), Greece, Cyprus and Netherlands	–	9	
Macário et al. (2015)	Transport	Portugal	–	1	

(continued)

Table 4.4 (continued)

Author (year)	Sector	Region/Country	N° of PPPs	N° of PPPs renegotiated	Percentage of PPPs renegotiated
Squeren and Moore (2015)	Transport	France	–	1	
Xiong and Zhang (2016)	Transport	Hypothetical	–	1	
Miranda Sarmento and Renneboog (2016a)	Transport	Portugal	–	2	
Domingues and Sarmento (2016)	Road and railway	13 European countries	–	32[d]	
Miranda Sarmento and Renneboog (2016b)	Roads, railway, ports, health, security	Portugal	35	26	74%
Neto et al. (2017)	Transports, Environment, Sports, Health, Security, Housing	Brazil	42	27	64%
Andrade et al. (2018)	Water	Portugal	31	n.a.	n.a.
Fernandes et al. (2019)	Transport	Portugal	1	1	

[a]This paper uses the Guasch et al. (2003) general data base
[b]Data base developed by the World Bank
[c]Four are early-termination contracts
[d]Data base developed by COST Publications
[e]This paper uses the Guasch (2004) data base
n.a.–Not available

The reality is that, even in the short-term, most contracts are renegotiated, even during the construction phase.

4.3.3 *Motives*

Table 4.7 presents an overview of the main motives for PPP renegotiation. As Engel et al. (2006) and Guasch and Straub (2009) argue, governments tend to change projects for political reasons, which inevitably leads to a renegotiation of the

Table 4.5 Initiator of PPP renegotiations

Author (year)	Sector		Government	Private	Both
Guasch (2004)	All sectors	Latin America	36%	61%	13%
	Water and sanitation		24%	66%	10%
	Transports		27%	57%	16%
Cruz and Marques (2013b)	Energy	Portugal	100%		
	Transportation		17.6%	76.4%	5.8%
	Water and sanitation		6.1%	89.8%	4.1%
	Health		100%		
Bitran et al. (2013)	Roads	Chile	84%	12%	4%
		Colombia	40%	20%	40%
		Peru	64%	23%	13%
Neto et al. (2017)	All sectors	Brazil	6%	12%	82%

Table 4.6 Timing of PPP renegotiations

Author (year)	Sector	Region/ Country	Average time until start of the first renegotiation (years)
Guasch (2004)	All sectors	Latin America	2.2
	Water and sanitation		1.6
	Transportation		3.1
Cruz and Marques (2013b)	Transportation	Portugal	3.3
	Health		1.0
	Water		1.5
	Energy		15
Bitran et al. (2013)	Roads	Chile	2.7
		Colombia	1.0
		Peru	1.4
Sarmento and Renneboog (2017)	All sectors	Portugal	3.5
	Road		3.4
	Rail		7.0
	Health		4.0
	Security		2.0
Neto et al. (2017)	All sectors	Brazil	n.a.
	Transportation		2.4
	Environment		1.1
	Sports		1.2
	Health		0.5
	Security		1.5
	Housing		0.5

Table 4.7 Motives for PPP renegotiations

	Changes in design/ scope	Demand/ consumption below forecast	Delay in expropriations and administrative permits	*Force majeure*	Others[a]
Cruz and Marques (2013b)	37%	49%	9%	2%	3%
Sarmento and Renneboog (2017)					
Andrade et al. (2018)	66%	32%	n.a	n.a	4%
Neto et al. (2017)	62%	3%	22%	2%	10%

n.a—not available
[a]Others include unilateral changes, comeptition issues, etc

contract. When analysing the motives that led to renegotiation in Brazilian PPPs, Neto et al. (2017) identified that the most common motives are precisely related with modifications in the project design/scope, its features, and requests for additional work. This is consistent with the evidence in the same study of extremely early renegotiations (as shown in Table 4.4). On the other hand, Cruz and Marques (2013b) found that the primary motive for PPP renegotiation was level of demand/ traffic below forecast, followed by changes in the design of the project. The same pattern was identified by Andrade et al. (2018) and Sarmento and Renneboog (2016b). Are these problems a result of specific characteristics of the projects, or a result of the economic and institutional context which renders proper planning incapable and prevents costly *ex-post* renegotiations? The next subsection analyses in detail the main determinants identified in the literature.

4.3.4 Outcomes

As discussed above, renegotiation is the process of the redesign and readjustment of a contract and, as such, once completed, it implies a change or an outcome in the initial contract. Table 4.8 summarises the main outcomes, which are divided into five main types: increase in users' tariffs; change in contract duration; direct payment from the government to the concessionaire; tax benefits, and; others.

As shown in Table 4.7, the large majority of outcomes are either an increase in users' tariffs or direct payments from the government. This is consistent with the previous findings in the literature, which show that the main motives for renegotiations are related to changes in projects' design and/or scope, as well as consumption/demand below that forecast. It is important to notice that these outcomes are not mutually exclusive, and that often the same renegotiation process can involve a mix

Table 4.8 Outcomes of PPP renegotiations

		Increase in users' tariffs	Change in contract duration[a]	Direct payment	Tax benefits	Others[b]
Guasch (2004)		62%	38%	n.a.	n.a.	n.a.
Cruz and Marques (2013b)	Transportation		4%	88%	4%	4%
	Energy	100%				
	Water	86%	14%			
	Health			100%		4%
Bitran et al. (2013)	Chile	24%	12%	82%		15%
	Colombia	1%	12%	48%		45%[c]
	Peru	14%		20%		77%[c]
Andrade et al. (2018)	Water	54%	20%	26%		

n.a—not available
Note: outcomes could be above 100% as one renegotiation can lead to one or several outcomes
[a]The change in contract duration can be an extension or a reduction, although the majority of the cases are extensions
[b]Others—includes not representing a direct cost, a reduction of contract scope, a tax benefit, or delaying some investments
[c]Without direct costs

of several outcomes. This evidence also confirms a biased distribution of benefits, where there is transfer of benefits from users and taxpayers to concessionaires.

4.4 Determinants of PPP Renegotiations

Acknowledging that renegotiations tend to occur very frequently and very early, according to the pattern identified before, many studies have focussed on understanding the factors that trigger renegotiations, mainly to analyse what the determinants are, i.e., what are the factors that positively or negatively impact on the probability of renegotiations. In this subsection we provide an answer to the research question of why some projects are more prone to renegotiation than others, and what are the underlying factors that influence the likelihood of renegotiation?

Most studies build on a similar hypothesis, based on the theoretical background. Using different models, several authors have attempted to identify the effects of a set of determinants. The first task was to exhaustively identify all determinants that have been used by all the authors. Table 4.9 presents the analysis of 11 studies which explicitly analysed the potential of determinants that increase or reduce the likelihood of renegotiation.

Second, it was necessary to create a taxonomy for classifying the determinants. In this chapter of the book we used the taxonomy presented by Sarmento and

Table 4.9 Determinants of PPP renegotiations

Determinant	Main conclusion	1	2	3	4	5	6	7	8	9	10	11
1 Contract/Project determinants (endogenous)												
1.1 Invest. requirements	Increase	+	+	+	+	+				+		
1.2 Contract duration	Not clear	n.s	–		n.s		n.s	+	–			+
1.3 Investment amount	Increase						+	+	n.s			–
1.4 High leverage	Reduce								–			
1.5 Availability Payments	Reduce								–		–	
1.6 Foreign shareholders	Reduce		+						–		–	
1.7 Operational stage	Increase								+	+		
1.8 EIB loans	Reduce								–			
1.9 Transport sector	Increase	+			+	n.s	+		n.s			
1.10 Excludes private financing	Increase	+	n.s	–	+	n.s						
1.11 Income guarantee	Increase	+	n.s	+	–							
1.12 Arbitration process	Not clear	n.s		–	n.s							
1.13 Construction delays	Increase							+				
1.14 Greenfield	Increase									+		
1.15 Renegotiations clauses	Increase									+		
2 Concessions and Renegotiations experience (endogenous)												
2.1 First renegotiation	Increase								+			–
2.2 Age at renegotiation	Increase	+		+	+	+	n.s	+	n.s			–
3 Institutional and governance context (exogenous)												
3.1 Bureaucratic quality	Reduce	–		–	–	–						
3.2 Government effectiveness	Increase						+			–		
3.3 Regulatory quality	Reduce						–					–
3.4 Price-cap regulation	Increase	+	+	+	+	+						
3.5 Regulatory body	Reduce	–	–	–	–	–		–				
3.6 Age of the regulator	Reduce							–				

(continued)

Table 4.9 (continued)

Determinant	Main conclusion	1	2	3	4	5	6	7	8	9	10	11
3.7 Autonomous regulator	Increase		+									
3.8 Specific legislation	Increase		+						+	−		
3.9 Rule of law	Increase	+							+	−		−
3.10 Corruption index (low corruption)	Reduce	−		−	−	−	−		−	−		−
3.11 Contract viability	Reduce								−			
3.12 Risk rating	Reduce								−			
3.13 Bidding process	Increase	−		+	n.s			+				
3.14 Number of bidders	Increase						+	n.s	+	n.s		
3.15 Award criteria	Increase		+	+								
3.16 Multi-criteria	Not clear		n.s				+					
3.17 Reputation	Increase		+									
4 Political and legal context (exogenous)												
4.1 Electoral year (+/− 1)	Increase	+		+	+	+			+		n.s	−
4.2 Right-wing government	Increase								+			
4.3 Government change	Not clear								n.s			
4.4 Majority government	Increase								+			
4.5 Political stability	Reduce								−			
4.6 Unemployment rate	Reduce						−					
4.7 Optimism bias	Increase							+				
4.8 Unilateral change	Increase							+				
5 Economic context (exogenous)												
5.1 Growth in GDP	Reduce	−	n.s	−	−	−			+	−		−
5.2 Deficit	Reduce								−	+		
5.3 Public debt	Increase								+			
5.4 Exchange rate	Increase	+	n.s	−	+							

(1) Guasch et al. (2003); (2) Guasch (2004); (3) Guasch et al. (2007); (4) Guasch et al. (2008); (5) Guasch and Straub (2009); (6) Estache et al. (2009); (7) Cruz and Marques (2013b); (8) Sarmento and Renneboog (2017); (9) Domingues and Sarmento (2016); (10) Neto et al. (2017); (11) Andrade et al. (2018)

n.s.—not significant

Renneboog (2016b). The determinants started by being classified according to two simple categories, which can be subsequently subdivided. The first are endogenous determinants, which are related to the specific characteristics of the project and/or contract. The second are exogenous determinants, which are associated with the overall external environment. Endogenous determinants were latter subdivided into contract/project determinants and experience, while the exogenous were subdivided into institutional & governance, political & legal, and economic.

The purpose of having a clear taxonomy is two-fold: first, given that a large number of determinants used by the various studies (46 variables), creating clusters enables a more precise understanding of the type of hypothesis under study, and, second, it facilitates the ability to link the determinants to the theoretical background. We attempted to summarise this link between theory and determinants in Table 4.9. The endogenous determinants, both those related with the contract/project (describing particular features and characteristics of the contract/project) and with the experience (describing the historical pattern of renegotiations of the contract), help to support and test the hypothesis which is built on the contract theory and the transaction cost theory. Simply put, the authors surmise that renegotiations are a consequence of the incomplete nature of contracts and/or the excessive transaction cost of increasing the contract detail in order to minimise its "incompleteness". The only dimension of the contract that constitutes an exogenous variable is the arbitration process. On the other hand, as expected, most of the exogenous determinants, whether implicitly or explicitly, enable the ability to test for the hypothesis raised by the institutional theory, i.e., that the likelihood and performance of renegotiations is more a problem of institutional and legal design, and also results from the economic situation.

Over the next subsections, we analyse in detail the results of the comparative analysis, using the data provided in Table 4.9.

4.5 Analysis of the Results

As previously mentioned, with a few exceptions, most studies are consistent regarding the influence of the main determinants for renegotiations. In relation to contract/project determinants, most studies found that the following factors all contribute positively to the likelihood of renegotiations: investment requirements, investment amount, operational stage, a project being in the transport sector, the exclusion of private financing, income guarantee, construction delays, being greenfield vs. brownfield, and renegotiations clauses. On the other hand, high leverage, availability payments, foreign shareholders and EIB loans, all tend to decrease the probability of renegotiations. The relationship between contract duration and the likelihood of renegotiation is not consensual, and, in reality, most studies found no relation at all. This is an interesting finding, as the theoretical background suggests that the long duration of contracts was one of the main reasons why such contracts are vulnerable to uncertainty and are not complete. With regards historical performance or experience of the project, only two determinants were

Table 4.10 Determinants of PPP renegotiations

	Endogenous		Exogenous		
	Contract/Project	Experience	Institutional & Governance	Political & Legal	Economic
Contract theory	1.1 Investment requirements	2.1 First renegotiation		1.12 Arbitration process	
	1.2 Contract duration	2.2 Age at renegotiation			
	1.3 Investment amount				
	1.4 High leverage				
	1.5 Availability Payments				
	1.7 Operational stage				
	1.8 EIB loans				
	1.9 Transport sector				
	1.10 Excludes private financing				
	1.11 Income guarantee				
	1.12 Construction delays				
	1.14 Greenfield				
	1.15 Renegotiations clauses				
Transaction cost theory	3.11 Contract viability		4.17 Optimism bias	3.8 Specific legislation	4.6 Unemployment rate
	3.12 Risk rating			3.9 Rule of law	
	3.13 Bidding process				
	3.14 Number of bidders				
	3.15 Award criteria				
	3.16 Multi-criteria				

(continued)

Table 4.10 (continued)

	Endogenous		Exogenous		
	Contract/Project	Experience	Institutional & Governance	Political & Legal	Economic
Institutional Theory			3.10 Corruption index	1.6 Foreign shareholders	5.1 Growth in GDP
			3.17 Reputation	3.1 Bureaucratic quality	5.2 Deficit
			4.8 Unilateral change	3.2 Government effectiveness	5.3 Public debt
				3.3 Regulatory quality	5.4 Exchange rate
				3.4 Price-cap regulation	
				3.5 Regulatory body	
				3.6 Age of the regulator	
				3.7 Autonomous regulator	
				4.1 Electoral year (+/− 1)	
				4.2 Right-wing government	
				4.3 Government change	
				4.4 Majority government	
				4.5 Political stability	

analysed—first renegotiation and age at renegotiation, both of which are positively correlated with the occurrence of renegotiations (Sarmento and Renneboog 2016b; Andrade et al. 2018).

Concerning the determinants related with the institutional and governance context, characteristics such as price-cap regulation, autonomous regulator, specific legislation, the rule of law, bidding process, number of bidders, and award criteria all have a positive influence on the probability of renegotiation. Bureaucratic quality has the opposite effect (reducing the likelihood of renegotiations), as does regulatory quality, the existence of a regulatory body or/and a corruption index (low corruption), the age of the regulator, contract viability, and risk rating. The existence of a multicriteria model in the public procurement appears not to be relevant (Table 4.10).

For the political and legal context, the electoral year (and the lag and lead—the year before and after elections), right-wing government, majority government, optimism bias, and unilateral change, all tend to increase the likelihood of renegotiation, whereas political stability and unemployment rate tend to reduce the likelihood of renegotiation, although only one study has focussed on each of these determinants (Estache et al. 2009). Finally, with regards to the economic context, GDP growth, and deficit, all have a negative impact (although this is not consensual, as some studies show a different effect, as seen in Table 4.8), whereas public debt and exchange rate increase the probability or renegotiation (although the latter is also not consensual).

4.6 Discussion of Results

The empirical literature on PPP renegotiations is growing and casts some light on a previously less-studied process. PPP renegotiations is still a subject that requires greater transparency. However, the literature is already starting to provide certain evidence of patterns regarding renegotiations that can help further enhance policy making and future research (which is to be discussed in the last section).

The contract theory and the transaction costs theory both provide an essential theoretical base for understanding the phenomenon of renegotiations, although they do not replace the real world evidence that can be extracted from empirical research. In the same way that experience in the use and operation of PPPs is growing, so is the historical operation period, and thus there is an increase in the respective available data and the number of empirical studies published, as seen in Sect. 3 of this chapter. Nevertheless, these are not as frequent as one would expect, and there are many countries with enormous experience in PPPs which still have very little relevant academic research on the topic of PPP renegotiations, e.g., UK, Canada, or Australia.

The main findings of the literature are summarised below, organised around our initial research questions which guided this literature review.

4.6.1 How Frequent Are Renegotiations in PPPs?

Renegotiations are very frequent. Most studies identify a renegotiation rate of above 50%, however, considering that some studies are already 10–15 years' old, it is extremely likely that many of the PPPs that still had not been renegotiated when the studies were carried out might have been renegotiated in the meantime. Regarding the occurrence of renegotiations, the literature shows that the question is not so much whether renegotiations will occur, but rather when. This empirical evidence is supported by the contract theory, which claims that renegotiations are inevitable at some point of the project (Tirole 1999), mainly because the incomplete nature of the contract will be tested by an unveiling circumstance.

4.6.2 Who Initiates the Renegotiation Process?

Typically, the private sector initiates the renegotiation process, in response to a change requested by the government or to a lower volume of demand and revenue than initially forecast. However, the literature also provides evidence that governments can also strategically use renegotiations to increase spending, as a way of bypassing State budgets and/or adjusting the projects due to political motivations (specially before elections), which can be verified by the main motives for renegotiations. The institutional theory also supports this evidence. The flaws in the institutional, governance, and legal contexts all help to justify strategic and opportunistic behaviours by agents, as argued by Guasch et al. (2003).

4.6.3 When Do Renegotiations Happen?

The literature shows that PPP renegotiations tend to occur very early in the contract, and therefore their occurrence cannot be linked exclusively to uncertainty regarding the project, although in capital-intensive construction projects, uncertainty is real and significant. Clearly, several pitfalls exist during the planning stage, which increase the probability of renegotiations.

4.6.4 What Are the Main Motives for the Occurrence of Renegotiations?

Two motives emerge as being the most common: projects and contracts changes and demand/consumption below the level forecast. There are technical and institutional reasons behind these motives. For example, they might be related to poor planning and bad preparation of the procurement process, or they can be politically motivated by excessive optimism and opportunism by governments. What is clear is that projects submitted for procurement lack the technical or political maturity to ensure that they perform well. The proof of this is that contracts fail too early on.

4.6.5 What Are the Main Results of Renegotiations?

The main results of renegotiations are an increase in users' tariffs and in the level of direct payments to the concessionaire, which can either be carried out by paying a lump sum, or by means of periodical payments for a certain time period, up until the end of the contract. This represents an asymmetric bias towards concessionaires. It is important to mention that while the contract award stage occurs in a competitive environment, renegotiations take place in a bilateral environment, with significant information asymmetry problems.

4.6.6 What Are the Main Determinants of Renegotiation Processes?

The identification of the determinants of renegotiation processes in PPP projects has been at the core of the empirical research on this subject. The consensual key factor regarding the determinants is the role played by a robust institutional and legal/ regulatory framework in reducing the likelihood of renegotiation. A structural improvement in the management of complex projects and capital-intensive large construction projects is only possible by improving the overall institutional, legal, and political context.

However, at project level, some important determinants also exist. Some are difficult to act upon, such as, for example, the fact that larger projects are more prone to renegotiation, although others can be redesigned. For example, the literature shows that with higher leverage, the likelihood of renegotiation decreases, or at least it is reduced when the level of risk transfer is mitigated by using, for example, availability payments. The evidence suggests that excessive risk transfer could have a significant *ex-post* cost in future renegotiations. These findings confirm the hypotheses of several authors who have been researching the topic of risk management in PPPs, such as Kumar et al. (2018), or Hodge and Greve (2009), who found that full risk transfer to concessionaires might not be the optimal solution. On the contrary, each party should bear the risks that they have the capacity to manage.

4.7 Main Literature Gaps

Both at the theoretical and empirical levels, renegotiations are attracting significant attention from researchers. Over the last 10 years, empirical research has been growing, which is a natural result of the PPP experience. Most countries developed PPP starting the mid-1990s and 2000s, and relevant databases are now available for analysis. However, certain literature gaps need to be addressed.

First, the fact that most empirical evidence targets Latin-American countries and Mediterranean countries. For there are no studies which examine the empirical evidence of renegotiations with large databases (of projects and time series) for Anglo-Saxon countries. Do these countries have the same patterns? Are there any changes in the determinants? This is more relevant, considering that the UK experience has inspired most PPP programmes around the world.

Second, little is known about the actual economic and social benefit of the changes made in renegotiations. The data shows that physical changes in the projects are one of the main reasons for renegotiations. What are the economic and social consequences of such changes? The literature also shows that these changes are carried out at the expenses of the public budget, however, what are the broader economic and social benefits (or costs) or such changes? Fernandes et al. (2019) analysed a case-study, and show that besides an increase in government costs, there might also be additional costs for users. Yet, more evidence based on a greater number of projects is fundamental to evaluate whether the costs of renegotiations are far more relevant than the increase in the government burden.

Third, in many cases, the changes that the literature presents as being strategic behaviour, are still not well understood. Campos et al. (2019) introduce a new perspective, questioning the link between renegotiations and corruption, using the case study of the Brazilian construction firm Odebrecht. This is a new and promising area of research, which should lead to surprising findings over the following years.

Fourth, the literature suggests the adoption of flexibility as a means to tackle renegotiations, although this trade-off "flexibility-adaptation" still lacks empirical validation. What is the effect of flexibility on competition for the project and on value for money? Are flexible contracts less vulnerable to renegotiations?

4.8 Policy Implications

Renegotiations will always be an important feature of PPP management, particularly when dealing with large public infrastructure which are subject to a high level of uncertainty. This potential inevitability of renegotiations does not necessarily mean that areas exist where it is possible to innovate and develop mechanisms to improve the performance of renegotiation processes.

The empirical evidence suggests that exogenous determinants play a fundamental role, and that therefore all the institutional and governance improvements that are carried out at a country-wide level that lead to an increase in the efficiency of the government, regulators, and the rule-of-law can all reduce the likelihood of renegotiations and/or improve a contract's performance. Nevertheless, these are changes that can take a generation to occur, and thus the influence of a project manager is practically null. Does this mean that little can be done to reduce the probability of renegotiations in the short term? Quite to the contrary.

This literature review provides evidence that endogenous determinants also play a fundamental role. For example, construction delays, risk-sharing, or financing structure can all be used to reduce the likelihood of renegotiation.

At the level of contract design, research is evolving towards the concept of "flexible contracts", as discussed, for example, by Xiong and Zhang (2014). In this case, the rationale is that if the future cannot be entirely predicted, then the contract should be as flexible as possible. This flexibility can be in the form of contractual flexibility, whereby, for example, a flexible payment mechanism could be implemented which can be adjusted to changing demand conditions. However, the potential impact of such contractual flexibility is more limited than the possibility of embedding options in the infrastructure design which can be exercised under new circumstances.

Future research in PPP renegotiation is expected to evolve in two directions. The first is to increase our knowledge of the patterns of renegotiations outcomes—which are still relatively unknown. Examples include knowing what determines opting for government payments, rather than contract extensions or an increase in users' tariffs, and also what are the dynamics of the renegotiation process, from a project management perspective. The second is to explore the concept of "flexible contracts" and to see how the recent trend towards digitalisation in construction and infrastructure can be used to reduce uncertainty, or to allow for a better adaptation to uncertainty in the long-term, which would thus minimise the need to renegotiate in an asymmetric environment.

References

Aghion, P., & Tirole, J. (1994). The management of innovation. *The Quarterly Journal of Economics, 109*(4), 1185–1209.

Andrade, I., Cruz, C. O., & Sarmento, J. M. (2018). Renegotiations of water concessions: Empirical analysis of main determinants. *Journal of Water Resources Planning and Management, 144* (11), 04018073.

Artana, D., Navajas, F., & Urbiztondo, S. (1998). *Regulation and contractual adaptation in public utilities: the case of Argentina* (p. 115). Infrastructure and financial markets division: Inter-American development bank, Sustainable development department.

Bae, D. S., Damnjanoic, I., & Kang, D. H. (2019). PPP renegotiation framework based on equivalent NPV constraint in the case of BOT project: Incheon Airport Highway, South Korea. *KSCE Journal of Civil Engineering, 23*(4), 1473–1483.

Bajari, P., & Tadelis, S. (2001). Incentives versus transaction costs: A theory of procurement contracts. *Rand journal of Economics*, 387–407.

Bitran, E., Nieto-Parra, S., & Robledo, J. S. (2013). Opening the black box of contract renegotiations: An analysis of road concessions in Chile., Colombia and Peru.

de Brux, J. (2010). The dark and bright sides of renegotiation: An application to transport concession contracts. *Utilities Policy, 18*(2), 77–85. https://doi.org/10.1016/j.jup.2009.07.003.

Campos, N., Engel, E., Fischer, R., & Galetovic, A. (2019). Renegotiations and corruption in infrastructure: The Odebrecht case (No. 0230). Dipartimento di Scienze Economiche "Marco Fanno".

Crocker, K. J., & Reynolds, K. J. (1993). The efficiency of incomplete contracts: An empirical analysis of air force engine procurement. *The RAND Journal of Economics, 24*, 126–146.

Cruz, C. O., & Marques, R. C. (2012). Using the economic and financial reequilibrium model to decrease infrastructure contract incompleteness. *Journal of Infrastructure Systems, 19*(1), 58–66.

Cruz, C. O., & Marques, R. C. (2013a). Endogenous determinants for renegotiating concessions: Evidence from local infrastructure. *Local Government Studies, 39*(3), 352–374. https://doi.org/10.1080/03003930.2013.783476.

Cruz, C. O., & Marques, R. C. (2013b). Exogenous determinants for renegotiating public infrastructure concessions: Evidence from Portugal. *Journal of Construction Engineering and Management, 139*(9), 1082–1090. https://doi.org/10.1061/(ASCE)CO.1943-7862.0000710.

Cruz, C. O., & Marques, R. C. (2013c). Integrating infrastructure and clinical management in PPPs for health care. *Journal of Management in Engineering, 29*(4), 471–481.

Cruz, C. O., Marques, R. C., & Franco, D. (2015). Road-network development in quickly-growing economies: Brazilian case study MG-050. *Journal of Infrastructure Systems, 21*(4), 05015002.

Dewatripont, M. (1988). Commitment through renegotiation-proof contracts with third parties. *The Review of Economic Studies, 55*(3), 377–390.

Dolla, T., & Laishram, B. S. (2018). Procurement of low carbon municipal solid waste infrastructure in India through public-private partnerships. *Built Environment Project and Asset Management, 8*(5), 449–460.

Domingues, S., & Sarmento, J. M. (2016). Critical renegotiation triggers of European transport concessions. *Transport Policy, 48*, 82–91. https://doi.org/10.1016/j.tranpol.2016.02.016.

Domingues, S., & Zlatkovic, D. (2015). Renegotiating PPP contracts: Reinforcing the "P" in partnership. *Transport Reviews, 35*(2), 204–225. https://doi.org/10.1080/01441647.2014.992495.

Edlin, A. S., & Hermalin, B. E. (1997). Contract renegotiation in agency problems (No. w6086). National Bureau of Economic Research.

Engel, E., Fischer, R., & Galetovic, A. (2006). *Renegotiation without holdup: Anticipating spending and infrastructure concessions*. National Bureau of economic research working paper series (vol. no. 12399). https://doi.org/10.3386/w12399

Engel, E., Fischer, R., & Galetovic, A. (2009). *Soft budgets and renegotiations in public-private partnerships*. National bureau of economic research working paper series (vol. no. 15300). https://doi.org/10.2139/ssrn.1460688

Estache, A., Guasch, J. L., Iimi, A., & Trujillo, L. (2009). Multidimensionality and renegotiation: Evidence from transport-sector public-private-partnership transactions in Latin America. *Review of Industrial Organization, 35*, 41–71. https://doi.org/10.1007/s11151-009-9225-0.

Estache, A., Guasch, J.-L., & Trujillo, L. (2003). *Price caps, efficiency payoffs and infrastructure contract renegotiation in Latin America*. World bank policy research working paper 3129. https://doi.org/10.1596/1813-9450-3129

Fernandes, C., Cruz, C. O., & Moura, F. (2019). Ex post evaluation of PPP government-led renegotiations: Impacts on the financing of road infrastructure. *The Engineering Economist, 64*, 116–141. https://doi.org/10.1080/0013791X.2018.1559384.

Green, J. R., & Laffont, J. J. (1992). Renegotiation and the form of efficient contracts. *Annales d'Economie et de Statistique*, 123–150.

Guasch, J. L. (2004). *Granting and renegotiating infrastructure concessions: Doing it right.* Washington, DC: The World Bank. Retrieved from www.worldbank.org

Guasch, J. L., Benitez, D., Portabales, I., & Flor, L. (2014). *The renegotiation of PPP contracts: An overview of its recent evolution in Latin America*. Discussion paper 2014–18, International Transport Forum, OECD.

Guasch, J. L., Laffont, J. J., & Straub, S. (2003). *Renegotiation of concessions contracts in Latin America*. Policy research working paper 3011, The World Bank.

Guasch, J. L., Laffont, J. J., & Straub, S. (2006). Renegotiation of concession contracts: A theoretical approach. *Review of Industrial Organization, 29*(1–2), 55–73. https://doi.org/10.1007/s11151-006-9109-5.

Guasch, J. L., Laffont, J. J., & Straub, S. (2007). Concessions of infrastructure in Latin America: Government-led renegotiation. *Journal of Applied Econometrics, 22*, 1267–1294. https://doi.org/10.1002/jae.

Guasch, J. L., Laffont, J. J., & Straub, S. (2008). Renegotiation of concession contracts in Latin America. Evidence from the water and transport sectors. *International Journal of Industrial Organization, 26*(2), 421–442. https://doi.org/10.1016/j.ijindorg.2007.05.003.

Guasch, J. L., & Straub, S. (2009). Corruption and concession renegotiations. Evidence from the water and transport sectors in Latin America. *Utilities Policy, 17*(2), 185–190. https://doi.org/10.1016/j.jup.2008.07.003.

Hart, O., & Moore, J. (1988). Incomplete contracts and renegotiation. *Econometrica: Journal of the Econometric Society*, 755–785.

Ho, S. P. (2006). Model for financial renegotiation in public-private partnership projects and its policy implications: Game theoretic view. *Journal of Construction Engineering and Management, 132*(7), 678–688.

Hodge, G. A., & Greve, C. (2009). PPPs: The passage of time permits a sober reflection. *Economic Affairs, 29*(1), 33–39.

Holmstrom, B. R., & Tirole, J. (1989). The theory of the firm. *Handbook of Industrial Organization, 1*, 61–133.

Howell, B., & Sadowski, B. (2018). Anatomy of a public-private partnership: Hold-up and regulatory commitment in Ultrafast Broadband. *Telecommunications Policy, 42*(7), 552–565.

Khallaf, R., Naderpajouh, N., & Hastak, M. (2016). A risk registry for renegotiation in public private partnerships (PPP) projects: ICRAM-PPP. In *Construction research congress 2016: Old and new construction technologies in historic San Juan* (pp. 2669–2678). American Society of Civil Engineers.

Khallaf, R., Naderpajouh, N., & Hastak, M. (2018). Modeling three-party interactional risks in the governance of public–private partnerships. *Journal of Management in Engineering, 34*(6), 04018040.

Klein, B., Crawford, R. G., & Alchian, A. A. (1978). Vertical integration, appropriable rents, and the competitive contracting process. *The journal of Law and Economics, 21*(2), 297–326.

Kumar, L., Jindal, A., & Velaga, N. R. (2018). Financial risk assessment and modelling of PPP based Indian highway infrastructure projects. *Transport Policy, 62*, 2–11.

Li, X., & Hao, S. (2017, July). The PPP project renegotiation analysis based on the asymmetric game model. In *2017 4th International conference on industrial economics system and industrial security engineering (IEIS)* (pp. 1–5). IEEE.

Lohmann, C., & Rötzel, P. G. (2014). Opportunistic behavior in renegotiations between public-private partnerships and government institutions: Data on public-private partnerships of the German armed forces. *International Public Management Journal, 17*(3), 387–410.

Lohmann, C., & Rötzel, P. G. (2018). The outcome of renegotiations between institutionalized public–private partnerships and their public clients: Data on the public–private partnerships of the german federal armed forces. *International Journal of Public Administration, 41*(9), 735–745.

Macário, M. D. R. M. R., Costa, J. D., & Ribeiro, J. A. M. (2015). Cross-sector analysis of four renegotiated transport PPPs in Portugal. *Transport Reviews, 35*(2), 226–244. https://doi.org/10.1080/01441647.2015.1012755.

Maskin, E., & Moore, J. (1999). Implementation and renegotiation. Review of Economic studies, 39–56.

Menezes, F., & Ryan, M. (2015). Default and renegotiation in public-private partnership auctions. *Journal of Public Economic Theory, 17*(1), 49–77.

Neto, D., Cruz, C. O., & Sarmento, J. M. (2017). Understanding the patterns of PPP renegotiations for infrastructure projects in Latin America: The case of Brazil. *Competition and Regulation in Network Industries, 18*(3-4), 271–296.

Nikolaidis, N., & Roumboutsos, A. (2013). A PPP renegotiation framework: A road concession in Greece. *Built Environment Project and Asset Management, 3*(2), 264–278.

Owusu-Manu, D. G., Edwards, D. J., Kukah, A. S., Parn, E. A., El-Gohary, H., & Hosseini, M. R. (2018). An empirical examination of moral hazards and adverse selection on PPP projects: A case study of Ghana. *Journal of Engineering, Design and Technology, 16*(6), 910–924.

Sarmento, J. M., & Renneboog, L. (2016a). Anatomy of public-private partnerships: Their creation, financing and renegotiations. *International Journal of Managing Projects in Business, 9*(1), 94–122.

Sarmento, J. M. & Renneboog, L. (2016b). *Renegotiating public-private partnerships*. European Corporate Governance Institute (ECGI)-finance working paper (461).

Sarmento, J. M., & Renneboog, L. (2017). Cost overruns in public sector investment projects. *Public Works Management & Policy, 22*(2), 140–164.

Sharafi, A., Taleizadeh, A. A., & Amalnick, M. S. (2018). Fair allocation in financial disputes between public–private partnership stakeholders using game theory. *Service Science, 10*(1), 1–11.

Shi, L., Zhang, L., Onishi, M., Kobayashi, K., & Dai, D. (2018). Contractual efficiency of PPP infrastructure projects: An incomplete contract model. *Mathematical Problems in Engineering, 2018*, 3631270.

Soliño, A. S., & Gago de Santos, P. (2016). Influence of the tendering mechanism in the performance of public-private partnerships: A transaction cost approach. *Public Performance & Management Review, 40*(1), 97–118.

Squeren, Z. L., & Moore, J. (2015). The political cycle of public-private contract renegotiations: Evidence from the French car park sector. In *19th Annual Conference of the international society for new institutional economics - ISNIE 2015* (pp. 1–43).

Sun, H., & Yin, X. (2017). Seek a positive renegotiation mechanism for PPP projects. In *Advances in public-private partnerships* (pp. 354–364). Reston, VA: American Society of Civil Engineers.

Tirole, J. (1999). Incomplete contracts: Where do we stand? *Econometrica, 67*(4), 741–781.

Valéro, V. (2015). Government opportunism in public-private partnerships. *Journal of Public Economic Theory, 17*(1), 111–135.

Wee, B. V., & Banister, D. (2016). How to write a literature review paper? *Transport Reviews, 36* (2), 278–288.

Williamson, O. E. (1976). Franchise bidding for natural monopolies – in general and with respect to CATV. *Bell Journal of Economics, 7*(1), 73–104.

Wu, S. & Yang, Y. (2016, May). Analysis and review of key factors at PPP project renegotiation. In *2016 International conference on education, management and computer science*. Atlantis Press.

Xiong, W., & Zhang, X. (2014). The real option value of renegotiation in public–private partnerships. *Journal of Construction Engineering and Management* (February), 4016021. https://doi.org/10.1061/(ASCE)CO.1943-7862.0001130

Xiong, W., & Zhang, X. (2016). The real option value of renegotiation in public–private partnerships. *Journal of construction engineering and management, 142*(8) 04016021.

Xiong, W., Zhao, X., & Wang, H. (2018). Information asymmetry in renegotiation of public–private partnership projects. *Journal of Computing in Civil Engineering, 32*(4), 04018028.

Xiong, W., Zhao, X., Yuan, J. F., & Luo, S. (2017). Ex post risk management in public-private partnership infrastructure projects. *Project Management Journal, 48*(3), 76–89.

Zhang, X., & Xiong, W. (2015). Renegotiation and early-termination in public private partnerships. *International Journal of Architecture, Engineering and Construction, 4*(4), 204–213. https://doi.org/10.7492/IJAEC.2015.021.

Chapter 5
Country Analysis

5.1 USA

5.1.1 Framework

There is a strong and urgent need for investment in infrastructures in the United States. The Report Card of the American Society of Civil Engineers (ASCE) gives the country's infrastructure a D+, and estimates that the sector will need US$3.6 trillion by 2020 (ASCE 2017).

Few areas within public policy have gathered such political consensus such as infrastructure investment. In 2014, President Obama announce a mega infrastructure plan worth over 300 bn to ensure the recovery of the infrastructure system, in particular transportation-related infrastructure; more recently, in February 2018, President Trump also presented an infrastructure plan with US$200 billion in federal funding, as well as an additional US$1.5 trillion from private sector funding.

Toll road projects were the first PPPs to be celebrated in the US, more commonly referred to as P3s. These started out as typical concessions, where the concessionaire was awarded the right to build and/or operate a road infrastructure, in return for receiving the revenues from the tolls for a certain period of time. A common example is the Chicago Skyway Toll Bridge—a 7.8 mile long road which was built back in 1958 by the City of Chicago and then transferred to the Skyway Concession Company LLC under a lease agreement for 99-years. This was considered to be the first case of the concession of an existing toll road in the US. Additionally, there has been an on-going trend over the last decade to witness pension funds to buy participations in infrastructure projects, particularly those under concession agreements, for which most of the risks no longer apply (e.g., construction and demand risk). In cases when such projects are performing poorly, with significant levels of debt and are incapable of generating revenues to cover the debt service and/or remunerate the shareholders, these funds often buy these assets with significant

C. Oliveira Cruz, J. Miranda Sarmento, *The Renegotiations of Public Private Partnerships in Transportation*, Competitive Government: Public Private Partnerships, https://doi.org/10.1007/978-3-030-61258-0_5

discounts. In effect, construction companies and banks often just want to cut their losses and walk away, accepting severe price cuts.

Nowadays, the US authorities are considering a much wider range of projects, including social infrastructure, such as power, waste and water, among others (PWC 2016; Casady and Geddes 2016). Over the last decade, there has been a growing interest from private investors and particularly from pension funds to invest in these infrastructure. Investors are looking for low risk and long term investments, and public infrastructure often meet both these criteria.

As in most countries, the US has used the PPP/concession model for large infrastructures, although, more recently, it has experimented using PPPs for smaller projects, which are bundled together to ensure a minimum viable dimension. An example is the Rapid Bridge Replacement Project in Pennsylvania, comprising a total of 558 bridges, with a total value of US$900 million.

5.1.2 Overall Legal and Regulatory Framework

It is very difficult to commonly characterise the legal framework in the US, because it varies significantly from state to state. As discussed by Mirchandani and Jacobo (2020), there is no uniform statutory definition of a PPP in the US, and thus the legal organisation of transactions has varied from state to state. In some states, the existing procurement regulations forced the separation of design from the procurement of the construction (Mirchandani and Jacobo 2020). The legislation applicable to PPP includes the general rules and regulations for procurement, as well as common law, unless the state has enacted PPP-specific legislation.

Several states have enacted legislation which enables the use of PPPs, with varying degrees of flexibility and complexity (see Fig. 5.1).

5.1.3 PPP Governance and Management

There is not a specific and centralised PPP unit. The administrative entities of the US do not facilitate the typical governance and management of PPPs which is in place in other countries. Nevertheless, some entities in the US exercise direct or indirect responsibilities over the management of PPP projects, namely the Federal Highway Administration (FHWA) of the Department of State, the Office of Global Partnerships, and the National Council for PPPs.

The Federal Highway Administration

In 2019, the FHWA released a guide entitled "Public-Private Partnerships (P3 Procurement: A Guide for Public Owners". The main objective was to

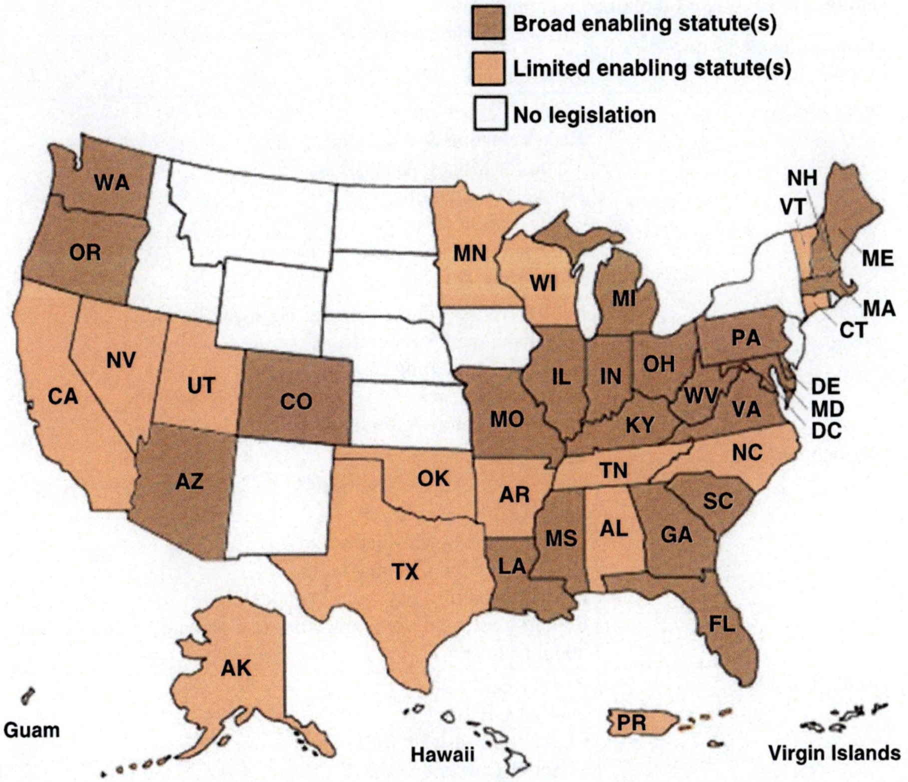

Fig. 5.1 States which have enacted legislation for PPPs (Source: FHWA, 2018)

> provide advanced guidance on procedures, issues, and considerations involved in public-private partnership (P3) procurement of surface transportation projects, in particular for highway and transit investments. This Guidebook is part of the P3 Toolkit that consists of P3 guidance documents and tools to assist in educating Federal, State, and local policy makers, legislative and executive staff, and transportation professionals. (Federal Highway Administration 2019)

The release of this type of guide is a typical function of PPP units—with the objective to contribute with knowhow and directives to facilitate and promote the development of PPPs. In fact, this procurement tool is part of a larger initiative which is designated the FHWA P3 Toolkit, whose main elements are summarised in Table 5.1.

Department of State; Office of Global Partnerships

The Office of Global Partnerships is located within the Department of State. Its objective is to enhance foreign policy through private sector engagement. It does not have any technical or operative role in the development and management of PPPs, but plays an important political and strategic role in identifying investment

Table 5.1 FHWA P3 toolkit core components

Core components of the P3 toolkit	Description
Fact Sheets	FHWA P3 Toolkit Risk Valuation & Allocation Value for Money Analysis Financial Structuring Analytical Studies Conducting Procurements Monitoring & Oversight
Primers	Public-Private Concessions for Highway Projects Establishing a P3 Program Financial Structuring & Assessment Risk Assessment Value for Money Assessment
Guidebooks	Risk Assessment Value for Money Assessment P3 Project Financing P3 Procurement (this document) Toll Concession Contract Guide Draft Availability Payment Contract Guide Benefit-Cost Analysis Framework to Compare P3 and Conventional Delivery
Analytical Tools	P3-SCREEN P3-VALUE 2.1 • Excel Spreadsheet Tool • User & Concept Guide • Quick Start Guide • FAQs

Source: FHWA

opportunities and in providing the roadmap and navigating instructions for the effective and successful implementation of the projects. Its remit is not limited to infrastructure projects and it has a specific accelerator programme for PPP projects which is designated "Boldline: The P3 Accelerator".

5.1.4 Projects Overview

The Chicago Skyway was a milestone in the US PPP market. However, since then, the market has grown significantly. According to Deye (2015), 48 infrastructure PPP transactions were carried out between 2005 and 2014, with an aggregate value of 61 billion dollars. The majority of transactions were successful, although there were a few failed transactions (e.g., Texas's US$3.5 billion SH-121 in 2007, the US$12.8 billion Pennsylvania Turnpike lease in 2008, the US$452 million Pittsburgh Parking concession in 2010, and the US$2.5 billion Chicago Midway Airport lease in 2009 and 2013) (Deye 2015). Recently, the ASCE (2017) estimated a need for investment totalling 1.6 trillion dollars over the next five years (which is an amount similar to Italy's GDP, as mentioned by Deloitte (2017)).

With public budgets under pressure, and an extremely high public debt, US Federal and State governments will struggle to keep pace with infrastructure investment. The ability of PPPs to raise private capital, will certainly provide an important incentive for decision makers.

5.2 UK

5.2.1 Framework

Anglo-Saxon experience is often cited as an important reference in the field of PPPs (perhaps even the most relevant and important) and has influenced many of the policy choices made in other countries (Osborne 2000; Li et al. 2005; Yescombe and Farquharson 2018). The beginning of PPPs, as we know them, is commonly positioned in the early 1990s in the United Kingdom—where it is also known as Private Finance Initiative (PFI), although the concept of concession dates back earlier (Hodge and Greve 2007; Cruz and Sarmento 2019). Furthermore, aware of the problems associated with the model, the governments of Anglo-Saxon countries have been carrying out reforms themselves and have implemented changes in the way partnerships are contracted and established (Froud 2003; Shaoul 2005).

For example, in 2012, the United Kingdom reviewed almost two decades of experience of using PFI, and defined a set of strategic guidelines for a new model which it dubbed PFI2 (known as PF2), i.e., a version 2 of the initial model, which seeks to address the main weaknesses identified and, at the same time, enhance the model's ability to generate Value for Money (VfM) for the public sector (Heald 2003; Li et al. 2005; et al. 2020; H.M. Treasury 2012). Another example is Canada, which changed structural aspects in how it allocated risk during the second wave of PPP (Siemiatycki 2015; Opara and Rouse 2019).

PF2 implied a series of structural changes to the PFI model (H.M. Treasury 2012; Richards et al. 2019). The following featured among the key changes:

- The Public sector taking around 10% of equity interest in PFI vehicles;
- Shorter tendering processes;
- The unbundling of soft facilities management services (and removal from the contract);
- The sharing of funding benefits in the long run;
- The promotion of funding contests for the private sector equity in PFI vehicles;
- Transferring more risk to the public sector, thus reducing the level of uncertainty for private investors, resulting in the potential impact of a reduction in financing cost;

- Greater transparency, in order to ensure public access to the following information for each project.[1]

5.2.2 Overall Legal and Regulatory Framework

The United Kingdom does not have specific PPP laws, as the Common Law system has sufficient flexibility to recognise and allow PPPs (Shadrina and Vinogradov 2013; Van Den Hurk and Verhoest 2016). Countries such as France, Portugal, and Spain all have civil law-based systems, featuring administrative laws which determine and develop a legal framework (including, for example, the right of the concessionaire to claim for a compensation, or the right of the grantor to unilaterally change the contract in order to protect the public interest).

Irrespective of the differences between the two systems, the risks, challenges, and the structuring of a PPP can be quite similar in different countries, and, as such, the UK experience has frequently served as a reference for civil law countries. In fact, many of the international private players in the PPP market often operate in both civil and common law countries, without any significant difference in terms of contractual structure and, more importantly, risk allocation (Roumboutsos and Anagnostopoulos 2008; Hodge and Greve 2007).

The lack of a specific legislation does not mean, however, that extensive technical, legal, and financial supporting documentation does not exist to guide all stages of the process and to ensure best practice and knowledge transfer. Indeed, such comprehensive documentation can be consulted in NAO website.[2] One of the most recent examples is the guide called "Standardisation of PF2 contracts", which addresses various issues related to the evaluation, design, implementation, and management of PFI/PPP projects.

Towards the end of the first decade of the twenty-first century, resulting from an in-depth analysis of the nearly 20-year experience of PPPs, the UK government understood that, despite the potential advantages of the PPP model, there had been less successful cases and not very positive experiences. From the public interest point of view, this negative experience, together with a substantial change in the market and the economic and financial context at the time, combined to justify a review of the way projects were evaluated and developed.

Accordingly, in 2012, HM Treasury released its vision for the PPP sector, identifying the various drivers of change. The review of the past experience

[1]A unique HMT project ID and project name; the sponsoring department and the procuring authority; the sector and region; key dates - such as the beginning and end of the procurement process; the duration of the contract; a balance sheet and budget control; the capital value; forecast annual payments, identification of the shareholders; the project company's name and address.

[2]https://www.nao.org.uk.

identified the following main weaknesses in the use of the PPP model (HM Treasury 2012):

- PFI procurement was, as a rule, very slow and costly for both the public and private sectors, with obvious consequences for reducing VfM;
- PFI contracts have proved to be too rigid during the operational period, making it difficult to adapt as a result of new service requirements;
- There was a lack of full transparency regarding the future charges generated by PFI projects to taxpayers and also about the actual returns of projects to investors, which in many cases are estimated to have been greater than commercially-acceptable values;
- Inappropriate risks were transferred to the private sector, which resulted in higher risk premiums and lower VfM;

In order to overcome the identified weaknesses, priority reform areas were defined, which were to constitute the strategic guidelines for a new wave called PFI2. These priority areas are as follows (HM Treasury 2012).

1. **Financing**—Government strategy should include:

   - Acting as a minority public equity co-investor in PF2 projects; and
   - The introduction of funding contests to attain a sufficiently good capital ratio to attract project investors before the financial closure.

2. **Contracting**—One of the problems with the PFI procurement processes was precisely the excessive duration and associated high costs, and thus there is a necessity to:

   - Improve the public sector procurement process management capacity through Infrastructure UK and develop centralised procurement units; the whole hiring process cannot exceed 18 months;
   - Standardise hiring procedures and reinforced the scrutiny of the process.

3. **Flexibility**—The rigidity of contracts is a problem during the operation phase, and therefore there is a need to introduce flexibility through, for example:

   - Soft services, such as cleaning and catering, need to be removed from projects, which will facilitate any changes to the requirements of these services;
   - Flexible options need to be established regarding whether or not to add or remove certain elective services, an example being light maintenance activities, once the contract is in operation;
   - The introduction of infrastructure-sharing mechanisms for lifecycle management;
   - The phasing in of periodic reviews of service delivery.

4. **Transparency**—Increasing project transparency has been identified as a critical

factor, with the associated following actions:

- Ensure full control and transparency for commitments under FP2 contracts;
- Require the private sector to provide accurate and real information on profitability;
- Publish an annual report detailing project and financial information for all projects where the government is a shareholder;
- Introduce follow-up mechanisms for the business case approval process on the Treasury website; and
- Improve information exchange at the contractual level.

5. **Risk Allocation**: To improve cost-effectiveness, a more optimised approach is required for when choosing the risks to be managed by the public sector, including the risk of additional capital expenditures arising from an unpredictable change in law, or service costs (i.e., energy, water, etc.), site contamination, or insurance premiums.
6. **Future debt financing**: it was decided that design of the financing structure of PF2 must allow access to long-term debt financing, especially to the capital market.
7. **VfM**: The VfM evaluation process should be reviewed with the aim to incorporate more accurate mechanisms and techniques for performing this test.

5.2.3 PPP Governance and Management

In the UK, the main Authorities (or public bodies) which have responsibility for PPP projects are the following (Richards et al. 2019):

- Her Majesty's Treasury, which controls public spending and sets the general direction and policy on PPP. It also approves the project business cases;
- the Cabinet Office, which oversees the standards and efficiency of government functions and procurement and approves procurement structures;
- The Infrastructure and Projects Authority (IPA), which helps translate long-term planning into successful projects. The IPA publishes National Infrastructure Delivery Plans to cover infrastructure policy over a five-year period;
- procuring bodies: the authorities that structure and procure projects. They are the contracting party and manage the project and pay the contractor;
- independent regulators: some areas of activity are regulated by a specific body, for example, gas and electricity, large airports, water, and environment;
- planning authorities that decide whether to grant development consent for a project. The size and location of the project will define who the relevant planning authority is; and
- the Controller and National Audit Office, which scrutinises government spending. The Comptroller and National Audit Office recently published a report on the costs and benefits of PFI/PF2.

As mentioned at the start of this UK subsection, PPPs are commonly referred to as PFIs (Private Finance Initiative) in the United Kingdom, and their initial use can be traced back to the early 1990s. Prior to 1989, there were formal limitations on private equity participation in public infrastructure financing, however these were removed later that year (Li et al. 2005).

One of the most distinguishing aspects of the UK experience in the use of PPP/PFI is that an early monitoring and continuous improvement of the contract design, implementation, and management process has been carried out. This resulted in the first formal use revision of the model being carried out in 1997, in what became known as the "Bates review", with a second review being carried out just two years later. One of the recommendations that emerged from these reviews was the need to set up a dedicated body to prepare, review, control, and monitor PPP projects. This organisation, later to be known as Partnerships UK, replaced the previously-existing Task Force. Partnerships UK was later absorbed by Infrastructure UK, which was set up as part of HM Treasury, which not only has the responsibility to ensure that PFIs are to be developed, but also to support public policy formulation in the areas of transport, energy, and the environment. In 2016, Infrastructure UK became part of the Infrastructure and Projects Authority.

This unit is responsible for the oversight of its portfolio of projects (both ones under development and prospective ones), although it does not necessarily manage the projects from a tactical and operational perspective. However, its approval is mandatory for the development of the projects.

This centralised strategic management of projects is highly beneficial, for several distinct reasons (H.M. Treasury 2010), as it:

(a) Consolidates the learning curve, and offers a "reservoir" of knowledge;
(b) Facilitates the identification of best practices and their roll-out to other projects;
(c) Ensures a benchmark of common projects, which thus pressurises project developers to achieve a higher value for money;
(d) Enforces a common evaluation approach for the portfolio of projects, which maximises the possibility of developing optimal portfolios from a public interest perspective;
(e) Decreases the likelihood of a potential optimism bias not only in terms of forecast revenue (Cruz and Sarmento 2019), but also in terms of the underestimation of construction costs (which is very common in large construction projects—see more in Catalão et al. 2019).
(f) Ensures an alignment of the portfolio with the overall strategy for infrastructure development and management.

Infrastructure UK establishes a roadmap for the management of complex capital investment programmes, in order to ensure robustness and efficiency in such processes (which is summarised in Fig. 5.2).

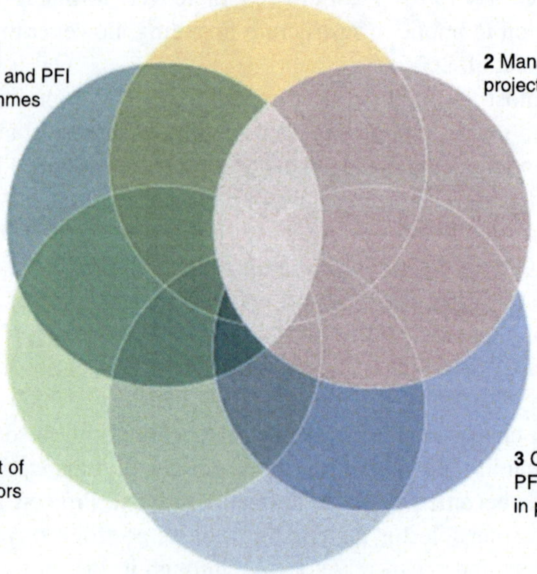

Fig. 5.2 Six basic functions for the management of complex capital investment programmes (Source: H.M. Treasury, 2010)

5.2.4 *Projects Overview*

Since the mid-1990s, there has been a notable increase both in the number of projects and also in the capital value of these projects (see Fig. 5.3). The most significant and structural decrease in the use of the model was at the beginning of the 2008 financial crises, when many projects were abandoned, the availability of capital was scarce, and the cost of capital was very high. Even with the surge of the PF2 initiative, the number (and value) of projects did not increase significantly.

Unlike most countries, where the transportation sector has been, by far, the major beneficiary of PPP projects, it is the Department of Education and Health and Social Care which takes the lead in the UK, both in terms of number of projects and capital value (see Fig. 5.4).

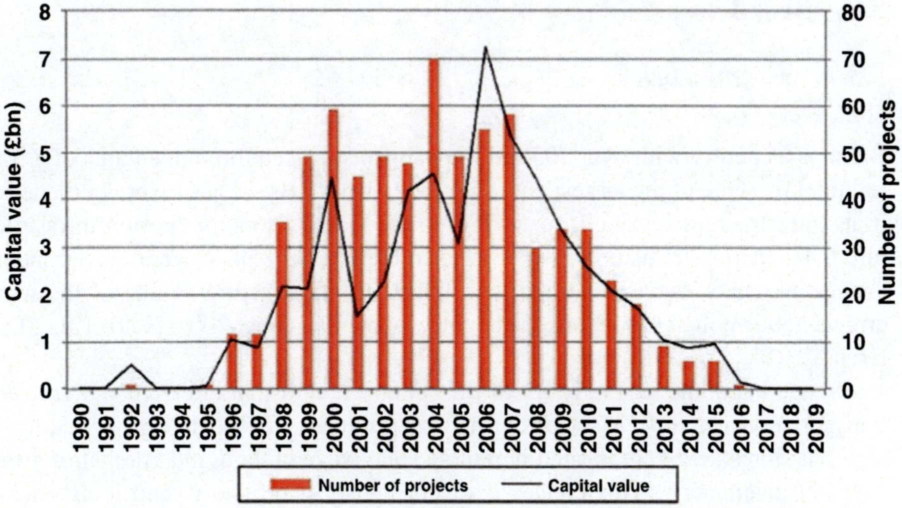

Fig. 5.3 Portfolio of current PFI and PF2 projects (number and capital value; Source: H.M. Treasury and Infrastructure and Projects Authority, 2019)

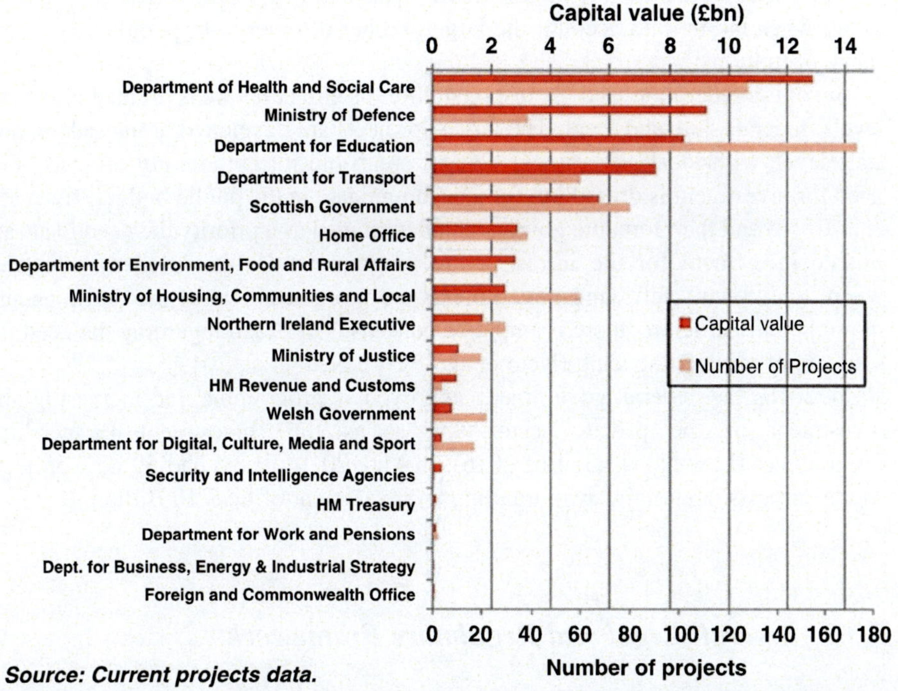

Fig. 5.4 Portfolio of current PFI and PF2 projects (number and capital value by Department; Source: H.M. Treasury and Infrastructure and Projects Authority, 2019)

5.3 Brazil

5.3.1 Framework

Brazil is a country with over 205 million habitants, spread through an area of 8.511 million km^2. One of the largest countries in the world, Brazil has severe bottlenecks in its infrastructure system. It ranks 78th in the World Economic Forum Infrastructure Index, and in terms of transport infrastructure ranks 85th. Several governments and "think tanks" have identified investment in infrastructure as one of the most critical public policies to unlock the country's potential (Baer 2001; Neto et al. 2020; Evans 2018).

On one hand, the vast territory of the country requires an effective and efficient transportation network. Most of the natural resources of Brazil (e.g., agricultural, minerals, forest, etc.) are located in remote areas, several thousand kilometres away from the main ports. This creates a severe logistical difficulty, and a significant burden for producers and, ultimately, consumers (Armijo and Rhodes 2017). On the other hand, airports and ports also lack capacity and require an upgrade of existing systems and processes (Wanke 2013; Wanke and Barros 2016; Fernandes and Pacheco 2018). Furthermore, at the urban level, significant difficulties exist, particularly when taking into account the large number of cities with populations in the range of millions.

Brazil is a federation, and the responsibility for infrastructure is divided into three levels: federal, state and local. The largest projects are developed at the federal and state level, with local government being responsible for community projects. The need for investment is difficult to fully accommodate in the public budget (Carranza et al. 2014) and therefore, the government determined as a priority the need to attract private investment for the infrastructure programme. Unlike in many countries where traditionally left-wing governments are more sceptical of private financing of public infrastructure, there is a relative consensus in Brazil regarding the need for a stream of private financing (Neto et al. 2017; e Neto et al. 2019).

In 2016, the federal government approved a programme for increasing the investment of the private sector—known as the 'Investment Partnerships Programme' (Law No. 13,334 of 2016). In May 2019, Brazil had 59 new projects (ports, airports, and highways), totalling an investment of US$ 10 Billion.

5.3.2 Overall Legal and Regulatory Framework

Brazil is a federation, where both federal and state government have legislative power. The PPP legislation is established for both levels. This section presents the main legal and regulatory framework, starting with the general rules, followed by an analysis at the state level.

The main piece of legislation on public-private partnerships is Law 11.079 of December 30, 2004, which "*establishes general rules for the bidding and contracting of public-private partnerships within the public administration*." This law establishes the principles under which all levels of public administration can establish PPPs. These principles are as follows:

(a) Efficiency in the fulfilment of state missions and the use of society's resources;
(b) Respect for the interests and rights of the recipients of the services and of the private entities responsible for their execution;
(c) Ineligibility of the functions of regulation, jurisdiction, the exercise of police power, and other exclusive activities of the State;
(d) Fiscal responsibility in the conclusion and execution of partnerships;
(e) Transparency of procedures and decisions;
(f) Objective risk sharing between the parties;
(g) Financial sustainability and socioeconomic advantages of partnership projects.

The Brazilian PPP law also contains a minimum level of requirements that any contract must comply with, for example:

(a) The term of the contract, being compatible with the amortisation of the investments made, should be not less than five (5), nor more than thirty-five (35) years, including any extension;
(b) The penalties applicable to the Public Administration and to the private partner in case of contractual default are always fixed in proportion to the seriousness of the misconduct committed and the obligations assumed;
(c) The apportionment of risk between the parties, including those related to 'acts of God', force majeure;
(d) The forms of remuneration and updating of contractual amounts;
(e) The mechanisms for the preservation of the current rendering of services;
(f) The facts that characterise the pecuniary default of the public partner, the modes and period of settlement, and, when applicable, the form of activation of the guarantee;
(g) The objective criteria for evaluating the performance of the private partner;
(h) The provision, by the private partner, of sufficient execution guarantees compatible with the guarantees and risks involved, observing the limits of §§ 3 and 5 of Art. 56 of Law No. 8666, of June 21, 1993, and the provisions of Item XV of Art. 18 of Law No. 8987, of February 13, 1995 in the case of sponsored concessions;
(i) The sharing with the Public Administration of the effective economic gains of the private partner which originate from the reduction of the credit risk of the financing used by the private partner;
(j) The carrying out of a survey of reversible assets, whereby the public partner may withhold payments to the private partner, in the amount required to put to right any irregularities detected.
(k) The schedule and milestones for the transfer to the private partner of the instalments of the funds during the investment phase of the project and/or after

the availability of services, whenever the hypothesis of § 2 of Art. 6 of this Law applies (included in Law No. 12,766 of 2012).

This law also establishes the criteria for setting up a PPP and a classification for the model. Regarding the former, the main criteria are a project with a contract value greater than ten million Reais (approx. $US 2.5 million) and a contract duration equal to, or greater than 5 years. The classification for the model is made based on the type of payment, as follows:

- Sponsored concession *(in Portuguese: Concessão patrocinada)*: the remuneration of the concessionaire consists of user tariffs, as well as a payment from the grantor;
- Administrative concession (*in Portuguese: Concessão administrativa)*: the remuneration of the concessionaire consists only of payments from the grantor;
- Common concession *(in Portuguese: Concessão comum)*: the remuneration of the concessionaire consists only of user tariffs.

Those concessions that do not involve any payment from the grantor are not considered by the Brazilian law to be a PPP and are thus not subject to the laws applicable to PPP projects. However the all-important law for PPP development is the Constitution of the Republic of 1988, which establishes the limits of the actions, objectives, and guidelines to be adopted in public procurement, public service provision, and State intervention in the economy, among other issues.

In the case of "stand-alone" projects (i.e., those that are economically self-sufficient), a specific law exists (8.987/1995) which applies to the case of common concessions. Several laws apply to PPPs (Ministry of Economy 2019).[3]

[3]Law No. 11,079, of 30 December, 2004 "establishes general rules for the bidding and contracting of public-private partnerships within the public administration."

- Law No. 12,766, of 27 September, 2012 "amends Laws No. 11,079, of 30 December, 2004, which establishes general rules for the bidding and contracting of public-private partnership within the public administration, to provide for the contribution of funds in favour of the private partner; No. 10,637, of 30 December, 2002; No. 10,833, of 29 December, 2003; No. 12,058, of 13 October, 2009; No. 9430, of 27 December, 1996; No. 10,420, of 10 April, 2002; No. 10,925, of 23 July, 2004; No. 10,602, of 12 December, 2002; No. 9718, of 27 November, 1998, and also; Provisional Measure No. 2, 158-35, of 24 August, 2001, as well as other provisions."
- Decree 5385, of 4 March, 2005 "establishes the Federal Public-Private Partnership Management Committee—CGP and makes other arrangements".
- Decree 8428, of 2 April, 2015 "provides for the procedure of expression of interest to be observed in the presentation of projects, surveys, investigations or studies, by individuals or legal entities under private law, to be used by the public administration."
- Decree No. 6037 of 7 February, 2007 "amends and adds to the provisions of Decree No. 5385 of 4 March, 2005, establishing the Federal Public-Private Partnership Management Committee—CGP".
- Ordinance MP 52, of 16 March, 2005 (designates members of the Federal Public-Private Partnership Management Committee—CGP).
- Ordinance No. 368, of 10 September, 2015.

One of the main challenges of Brazil is to protect the private partners, including, in particular, international financing institutions, by ensuring that the public sector (federal, state, local, and all indirect public administrations) is able to comply with its contractual obligations and associated payments.

To protect the private partners, Law No. 11,079 of 30 December, 2004, created the opportunity for the Federal Government, municipalities, and public foundations to create and participate in a Guarantee Fund for PPPs (*Fundo Garantidor das PPPs*). The objective of this Fund is to ensure that all public obligations regarding future payments are risk-free. The Fund is managed by the Bank of Brazil, an independent and politically-autonomous institution, and any public institution (e.g. distinct levels of governments, public institutes, or public companies) can become a shareholder of the Fund. The revenues of the Fund are considered to be federal revenues, and the law stipulates that its portfolio cannot be worth less than 6 billion Reais (Approx. $US 1.5 billion).

This Fund constitutes an opportunity to accelerate the infrastructure development plan of Brazil, by reducing uncertainties and unnecessary costs, as well as the related cost of capital. It has also helped attract more international partners.

As mentioned above, the Brazilian government created a specific programme to increase private sector participation in infrastructure projects (the Investment Partnership Programme created by Law No. 13,344, 2016).

This investment programme's main objectives are as follows[4]:

- Expand investment and employment opportunities and stimulate technological and industrial development, in line with the country's social and economic development goals;
- Ensure the quality of the expansion of public infrastructure, with appropriate tariffs for users;
- Promote broad and fair competition in the celebration of partnerships and the provision of services;
- Ensure the stability and legal certainty of contracts, ensuring minimal intervention in business and investments;
- Strengthen the regulatory role of the State and the autonomy of State regulators.

Two entities have been created in parallel with the programme, namely: the PPI Council and the PPI Secretariat. The Council functions as a collegiate body—whose main mission is to advise the President of the Republic[5] on issues related with the selection of projects which should be part of the PPI, and also on matters regarding their execution and implementation. The Secretariat has a more executive role in terms of the execution and implementation of the PPP programme.

Those projects which are selected and classified as part of the Investment Partnership Programme have priority over other projects, in terms of assessment, licensing, procurement, etc.

[4]https://www.ppi.gov.br/about-the-program.

[5]In Brazil the President of the Republic holds the executive power.

Recently, the Brazilian federal government initiated a programme designed to encourage the adoption of PPPs and concessions, which is entitled "*A Política Pública de Fomento às Concessões e Parcerias público-privadas dos Estados, do Distrito Federal e dos Municípios*". This programme includes the following activities: Technical Assistance; Document Standardisation; Simplification of Legislation; Training of Public Agents; Technical and Economic Regulation; Public Guarantees, and; the Source of Financing.

The programme is coordinated by the Special Secretariat of the Investment Partnership Programme of the Presidential Office of the Civil House. In addition, it counts with the support and partnerships of the Ministry of Regional Development—which is the sectoral body responsible for urban issues, the National Confederation of Municipalities, and the National Mayors' Association.

5.3.3 PPP Governance and Management

Federal Government

The Federal Government created (Decree No. 5385, of March 4, 2005) the Federal Public-Private Partnership Management Committee—CGP, whose main objective is to select priority projects for investment through the Public-Private Partnerships Law—PPP.

The Ministry of Planning acts as the Coordinator of the Committee which also includes representatives from the Ministry of Finance and the Civil House of the Presidency of the Republic.

The Management Committee is responsible for approving the Public-Private Partnership Plan—PLP, which contains a PPP implementation schedule, the definition of priority sectors, and projects. In addition, the Management Committee establishes procedures for the conclusion of contracts, authorises the opening of tenders, and approves the public notices which are prepared by the sectoral bodies.

The decree provides for the creation of a Technical Commission to advise the Management Committee, which also includes two representatives from the Ministries of Planning and Finance, the Civil House, the Ministries of Development, Industry Foreign Trade, Transport, Mines and Energy, National Integration, and Environment, in addition to two technicians from BNDES, Banco do Brasil, and Caixa Econômica Federal.

The Economic Advisory Office of the Ministry of Planning acts as the Executive Secretariat of the Steering Committee and the Technical Commission, which is responsible for organising and preparing the meetings and for providing technical advice, as well as monitoring the implementation of the deliberations and guidelines set by the Steering Committee.

Furthermore, the Committee also establishes the prioritisation of the projects, based on the following criteria: integrate the federal government development strategy which is identified in the Multi-Year Plan; ensure revenue generating

Table 5.2 Profile of the analysed Brazilian states´ PPP units

Profile	Number (unid.)
Dedicated PPP units identified in Brazilian states' governments	19
Sponsoring departments identified in Brazilian states' governments	22
Staff members working in the PPP units or sponsoring departments	93
Published PPP laws	25
Already appraised PPPs projects	205
PPP project sectors	19
Types of PPP projects	27
State PPP contracts signed from 2006 to 2016	13
State PPP contracts signed from 2006 to 2016	49
PPP contracts in operation	43
Non-operational PPP contracts	05
Amended PPP contracts	14
PPP contractual amendments	48
Terminated PPP contracts	01

Source: e Neto et al. (2019)

capacity; encourage an interest from the private sector, and; achieve a reasonable level of project development.

The Economic Advisory Office of the Ministry of Planning has a PPP Unit, which has been in operation since 2018 and has three teams: Legal; Project evaluation; Economic and financial modelling.

State Government

At the level of the state government, the governance of PPP projects is usually the responsibility of specific PPP units, created by the state governments, with distinct configurations and locations within the government administrative structure.

e Neto et al. (2019) carried out research focussed on understanding the existing situation in terms of PPP units at the state level. As of 2018, 19 PPP units existed, which are responsible for the analysis of 205 projects, of which 49 were signed (Table 5.2).

5.3.4 *Projects Overview*

According to the World Bank (PPP Knowledge Lab, 2019), Brazil has developed a total of 951 PPP/concessions projects since 1990, which represents an accumulated investment of over 360,000 Million US$. Tables 5.3 and 5.4 presents the largest projects which have been developed so far, as well as the most recent projects (classified by sector, financial closure year, and level of investment).

Table 5.3 Largest PPP Projects in Brazil

Project name	Sector	Financial closure year	Investment ($US million)
Belo Monte Hydro Power Plant	Electricity	2012	$14,800.00
Rio de Janeiro Airport	Airports	2014	$10,508.00
Guarulhos Airport	Airports	2012	$9366.00
Companhia de Electricidade do Estado da Bahia (COELBA)	Electricity	1997	$7141.90
Santo Antonio Power Plant	Electricity	2009	$6800.00
Eletropaulo Metropolitana de Eletricidade	Electricity	1998	$6292.09
MRS Logistica SA	Railways	1996	$5305.20
Jirau Power Plant	Electricity	2009	$5300.00
Gasoduto Sudeste	Natural Gas	2016	$5190.00
Companhia Paulista de Forca e Luz (CPFL Paulista)	Electricity	1997	$5188.10

Source: World Bank (2019)

Table 5.4 Most recent PPP Projects in Brazil

Project name	Sector	Financial closure year	Investment ($US million)
Port of Acu I LNG-to-Power plant	Electricity	2019	$1200.00
Lagoa dos Ventos Wind Farm	Electricity	2019	$700.00
VSM 2 wind power plant	Electricity	2019	$348.51
Pernambuco Sanitation System Expansion	Water and sewerage	2019	$268.27
Equatorial 4 Transmission Line	Electricity	2019	$265.62
Equatorial 6 Transmission Line	Electricity	2019	$132.11
Tropicalia Transmission Line	Electricity	2019	$127.39
City of Sao Paulo waste management services Lot 2	Collection and Transport	2019	$116.90
City of Sao Paulo waste management services Lot 1	Collection and Transport	2019	$107.70
City of Sao Paulo waste management services Lot 3	Collection and Transport	2019	$101.90

Source: World Bank (2019)

5.4 Chile

5.4.1 Framework

Chile has been one of the leading countries in the use of PPPs as a procurement tool to deliver and upgrade public infrastructure projects. The first PPPs were developed in the 1990s, in the road sector, to deal with a surge in the number of private vehicles (over one million vehicles), which nearly doubled from the early 1980s to the 1990s

(Lorenzen et al. 2001). During this period, ports and airports were also subject to the involvement of the private sector, as a response to a growing economy which placed a significant burden on an ageing transportation system which also lacked the capacity to accommodate the increasing growth in the movement of people and cargo (Engel et al. 2014a, 2019).

As in most countries, the Ministry of Public Works historically assumed the investment, management, and operation of public infrastructure directly, through its different departments and agencies.

The Chilean Government decided to use concessions to build, operate, and maintain the transportation infrastructure, and thus bypass public budgetary constraints. The programme targeted over 2000 km of expressways, raising over US3$ billion in investment (Lorenzen et al. 2001). The level of required investment was out of reach of the Government, and the most desirable strategy to enable the financing of urgent infrastructure proved to be the concession model, which came to unlock a programme for improving infrastructure, while freeing up government resources (Engel et al. 2011).

Between 1995 and 1998, the Government awarded 12 concessions, covering 1954 km of highways, with a total investment of more than US$3200 billion. It is important to mention that the Chilean road system was primarily composed of non-paved, or partially-paved roads, and that the expressways were the backbone of the transportation system. Counting with regional roads and airports, the total value of concessions awarded between 1993 and 2001was 30, with a total investment of over US$ 5 billion.[6] This investment provided an important boost to the Chilean economy, but was not free from criticism. For example, even though the design of tender processes did indeed reduce competition, this had an *ex-post* negative impact on performance, which led to significant renegotiations which eroded the welfare (Bitran et al. 2013; Engel et al. 2014b, 2015; Guasch et al. 2003, 2006; Guasch and Straub 2009).

Despite the significant investment made in the past, the Chilean Government is still eager to invest in and update the country's infrastructure systems, particularly its road network. In 2019, the President of Chile announced an investment plan for the road infrastructure sector, which foresees the construction of almost 17,000 km of roads (highways, new lanes in existing roads, rural roads, and the expansion of the barrier-free toll system).

5.4.2 Overall Legal and Regulatory Framework

Several laws and regulations exist in Chile which establish the legal basis for designing, awarding, and managing PPPs, the most relevant being the Concessions

[6]Data from http://www.concesiones.cl/.

Law.[7] This piece of legislation has been widely adopted by distinct political stakeholders. It stipulates the rules and regulations for the adjudication, execution, and the repair or conservation of public works granted as a private concession. The Concessions Law does not represent any impediment to foreign companies participating in tender processes.

The Chilean regulatory framework enables project proposals to have either a public or private origin. In the case of public projects, the government, or the governmental body, selects, prepares, and evaluates the project, whereas in the case of private projects, the private sector can identify and analyse a certain project, which can later be used by the public sector, should the government decide to advance with the project. In this case, the government is prohibited from awarding the concession to the company which originally proposed the project, with the new company having to go through a typical procurement process, and be subject to all the principles and criteria of fairness, transparency, and equity.[8]

Should the government decide to advance with the project, it can compensate the company which took the initiative to propose the project by providing a bonus within the scope of the bidding evaluation model, albeit subject to clear and pre-determined rules.

A potential interest in a project needs to be verified by the relevant public bodies and has to be considered and integrated into the government's project portfolio. Next, the project is put out to an open tender, where any potential bidder can be a potential winner (upon due technical and financial qualification, if applicable).

The concession contracts are generally long, with durations between 20 to 30 years, although the Concessions Law permits a maximum duration of 50 years. The same law establishes that the income from the project should cover the capital and operational expenditure, and as such it allows for the development of a system of guarantees and insurances to protect all those agents involved in the construction, operation, and maintenance of the concession contract, and a financial scheme which enables diversifying the investment risks.

The use of the concession system in Chile has been accompanied by the introduction of a series of financing instruments, namely: a Minimum Guaranteed Income; an Infrastructure Bonus; an Exchange Coverage Mechanism, and; an Income Distribution Mechanism.

The concessions model used in Chile does not transfer the ownership of the asset to the concessionaire, but rather the ownership remains within the sphere of the government.

[7](DS No. 900 of 1996 of the Ministry of Public Works and its Regulations, Supreme Decree No. 956, from 1997).

[8]Data from http://www.concesiones.cl/.

5.4.3 *PPP Governance and Management*

General Directorate of Concessions

The governance of the PPP projects is ensured by the General Directorate of Concessions, which is part of the Ministry of Public Works. The General Directorate of Concessions is responsible by the following tasks[9]:

- The acceptance or rejection of proposed private concession initiatives presented by individuals, by virtue of the terms established in Article 2 of the Concessions Law.
- The programming of the tender procedures for the contracting of studies, projects, and the execution of public works through the Concession System.
- The administrative and economic conditions governing the tender processes for the granting of a concession for public works, in accordance with the current rules and regulations.
- The rules and regulations for the control of concession contracts, in accordance with the current legislation.
- Any modification which needs to be incorporated into concession contracts already under construction or in operation, subject to the current rules and regulations.

The General Directorate of Concessions has an active role in the different development phases of an infrastructure. For example, even when a project is proposed by the private sector, the Ministry of Public Works, through the General Directorate of Concessions, is responsible for ensuring the economic and public interest of the project.

Five distinct phases can be identified,[10] namely:

- Pre-feasibility Study: the Ministry of Public Works develops engineering specifications to define the demand and also carries out a social evaluation and verifies the private profitability of the project.
- Business Study: the Ministry of Public Works defines the engineering aspects with regards the tender, the model for the operation of the concession; the degree of commitment of the agents to the business risks, and; other important technical-economic aspects.
- Preparation of the Business Prospectus: the Ministry of Public Works prepares a document detailing the basic background of the concession. This document describes the details of the project and enables potential investors to carry out their preliminary evaluation of the project.
- Pre-qualification process: this is the stage when project is put out to public tender. According to the Law and the Concession Regulations, the Ministry of Public

[9]Source: Website of the General Directorate of Concessions, Ministry of Public Works.

[10]Source: Dirección General de Concesiones (Ministerio de Obras Públicas, Gobierno de Chile) [website: www.concesiones.cl].

Works selects a consortia which meet the legal and financial requirements to participate in the tender process. The parties analyse and discuss the main aspects of the work, such as engineering designs, demand studies, and legal, administrative, economic and financial aspects.

- Preparation of the Tender Terms: this phase involves the definition of the detail of all the administrative, technical, and economic legal parameters which the pre-qualified consortia need to consider in order to be able to formulate their technical and economic proposals. Ultimately, these are the parameters which enable the evaluation, adjudication, control, and supervision of the execution and operation of the concession.

The procurement process is initiated by a publication in the Official Gazette, and is generally divided into two phases for the evaluation of proposals. The first phase consists of a technical evaluation, which can lead to the exclusion of proposals which fail to meet the necessary (and minimum) technical requirements. The second phase is an economic evaluation, which is generally based on a multicriteria evaluation model, where the following criteria are the most commonly-used:

- Rate structure;
- State subsidy to the Consortium;
- Concession term;
- Minimum income guaranteed by the State;
- Payments offered by the consortium to the State for operating an existing infrastructure;
- The degree of risk commitment assumed by the Consortium during the construction of the work;
- The quality of the technical offer regarding the basic and conceptual engineering;
- The Consortium offers to pay extraordinary amounts to the State, or to reduce the price of fee when the return on equity over assets exceeds a contractually-agreed rate of return;
- The qualification of other necessary additional services.

By the end of the procurement process, a concessionaire is selected which is then required to create the "Concessionaire Corporation" or SPV in order to initiate the construction/operation of the project.

Concessions Board

Chile has a Concessions Board, which is a consultative body of the Ministry of Public Works (MOP), with overall responsibility for identifying the type of infrastructure/projects which need to be developed under the Concessions Law and the type of concession employed. This Board is composed of the Minister of Public Works and five Board Members. The Board is responsible for drawing up the regional urban development plans and also the community, inter-community, and metropolitan regulatory plans, as well as the social assessment, which has to be approved by the competent planning body.

5.4.4 *Projects Overview*

According to Deloitte (2016) from 1994–2016, the total investment in concessions in Chile amounted to YS$16 billion, covering several sectors such as roads (81%), public buildings (11%), airport infrastructure (7%), and social infrastructure (1%). One interesting example of Chile's engagement with concessions, is Route 5—the main highway in Chile, which connects the North with the South, which is divided into 11 concessions (with each concession operating a section of the highway).

In the airport sector, 11 airport concessions had been awarded up until 2016, all of which had varying dimensions and relevance. For example, the Airport of Santiago alone represents 60% of all passenger traffic in Chile, and over 66% of revenues (Deloitte 2016), operating under a 25-year concession which was awarded to a consortium composed of ADP, Vinci Airports, and Astaldi. In the port sector, Chile has over 52 ports, with the Port of San Antonio, located in the Central zone, being the most important, with a total market share of 39.7% of traffic in 2015. Most of the Chilean ports are operated on the landlord port model—whereby concessions are awarded (some within the same port) to build and/or operate and maintain specific port areas or terminals. The length of the concession contracts in the port sector vary from 7 to 42 years.

5.5 Portugal

5.5.1 *Framework*

Over the last 30 years there has been a high investment in infrastructure in Portugal, especially since 1986, with the entry of Portugal in the then European Economic Community (EEC, nowadays the European Union) (Pereira and Andraz 2005; Cruz and Sarmento 2018). Portugal has moved from a country with many delays and deficiencies in many areas (e.g., roads, water and sanitation, electrification, etc.) to a position of high development. Much of this investment was made directly by the State, using Community funds. A high level of investment and infrastructure took place between 1980 and 2009, with an average of 4% GDP/year (Pereira and Pinho 2008; Andrade and Duarte 2016).

From the 1990s onwards, the reduction of Community funds for infrastructure (which was redirected to training and qualification) led to the development of PPP as a mechanism for leveraging public investment.

The Portuguese experience has been marked by several criticisms (Cruz and Marques 2011; Macário et al. 2015; Sarmento 2010; Sarmento and Renneboog

2016a; Silvestre and Araújo 2012). The main one, which also occurs in other countries, is that PPPs are used as a way of de-budgeting public investment (Araújo and Silvestre 2014). This is because the EU accounting rules mean that the investment made through PPPs is not considered to be a public expenditure at the time it is made (since it is accounted for as an investment by the private entity). It is thus possible to defer these investments in terms of their impact on the budget deficit, and consequently on public debt. The OECD (Curristine et al. 2008) recommended that "Information on PPPs should include a risk analysis for all PPPs throughout the their useful life. . . . expanding the analysis and evaluation of PPPs to public companies and to regional and local administration,. . . . greater clarity and consistency in the rules applied to public companies regarding their indebtedness capacity, levels of indebtedness should be guaranteed and the contracting of PPP".

Although budgetary treatment varies from country to country (as each country presents its budget differently), the recording of investment in PPPs in the national accounts (in accordance with the rules that determine the value of the deficit and public debt in reporting to Brussels) has a defined process Eurostat rules (Sarmento 2018). In 2004, Eurostat published the accounting rules for PPPs, which remains practically unchanged to this day. These rules determine that, in terms of national accounting, the key issue is to determine whether the assets involved in the PPP are to be recorded as government assets (with a consequent reflection on the deficit and public debt) or as assets of the private partner (with no impact on the deficit and public debt). It is noteworthy that Eurostat only allows assets to be registered as assets of the private partner (with no impact on the deficit and debt) if the private partner bears most of the risks involved in the partnership, in accordance with a "risk and reward" criterion through an analysis of the risk distribution. If the construction risk and one of the two following risks (availability/demand) is allocated to the private sector, then the PPP is considered to be outside the scope of the public accounts. If this is not the case, then it will integrate that perimeter.

What is the consequence of either situation? If the PPP is not recorded in the government accounts during the investment phase, then there is no public expenditure, as the investment and financing are provided by the private sector. Only after the construction phase, already during the operation phase, do payments from the State to the private sector begin. These payments will already be considered public expenditure. That is to say that during the construction phase there is no impact on the budget deficit.

Other relevant and potentially negative topic has been renegotiations. According to Sarmento and Renneboog (2016a), between 1995 and 2012 there were 254 renegotiation events. These events have already meant that there has been a very significant increase in payments for PPPs. Some of these are high "contingent liability" events, given that the vast majority of the 254 events are still in the negotiation/litigation phase. The resolution of litigation, if it implies giving reason to the private sector (total or partial), could represent an increase in future charges to the value of hundreds of millions of Euros.

5.5.2 *Overall Legal and Regulatory Framework*

Central PPP

As in other European Union countries, a distinction in Portugal is also made between PPP and concessions. PPP is considered to be concessions in which almost all the private revenue is generated from public money, either from the Government Budget (Central Administration), or at the level of regional governments or municipalities (Cruz and Marques 2013a, b). It should be remembered that in the case of the payment mechanisms, the fact that the revenues are guaranteed by a public entity does not necessarily mean that the risk has been allocated to the public sector, as the public payment may be dependent on the demand/quantity. Concessions, on the other hand, are those where the private revenue is generated by commercial revenue, that is to say, from revenue generated by users, and, as a rule, there is no counterpart contracted with the public sector (Cruz and Marques 2013c, 2014).

The PPP legal regime was established by Decree-Law No. 86/2003, of 26 April, subsequently revised by Decree-Law No. 141/2006, of 27 July, and by Decree-Law No. 111/2012, of 23 May. Previously, the signing of the PPPs followed specific regimes approved for each contract, although, at least with regard contracting procedures, the current legislation was also applicable. In the Portuguese legislation, which has been in force since 2003, a PPP is understood to be "the contract or the union of contracts, whereby private entities, designated by private partners, are obliged, in a lasting way, before a public partner, to ensure the development of an activity aimed at satisfying a collective need, and in which the financing and the responsibility for investment and exploitation rest, in whole or in part, with the private partner".

Decree-Law No. 86/2003 regulates the public procurement regime for PPP. This diploma, which is horizontal to all sectors, aims to define the general rules applicable to State intervention in the definition, design, preparation, tender, award, amendment, inspection, and global monitoring of PPPs. As mentioned above, in 2006 this Law was amended by Decree-Law 141/2006 with a view to simplifying and better safeguarding the public interest, namely with regards to the effectiveness of sharing the risks and benefits achieved.

Two main phases are distinguished in the PPP procedure, each of which, in turn, is composed of distinct stages (Sarmento and Renneboog 2016b): the first is called the preliminary phase, which runs from the moment of identifying the need to be met up until the launch decision is made regarding the PPP. The second phase is called the pre-adjudication phase, which runs from the time that the decision was made and published in the Official Journal, up until the award and subsequent conclusion of the contract. The decision on launching the partnership is the responsibility of the finance ministers and sectoral advisors. The launching of the partnership is carried out by using the applicable adjudication procedure, in accordance with the current legislation on public procurement. The powers of inspection and control are vested in the entities or services designated by the Minister of Finance for economic and financial matters, and the sectorial Minister for other issues.

Municipal PPPs

In Portugal, the local government have a wide range of competences in the following areas: rural and urban equipment; energy; transport and communications; education; heritage, culture and science; leisure and sport; social action; housing; civil protection; the environment and basic sanitation; consumer protection; land planning and urbanism; municipal policy, and; external cooperation. In many of these areas there is a clear overlap with the competences of the Central Administration, as the planning of certain services, such as health, requires a degree of analysis which does beyond the administrative capabilities of the municipality.

The way that municipalities organise the provision of services in their areas of competence is very variable, but can be summarised in the following models: (a) direct provision through its own services; (b) the creation of municipal services; (c) the creation of municipal companies, and; (d) contractual and institutional PPPs.

As previously mentioned, contractual PPPs involve the establishment of a contract between the private entity (concessionaire) and the public entity (grantor) and is the most commonly-used type of PPP. Institutional PPPs are characterised by the creation of a company where the capital is simultaneously owned by both the public and the private entity. Companies with joint private and public shareholders are also formed, in the sense that entities of a different nature coexist in the shareholder structure (da Cruz and Marques 2012). Unlike the Central Administration, the Local Administration has resorted to the use of mixed companies on several occasions, in areas as different as the environment, transport, tourism and culture, and sport and leisure.

The use of mixed companies is mainly due to two reasons: the first concerned the possibility of being able to avoid consolidating such a company's debt in the municipal accounts, whilst assuming a minority stake in the shareholder structures; the second was due to the fact that revenue is earned by the municipality when such a company's capital is sold to the private partner. However, experience in using this model has revealed several difficulties. First of all, because it enables the creation of high volumes of debt, which, at the time, were not being properly accounted for, which, to a certain degree, is the same mechanism as that of "budget temptation", which has already been discussed above, which occurred in the contractual type of PPPs or concessions (Sarmento and Renneboog 2016a). However, the management of this type of PPP proved to be much more complex than that of concessions. In the case of institutional PPPs, a clear overlap of roles of the public entity exists, since the municipality is in effect the manager of the public cause, and is thus obliged to monitor the service provided by the joint venture, and, if necessary, must apply sanctions when non-compliance is verified. Nowadays, the municipality is also a shareholder, and accordingly is represented in the company's management bodies, and thus, in effect, could find itself subject to the application of the very same sanctions and is liable for the management acts.

In the case of the contractual PPP model, or concessions, its use has been more prevalent in the areas of the environment (water and sanitation) and transport (public transport and car parks), although it also applied to other types of infrastructure, such as crematoriums and cemeteries. Among the various types of project developed under contractual PPPs, water and sanitation concessions are those which are most relevant, both in terms of the number and the volume of investment involved. The first contractual concession developed was in Mafra, in 1993. The current legislation limits the maximum period for these concessions to 30 years, although some cases lasting 35 years are in force, which were negotiated prior to the current defined limit. All the municipal water and sanitation concessions currently in operation have been the subject to renegotiations for several reasons, the most important being unrealistic forecast water consumption—which has been well above actual consumption, and also changes to the original project. These renegotiations often result in tariff increases, with the user ending up paying for the cost of poorly-designed processes and contracts.

5.5.3 PPP Governance and Management

The frequent use of PPPs by many of countries at the international level has posed new challenges from the point of view of the Courts of Accounts. Equipped with juridic and financial control powers, the Courts of Accounts monitor the legality and regularity of public revenues and expenditures, and also assure the good financial management and effective responsibility for financial infractions, all of which are key for PPPs (Zymler and Almeida 2008).

The audit of PPPs by the Courts of Accounts occurs at different times throughout the life cycle of the contracting and implementation of a PPP. On the one hand, whilst in most countries a PPP contest requires the approval of the Court of Auditors at the end of the procedure, that is to say, after the final decision of the State regarding the award of the concession, the PPP still has to be validated and approved by the independent public sector audit entity, which assures compliance with the norms in force for governing the contracting procedure. On the other hand, the role of all Courts of Auditors is to evaluate the effectiveness, efficiency, and economic feasibility of decisions made regarding public acts. Finally, auditing entities are increasingly paying more attention to performance auditing. In addition, the Courts of Accounts frequently audit PPPs throughout their life cycle and at times when financial renegotiations and re-negotiations occur, especially in cases when there is an increase in the expenditure or contingent liability of the public entity in relation to project, or when an event warrants the carrying out of an audit.

Portuguese Court of Auditors provide these different types of best practice audits, which, as a rule, are described in internal procedures manuals. They also respect internationally-accepted practices and standards of control, such as those of

INTOSAI (the International Organization of Supreme Audit Institutions, which was created in 1953 within the UN, with the aim to unite all the Supreme Financial Control Institutions from all over the world), in particular the best practice guidelines defined by this entity for PPP audits. In this area, the example and documentation published by the National Audit Office (NAO) of the United Kingdom is also extremely relevant.

PPP Unit

PPPs developed by the Portuguese Central Government are monitored by a PPP unit which is designated UTAP—*Unidade Técnica de Acompanhamento de Projectos* (the Technical Project Monitoring Unit).

The Technical Project Monitoring Unit (UTAP) is an administrative entity which is endowed with administrative autonomy, under the responsibility of the Ministry of Finance. It is responsible for the global monitoring of PPP processes and provides specialised technical support, especially in matters of an economic, financial, and legal nature. UTAP should be involved in all projects which have a discounted value of future payments or investment greater than €ten million, or €25 million respectively. More precisely, the role of UTAP is to be involved during the following phases of a PPP project:

- The project identification and preparation phase: UTAP appoints members of the project preparation team and provides technical support for the process;
- The procurement phase: UTAP leads and appoints some of the members of the committee established to oversee the development of the contract and to evaluate PPP tender submissions;
- The implementation and monitoring phase: in addition to providing support for contract management, UTAP also appoints and heads up the team established to manage contract renegotiations, if so requested by the Ministry of Finance. This represents a significant part of UTAP's current activity.

UTAP's main mission is to participate in *the preparation, development, execution and global monitoring of PPP processes, providing the necessary specialised technical support to the Government and other public entities* (UTAP 2019).

The main tasks of UTAP currently include (EPEC 2014):

- Provide technical support to, *inter alia*, the various project teams and committees for the development, contracting, and monitoring of PPPs (and large infrastructure projects which are not necessarily defined as PPPs in the legislation), to the Ministry of Finance and, if so requested by the Ministry of Finance, to other entities;
- Monitor the public sector financial obligations of PPPs and provide real time information to the Ministry of Finance Treasury and Budget Directorates;
- Publish a quarterly report on financial obligations and other updates regarding contracts and make these publicly available on the UTAP website;

- Act as the central information point for all PPP contracts and collect, analyse, and archive all economic and financial information regarding PPP contracts;
- Appoint and, in certain cases, lead the various project teams and committees throughout the project cycle;
- Monitor and provide technical support for contract management negotiations and other issues, and, when necessary, assume the role of the contract manager;
- Share know-how regarding PPPs, and promote and provide training in PPPs.

The Technical Unit can also provide technical support in the development, contracting, and monitoring of large infrastructure projects which are not defined as a public-private partnership, which may be financed by the public sector, or result in charges for the public sector.

5.5.4 Projects Overview

Portugal currently has a total of 35 PPPs. Of these, 22 (62%) are in the road sector, 10 (27%) in the health sector, 2 (8%) in the railway sector, and 1 in the security sector (Siresp—Digital Security and Surveillance Networks).

These 35 projects represent a total investment of approximately €16 billion over the past 20 years. This investment has naturally been concentrated in the road sector, which represents 80% of total PPP investment, followed by the railway sector, with 18%. The remaining investment in the health and safety sector represents 2% and 1%, respectively. The use of PPP in Portugal has generated a significant burden for the public accounts for the next decades, as can be seen in Fig. 5.5. By 2030, the annual value of PPP-related charges is expected to exceed 0.5% of GDP, with this value representing 1% of GDP between 2014 and 2020. Applying a discount rate of 6% (which is the legal discount rate for PPPs in Portugal), the net present value of these charges amounts to 12% of GDP. It can thus be seen that PPPs represent a strong constraint on the process of consolidating public finances in Portugal. The large majority of the expenditure is related with road projects, which represent, on average, two thirds of the total expenditure on PPPs, followed by the health sector, with 28% (Sarmento and Renneboog 2015).

5.6 Spain

5.6.1 Framework

Spain has had a long tradition in PPP concessions (Allard and Trabant 2008; Carpintero and Ole 2014). The Spanish National Association of Construction Companies registered over 500 PPPs in the years between 2003 and 2011, with a total value of €50 billion (Fraga and Ortiz 2019). Similar to the UK, Spain has also

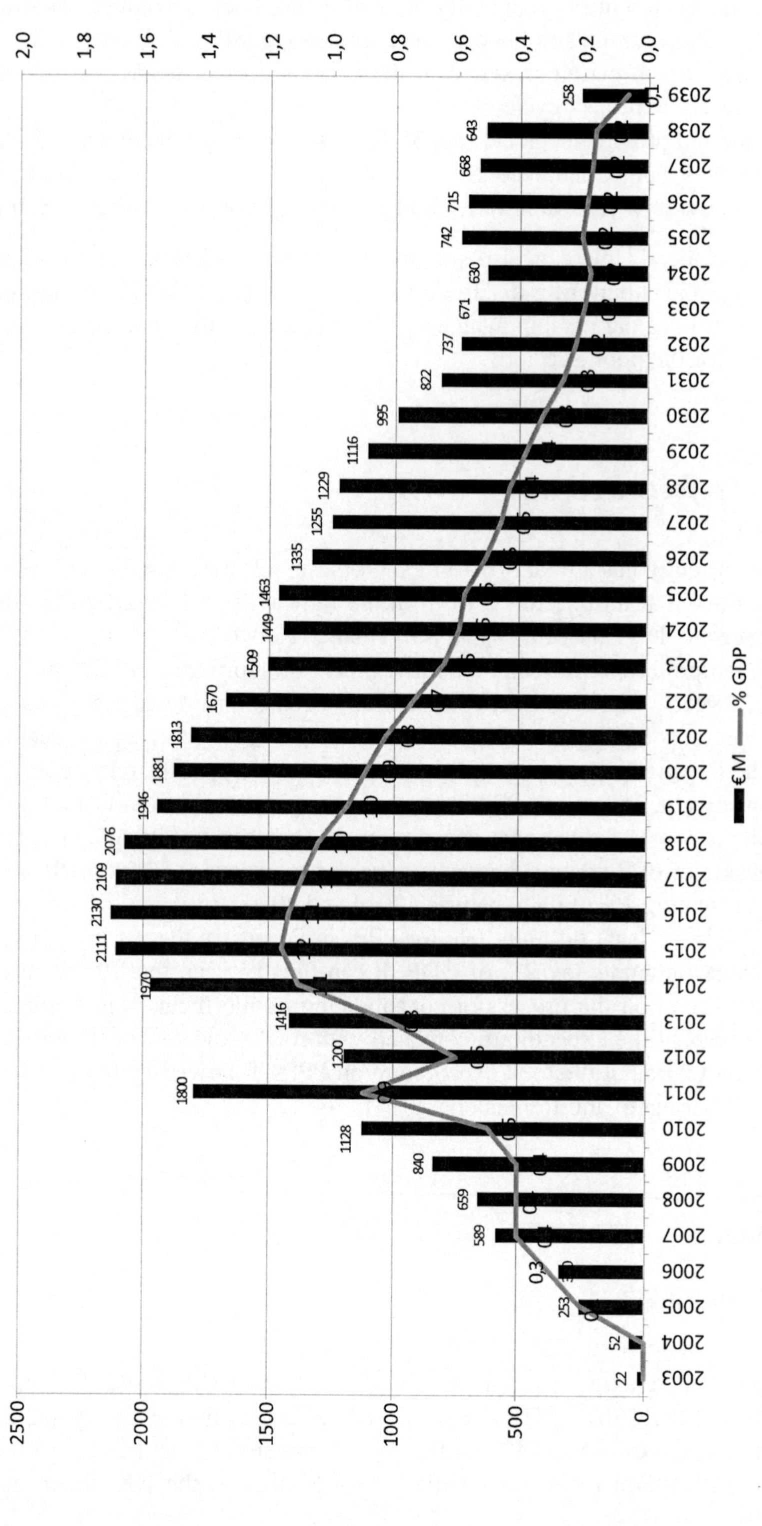

Fig. 5.5 PPP Gross payments (left axis—Euros; right axis—% of GDP)

experienced a significant decrease in PPP activity since the beginning of the financial crisis, which impacted Spain particularly after 2010 (Martín-Oliver et al. 2017; Garrido et al. 2019).

The use of PPP in infrastructure begun in the road sector (Pereira and Roca-Sagalés 2003). The first road planning project in Spain was developed in the late 1960s during the regime of Franco. Unlike most European countries which started developing their road networks based on State-owned enterprises, Spain was a pioneer in the use of concessions to build and operate its road network. The first project developed under a concession regime was the "Guadarrama Tunnel" in 1953 (Martinez and Queiroz 2017).

Spain has suffered from an asymmetric investment policy, which is biased towards transportation infrastructure. With an extremely modern and efficient national/regional transport network, which is composed of high-speed train lines, a dense network of airports ports, and other logistical infrastructures, the country's water, energy, urban transport, and social infrastructure still need significant investment. Several studies have highlighted that these types of infrastructure have a critical medium to long term priority (e.g., Sener and Seopan 2017). In 2015, A.T. Kearney also identified a country-wide need in Spain to increase the spending on infrastructure to a value of between €38,000 and €54,000 million annually. This represents 1.7 to 2.1 times the existing level of investment (A.T. Kearney 2015).

At a different level, there has been political pressure, especially from the European Commission, to limit public investment in infrastructure, on account of the Community's fiscal objectives for the deficit and debt reduction (Sarmento 2018). However, in the case of such fiscal restriction, it is difficult to carry out all the necessary investment and infrastructures through resorting to public expenditure.

The experience of the use of PPPs is often a mixture of successes and failures, and Spain is no exception. Deloitte, Uria Menéndez, and Seopan (2017) identified a number of "inefficiencies" along the contracting cycle, namely:

- In the preparation phase of the contracts, highlighted as inefficiencies are: the lack of maturity, which requires the greatest concentration in its definition, including a value for money analysis; the small size of some projects and the limited capacity of some contracting entities; the insufficient contractual definition of risk sharing between the public and private sectors;, and; uncertainty about the future project's projection as a public deed, with the consequent impact on the public deficit.
- In the bidding phase and awarding of contracts, an excessive speed of procedures is usual, which penaliszes competence and hinders the performance of the best offers and the financing of projects. Likewise, the lack of adaptation of the procedure for the type of APP project that is involved and the adequate technical valuation of the projects, which are inefficiencies that stimulate the abnormally low offers in highly complex projects.
- In the phase of contract execution, the contractual regulation of essential aspects is detected, such as the distribution of risks and the supposition of rebalancing, the inexistence of agile mechanisms for resolving disputes and the tendency of contracting entities to impose changes to the contract. That change the conditions

of departure for financing and put in risk the economic-financial viability of the contract.

- During the phase of termination of contracts, the abstract and insufficient definition and form of determining the compensation that proceeds on the basis of anticipated termination of contracts has been proven.

The early adoption of concessions for the delivery of public infrastructure leveraged the development of know-how which was later used by Spanish companies to operate in other countries, particularly after joining the European Union in the mid-1980s, benefitting from a larger, border-free market. Spanish companies are among the world leading companies. Kurihara (2016) argues that "*what lies behind today's large presence of Spanish construction companies in the global PPP market with a focus on the field of transportation infrastructure is a history of development of road infrastructure in Spain*".

5.6.2 Overall Legal and Regulatory Framework

Spain is a regional state, comprised of 17 regions, each with a significant degree of autonomy in terms of the management of public services and infrastructure. Below the regional government, local authorities with elected officials also have a certain degree of administrative authority. As discussed above, Spain has used concessions and PPPs as a public policy tool to develop its infrastructure network. The Spanish Public Procurement law identifies three types of PPP contracts: (1) public works concession contracts: where the concessionaire is responsible for building, financing, operating, and maintaining a public infrastructure, for which it receives a service fee (or toll), assuming all commercial/demand risk; (2) public service management contracts: where the public partners entrust the concessionaire with the responsibility for managing a service, whereby, unlike public works concession contracts, this does not involve a large share of construction works, and; (3) partnership agreements between the public and the private sector.

The bidding process for PPPs in Spain is organised around three distinct phases, as pointed out by Corral et al. (2006), namely:

> The public disclosure of feasibility studies. Depending on the project, economic-financial studies and preliminary design can also be disclosed. The standard bidding document that will be used during the process is disclosed at this phase; once the comments and recommendations made during the public disclosure phase have been taken into consideration, the detailed design process starts, under the supervision of the "Dirección General de Carreteras"; final phase is the actual bidding that must be publicly announced according to the law. Tenders are generally evaluated taking into account: (i) technical quality; (ii) feasibility of the proposal and technical and financial solvency of the concessionaire, and (iii) efficiency of the concession scheme.

5.6.3 PPP Governance and Management

In Spain there is no specific PPP unit or authority which is responsible for, or has centralised oversight of PPP projects. The reform of the Procurement Law (TRLCSP) created a new unit—the National Evaluation Office—which is responsible overall for the investments made by public authorities, albeit not necessarily under PPP regimes. The purpose of this unit is to analyse the financial sustainability of projects and support national and regional authorities to correctly assess the feasibility of public projects. This specific concern regarding the financial sustainability of projects is grounded on Spain's experience over the past 20 to 25 years, which saw a massive investment in transportation projects, some of which failed to deliver economic value, as discussed by Albalate et al. (2015) and Albalate and Bel-Piñana (2019).

The structure and composition of the National Evaluation Office is still unclear, and the unit is not regulated by a specific law. The responsibility for the definition of its composition should rest with the *Ordem del Ministerio de Hacienda y Administraciones Públicas* (the Ministry of Finance), however this has not been the case since 2019.

Some of the expected deliverables from the unit include the following (Deloitte, Uría Menéndez and Seopan 2017): if a project's profitability is reasonable, given the risk of demand assumed by the concessionaire has, then the mitigation of the State participation of risks other than demand which are usually supported by the economic operators must be taken into account; in the case of the concession of contracts for works where the concession fee is payable to the adjudicating power, the demand risk is transferred to the concessionaire, and; in cases of re-negotiation, the agreed financial compensations should maintain a reasonable profitability.

5.6.4 Projects Overview

Table 5.5 summarises the investment in PPPs and concessions in Spain between 2003 and 2018, organised by sector. Some interesting trends emerge from the Table, namely:

- Although there are significant variations from one year to the following, there is a clear trend of an increae in investment from 2003 until 2010;
- 2010 represents a profound change in the market, whereby after a peak of investment of €10.5 billion in 2010, investment decreased to €97.2 million in 2018, which represents a 99% reduction.
- As mentioned above, Spain has focussed most of its investment in transport-related infrastructure: the road sector—new roads (37%) and upgrading/maintenance (16%); urban mobility (11%); other transport related projects—such as railways, airports, carparks (6%); other related public infrastructure (17%).

Table 5.5 Public investment in concessions by type of infrastructure per year (Source: adapted from Seopan) € million

Infrastructure	2003	2004	2005	2006	2007	2008	2009	2010	2011	2012	2013	2014	2015	2016	2017	2018	TOTAL	%
Ports	100.1		292.4	7.5			56.7	126	106.7	20				16.7	3.3	6.6	736	1%
Roads																	0	0%
New	2321.1	259.3	1632.8	417.3	2723.9	481.1	458.2	6218.4	2924.3	430							17,866.4	32%
Upgrading		1513.4	697.5		5689.4				1151.4								9051.7	16%
Railways	1068.9																1068.9	2%
Airports	113.8			185.2													299	1%
Water				195.7	12.8						147.5					17.3	3,73.3	1%
Desalinization	199.7		35.9	947.1	1,52.8	31											1366.5	2%
Urban mobility	374.2	104.4	422.6	944.1	363.3	2490.4		1410.9									6109.9	11%
Parking	33.3	78.2	193.1	284.6	85.9	174.9	120.8	246.5	46.3	121.3	29.7		38.7		3.7	1.6	1458.6	3%
Waste water		431.3	1422.3		48.5	68.1	700	1379				1947.1	451.2				6447.5	12%
Social services	792.1	26.6	265.5	9.1	26.1	21.2	71.3	15.3		9.3					21.8		1258.3	2%
Urban infrastructure	670.3	367.7	1931.3	1542.5	552.3	1642.3	452.3	1098.7	197.7	32.9	205.6	279.9	129.2	405.3	66.3	71.7	9646	17%
Total	5673.5	2780.9	6893.4	4533.1	9655	4909	1859.3	10494.8	4426.4	613.5	382.8	2227	619.1	422	95.1	97.2	55,682.1	100%

Table 5.6 Priority investment (Source: adapted from Seopan)

Areas		No. of Projects	Investment per type of infrastructure				Total
			Roads	Railways	Water	Industrial	
Water	Supply	33			636		12,014
	Treatment	193			4354		
	Distribution	205			4942		
	Regulation	79			2082		
Transport	Cargo and logistics	8		699			70,344
	Urban accessibility	65	7625	15,765			
	Capacity management	144	24,256	3631			
	Secondary network	18		18,368			
Urban infrastructure	Urban mobility	37		14,900			14,900
Environment	Waste management	17				1304	6522
	Protection and regeneration	15				5218	
Total		814	31,881	53,363	12,014	6522	103,780

Spain has gained a mature infrastructure system based on the significant level of investment made in infrastructures up until 2010, however there has been a lack of significant investment since then, which is accordingly eroding the quality of Spain's infrastructure. Certain critical infrastructures have been identified which will require a significant investment (amounting to more than €100 billion—see Table 5.6). Once again, the same challenge which has also been identified in other countries emerges, whereby it will be very difficult to ensure that Spain's government will be able to leverage the necessary capital to finance the required portfolio of infrastructure projects. Private capital will be necessary.

Appendix

Table A1 PPP status in the US by State

State	Category	Allows for unsolicited proposals?	Statute(s)	Short summary
Alabama	Broad	No	Ala. Code §§ 23-1-40	Describes State DOT duties and powers generally. The statute gives the DOT the authority to enter into contracts with public or private entities for the construction of a public road, bridge, or tunnel.
Alabama	Broad	No	Ala. Code §§ 23-1-81	Authorises county commissions and the State DOT to licence private entities to establish or operate toll roads, toll bridges, ferries, or causeways. Allows the authorisation of a licensee to establish and fix the toll rates.
Alabama	Broad	No	Ala. Code §§ 23-2-140 to 163	Authorises the Alabama Toll Road, Bridge and Tunnel Authority to enter into agreements for design-build, design-build-operate, design-build-own-operate, or design-build-own-operate-maintain contracts, or other similar arrangements or agreements.
Alaska	Limited	No	Alaska Stat. §§ 19.75.011 to 990	Authorises the Knik Arm Bridge and Toll Authority to enter into P3s in any form to finance, design, construct, maintain, improve, or operate the Knik Arm Bridge. Allows the authority to issue bonds or incur other forms of indebtedness to finance the project and to fix and collect tolls for the use of the bridge; these tolls may exceed operating costs.

(continued)

Table A1 (continued)

State	Category	Allows for unsolicited proposals?	Statute(s)	Short summary
Arizona	Broad	Yes	Ariz. Rev. Stat. §§ 28-7701 to 7710 A	Comprehensive statute which authorises P3s for transportation projects. Allows for availability payments and revenue sharing. Limits agreements to no more than 50 years, which may be extended by the DOT. Allows for solicited and unsolicited proposals.
Arkansas	Limited		Ark. Stat. Ann. § 14-305-102	The law authorises the use by counties of P3s for the development of unpaved roads.
Arkansas	Limited	No	Ark. Stat. Ann. §§27-86-201 to 211; Ark. Stat. Ann. §27.76.402	Allows counties to grant franchises to private entities to build toll bridges, turnpikes, or causeways over or along swamps, watercourses, lakes or bays, whenever it is in the public interest.
Arkansas	Broad		Ark. Code §§ 22-10-101 to 22-10-505	Authorises county and local government to use P3 for projects that have a long-term operations agreement. Eligible projects include: ferries, mass transit facilities, vehicle parking facility, port facilities, power generation facilities, and fuel supply facilities, among others.
California	Limited	Yes	Cal. Gov. Code §§ 5956 to 5956.10	Authorises local governmental agencies to enter into agreements with private entities to study, plan, design, construct, develop, finance, maintain, rebuild, improve, repair, and/or operate a variety of fee-producing infrastructure facilities, including rail, highway, bridge, tunnel or airport

(continued)

Table A1 (continued)

State	Category	Allows for unsolicited proposals?	Statute(s)	Short summary
				projects. Allows for solicited and unsolicited proposals. Prohibits the use of the authority in this section to design, construct, finance, or operate a toll road in a State highway.
Colorado		No	Colo. Rev. Stat. § 32-9-128.5	This statute describes how the Regional Transportation District can load the net revenue of private activity or can exempt facility bonds to a private entity to finance all or a portion of a project.
Colorado		Yes	Colo. Rev. Stat. §§ 43-1-1201 to 1209	Allows the state DOT to enter into agreements for public-private initiatives, including for the design, financing, construction, operation, maintenance, and/or improvement of toll roads, turnpikes, and high-occupancy toll lanes. Allows for solicited and unsolicited proposals.
Colorado			Colo. Rev. Stat. § 43-2-219	Authorises a board of county commissioners to enter into public-private initiatives for county highways and bridges, to privatise any county highway or bridge, or to charge tolls for such facilities.
Colorado			Colo. Rev. Stat. §§ 43-3-202.5	Authorises the State DOT to make or enter into contracts or agreements with one or more public or private entities to design, finance, construct, operate, maintain, reconstruct, or improve a turnpike project by means of a public-private initiative.

(continued)

Table A1 (continued)

State	Category	Allows for unsolicited proposals?	Statute(s)	Short summary
				Finds that privately-developed transportation projects can result in time and cost savings and are able to reduce risk and enable new tax revenues. Requires that the public or private entity secures and maintains liability insurance coverage.
Colorado			Colo. Rev. Stat. §§ 43-4-413-414	Authorises the Transportation Commission, with the approval of the Governor, to enter into a contract with a private individual, firm or corporation for the construction, maintenance, and operation of one or more toll tunnels. Requires that all rates for tolls or fees to be charged by a private contractor have to first be approved by the Commission.
Colorado			Colo. Rev. Stat §§ 43-4-801 to 812	Creates and authorises a State-wide Bridge Enterprise to enter into P3s to design, develop, construct, reconstruct, repair, operate, or maintain bridge projects. Also creates the High-Performance Transportation Enterprise (HPTE) to procure and enter into P3s and other innovative means of completing surface transportation infrastructure projects.
Connecticut	Limited	No	Conn. Gen. Stat. §§ 4-255 to 4-263	This statute authorises the Governor to approve up to five projects to be implemented as P3 projects prior to January 2016. The statute limits State support for a

(continued)

Table A1 (continued)

State	Category	Allows for unsolicited proposals?	Statute(s)	Short summary
				partnership agreement to 25% of the total cost of the project.
Delaware	Broad	Yes	Del. Cod. Ann. Tit. 2, §§ 2001 to 2012	Authorises the secretary of transportation to enter into agreements with private entities to study, plan, design, construct, lease, finance, operate, maintain, repair, and/or expand transportation systems. Establishes the Public-Private Initiatives Program Revolving Loan Fund, which provides funds for financing such projects. Allows for solicited and unsolicited proposals.
Florida	Broad	Yes	Fla. Stat. Ann. § 334.30	Authorises the State DOT, with legislative approval, to enter into agreements with private entities to build, operate, own, or finance transportation facilities. Exempts private entities from certain taxes. Allows the DOT to lease existing toll facilities (except the Florida Turnpike System) through P3s with legislative approval; the DOT can also develop new toll facilities or increase the capacity of existing toll facilities through P3s. Allows for solicited and unsolicited proposals.
Florida	Broad	Yes	Fla. Stat. Ann. § 337.251	Authorises the State DOT to lease to public or private entities, for a term not exceeding 99 years and the use of DOT property, including rights-of-way. Allows for solicited and unsolicited proposals.

(continued)

Table A1 (continued)

State	Category	Allows for unsolicited proposals?	Statute(s)	Short summary
Florida	Broad	No	Fla. Stat. Ann. § 338.22 to 2511	Creates the Florida Turnpike Enterprise, which operates in the same way as a private-sector business within the State DOT to plan, develop, own, purchase, lease, or otherwise acquire, demolish, construct, improve, relocate, equip, repair, maintain, operate, and manage the Florida Turnpike System. Allows the enterprise to cooperate, coordinate, partner, and contract with other entities, both public and private, to accomplish its purposes.
Florida	Broad	Yes	Fla. Stat. Ann. § 343.962	Authorises the regional transportation authority to receive or solicit proposals and enter into agreements with private entities or consortia thereof for the building, operation, ownership, or financing of multimodal transportation systems, transit-oriented development nodes, transit stations, or related facilities
Florida	Broad	Yes	Fla. Stat. Ann. § 343.875	Authorises the Northwest Florida Transportation Corridor Authority to enter into agreements with private entities to build, operate, own or finance transportation facilities within its jurisdiction. Allows for solicited and unsolicited proposals.
Florida	Broad	Yes	Fla. Stat. Ann. § 348. 0004	Authorises any expressway authority, transportation authority, bridge authority, or toll authority to enter into agreements

(continued)

Table A1 (continued)

State	Category	Allows for unsolicited proposals?	Statute(s)	Short summary
				with private entities to build, operate, own, or finance transportation facilities within the jurisdiction of the authority. Allows for solicited and unsolicited proposals.
Florida	Broad	Yes	Fla. Stat. Ann § 287. 05712	County, municipality, or special district has the authority to establish P3 for a project which serves a public purpose, including, but not limited to, any ferry or mass transit facility, vehicle parking facility, airport or seaport facility, rail facility or project, and fuel supply facility, among others. Allows for solicited and unsolicited proposals.
Florida	Broad		Fla. Stat. Ann § 255.065	Exempts unsolicited proposals for P3 projects from public record and public meeting requirements for 180 days after receipt, if the public entity does not issue a competitive solicitation, or until the end of any competitive solicitation or promptly-reissued competitive solicitation.
Georgia	Broad		Ga. Code Ann. §48-5-41; Ga. Code Ann. §48-5-421.1	Exempts a property which qualifies as a public-private transportation project from ad valorem taxes. Section 48–5-421.1 provides that such projects shall not constitute special franchises.
Georgia			Ga. Code Ann. § 32-10-76	This statute establishes a grant programme for P3 streetcar development and provides assistance to local government entities.

(continued)

Table A1 (continued)

State	Category	Allows for unsolicited proposals?	Statute(s)	Short summary
Georgia			Ga. Code Ann. §32-2-41 (b)(6)	This statute allows the Commissioner to establish a Public-Private Initiatives Division within the State DOT.
Georgia	Broad	No	Ga. Code Ann. §§ 32-2-78 to 80	Authorises the DOT to solicit and accept proposals for projects which are funded or financed in part or in whole by private sources. Requires all future P3 projects to be solicited by the DOT. Includes public comment requirements and criteria for the DOT to use in awarding contracts. Authorises contracts to include tolls, fares, or other user fees and tax increments for use in the project. Final approval of P3 contracts is limited to the action of the State Transportation Board.
Georgia	Broad	Yes	Ga. Code. Ann. §§ 36-91-110 to 36-91-118	The Partnership for Public Facilities and Infrastructure Act establishes guidelines for local government for P3 procurement. The statute also outlines procedures for the review and analysis of each proposal. A 'Qualifying project' means any project which is selected in response to a request from a local government or submitted by a private entity as an unsolicited proposal and subsequently reviewed and approved by a local government, within its sole discretion, as meeting a public purpose or public need. This term shall not include and shall have no

(continued)

Table A1 (continued)

State	Category	Allows for unsolicited proposals?	Statute(s)	Short summary
				application to any project involving (a) the generation of electric energy for sale, (b) communication services, (c) cable and video services, and, (d) water reservoir projects.
Illinois	Limited		Ill. Rev. Stat. ch. 20, § 2705/2705-450	Authorises the State DOT to enter into agreements with any public or private entity for the purpose of promoting and developing high-speed rail and magnetic levitation transportation within the state.
Illinois	Limited		Ill. Rev. Stat. ch. 620 § 75/2-35	The South Suburban Airport Act gives general powers to the airport authority, specifically for P3. Any combination of design, build, finance, operate, and maintain can be authorised. The term of a P3 agreement is limited to 75 years, although the term may be extended by the General Assembly by law. The statute describes the prequalification and procurement processes. The statute also describes the provisions to be included in the P3 agreement. The P3 developer is unable to impose user fees outside the P3 agreement.
Illinois	Limited		Ill. Rev. Stat. ch. 605, § 5/10-802	Authorises municipalities to celebrate contracts "of every kind and nature" to acquire, construct, reconstruct, improve, enlarge, better, operate, maintain and/or repair any bridge within five miles of the corporate limits of the

(continued)

Table A1 (continued)

State	Category	Allows for unsolicited proposals?	Statute(s)	Short summary
				municipality, and to fix and apply tolls and fees for the use of such a bridge.
Illinois	Limited		Ill. Rev. Stat. ch. 605 §§ 130/1 to 130/999	Authorises the State DOT to enter into a P3 to develop, construct, manage or operate the Illiana Expressway. Limits the contract term to 99 years, including extensions. Requires legislative approval for all extensions. Chapter 820, Section 130/2 celebrates a P3 for the Illiana Expressway subject to the State Prevailing Wage Act (this section is also applicable to the lease of a facility at Chicago Midway International Airport).
Illinois	Broad		Ill. Rev. Stat. ch. 630 §§ 15/5	The Public-Private Partnership Act provides a broad authority for the development of new P3 projects by the DOT and Tollway Authority. Eligible projects include roads, bridges, intermodal facilities, intercity or high-speed passenger rail or other transportation facilities. Airports and toll roads are not eligible, unless authorised by Law. The Act can be applied to the reconstruction or expansion of existing assets. The Act describes project identification processes and the need for legislative authorisation by the joint resolution of the Illinois House and Senate. The Act describes three types of

(continued)

Table A1 (continued)

State	Category	Allows for unsolicited proposals?	Statute(s)	Short summary
				procurement processes, namely: sealed bidding, sealed proposals, and design-build. A preferred proponent's proposal is subsequently reviewed by the State's Commission on Government Forecasting and Accountability. The Governor makes the final award decision.
Indiana	Broad	No	Ind. Code Ann. §§ 5-23-1-1 to 5-23-7-2	Authorises governmental bodies to enter into P3 agreements with private entities for the acquisition, planning, design, development, reconstruction, repair, maintenance, or financing of public facilities. Applies to the State, a political subdivision in a county containing a consolidated city, or a political subdivision in a county which adopts these provisions by resolution or ordinance. Limits the original terms of P3 agreements to no more than five years with Board approval; a term in excess of five years requires the approval of the Board, the Governor and/or the fiscal body of a political subdivision. Requires a public hearing. Allows for solicited proposals only.
Indiana	Broad	No	Ind. Code Ann. §§ 8-15.5-1-1 to 8-15.5-13-8	Authorises the Indiana Finance Authority to enter into P3 agreements with private entities to plan, design, acquire, construct, reconstruct, improve, extend, expand, lease, operate, repair, manage, maintain, or

(continued)

Table A1 (continued)

State	Category	Allows for unsolicited proposals?	Statute(s)	Short summary
				finance toll road projects. Prohibits the State DOT or the Authority from issuing a request for proposals or from entering into a P3 for a toll road after 1 August, 2006, unless the General Assembly adopts a statute authorising the imposition of tolls. Exempts certain projects from the legislative approval requirement, including the Illiana Expressway under legislation enacted in 2010 (Senate Bill 382; 2010, Ind. Acts, P.L. 85). Requires public hearings to be held in affected counties and also requires certain preliminary studies. Limits lease terms to no more than 75 years. Allows for solicited proposals only.
Indiana	Broad	No	Ind. Code Ann. §§ 8-15.7-1-1 to 8-15.7-16-8	Authorises the State DOT to enter into P3s to develop, finance, or operate transportation projects, including tollways, roads and bridges, and some rail projects. Prohibits the DOT or the Indiana Finance Authority from issuing a request for proposals or entering into a P3 agreement unless the General Assembly adopts a statute authorising the activity. Exempts certain projects from the legislative approval requirement, including an Interstate 69 project and the Illiana Expressway under new legislation enacted in

(continued)

Table A1 (continued)

State	Category	Allows for unsolicited proposals?	Statute(s)	Short summary
				2010 (Senate Bill 382; 2010 Ind. Acts, P.L. 85). Allows for solicited proposals only.
Kentucky	Broad	No	Ky. Rev. Stat. § 45A. 077	The statute establishes an 11-member Kentucky Local Government Public Private Partnership, which will approve review and approve certain P3 agreements. The law also directs the Secretary of Finance and the Administration Cabinet to establish regulations in order to determine when a P3 may be used for a particular project, and the respective local governments must follow P3 agreements. The law sets forth regulations stipulating what should be contained in an RFP and establishes procedures regarding unsolicited proposals.
Louisiana	Broad	No	La. Rev. Stat. Ann. § 48:250.	Authorises the DOT to solicit and enter into P3 contracts for a transportation facility. 25% of P3 projects undertaken by the DOT should be located outside the boundaries of a metro area. Rural projects are subject to approval of the House and Senate committee on agriculture and rural development.
Louisiana	Broad	No	La. Rev. Stat. Ann. § 48:1660.1	Competitive bidding for contracts provides broad authority to the Regional Transit Authority to enter into P3 contracts for transportation facilities, which is unable to accept

(continued)

Table A1 (continued)

State	Category	Allows for unsolicited proposals?	Statute(s)	Short summary
				an unsolicited proposal. The statute refers to the procedural requirements previously enacted.
Louisiana	Broad		La. Rev. Stat. Ann. §§48:2020 to 2037	Encourages parishes and municipalities to use P3s to help the State finance improvements to the State highway system and to meet local transportation needs. Authorises parishes and municipalities to create transportation authorities, which can enter into agreements with public or private entities to construct, maintain, repair, and/or operate transportation projects. Allows transportation authorities to authorise the investment of public and private money to finance such projects, subject to compliance with the State law for the use of public funds.
Louisiana	Broad	Yes	La. Rev. Stat. Ann. §§48:2071 to 2074; La. Rev. Stat. Ann. §48:2077; La. Rev. Stat. Ann. §§48:2084 to 2084.15	Creates the Louisiana Transportation Authority to pursue alternative and innovative funding sources—including P3s, tolls, and unclaimed property bonds—to supplement public revenue sources and to improve Louisiana's transportation system. Allows the Authority to contract with a public or private entity to construct, maintain, repair, or operate authority projects, and to authorise the investment of public and private money to finance such projects, subject to compliance

(continued)

Table A1 (continued)

State	Category	Allows for unsolicited proposals?	Statute(s)	Short summary
				with the State law for the use of public funds. Allows a private entity to impose user fees, but prohibits a private entity from imposing tolls or user fees on any existing free transportation facility, unless the facility is improved or expanded. Allows for solicited and unsolicited proposals.
Maine	Broad	Yes	Me. Rev. Stat. Ann. Title 23, § 4251	Authorises the State DOT—with legislative approval—to enter into P3s for transportation projects with an estimated cost of more than US$25 million, or when a project proposal includes establishing tolls for existing transportation facilities which were not previously subject to tolls. Allows for solicited and unsolicited proposals. Sets standards and requirements for P3 proposals, including the carrying of certain studies. Requires P3 proposals to limit the use of State capital funding to less than 50% of the initial capital cost of the facility, and to the extent the practicable minimal use of public transportation funding sources. Allows a P3 agreement to authorise a private entity to impose tolls or fares, subject to certain requirements. Limits term length to 50 years, unless the Legislature approves a longer term., upon the recommendation of the Commissioner for Transportation.

(continued)

Table A1 (continued)

State	Category	Allows for unsolicited proposals?	Statute(s)	Short summary
Maryland		No	Md. Code Regs. § 23.3.05.05	County or local educational agencies can establish a P3 for the shared-use arrangements of school facilities in exchange for school property enhancements and/or revenue.
Maryland	Broad		Md. Code Ann., State Fin. & Proc. §§ 10a-101 to 10a-403	This statute provides authority to reporting agencies for State finance and procurement to enter into agreements for P3 project delivery. The statute allows agencies to determine their own regulations and processes for the procurement, development, and delivery of P3 projects. Eligible projects are those which "develop and strengthen a public infrastructure asset, in conjunction with a public-private partnership."
Maryland	Broad	Yes	Md. Code Regs. §§ 11. 07.06.01 to 14	This law establishes the Maryland Transportation Authority's programme for P3s. It describes the steering committee and the identification process, as well as the screening process, procurement steps, and delivery procedures. Allows for unsolicited proposals only.
Massachusetts	Broad	Yes	Mass. Gen. Laws Ann. Ch. 6C, §§1 to 74	MassDOT can solicit proposals and enter into contracts for design-build-finance-operate-maintain or design-build-operate-maintain services with the responsible and responsive bidder which submits the proposal which is the most

(continued)

Table A1 (continued)

State	Category	Allows for unsolicited proposals?	Statute(s)	Short summary
				advantageous for the department through the sale, lease, operation, and maintenance of a transportation facility within the Commonwealth. A Special Public-Private Partnership Infrastructure Oversight Commission is established, which must comment on and approve all requests for proposals.
Michigan	Broad	No	Mich. Comp. Laws § 124.401 to 426	This statute provides broad procurement authority to metro transportation authorities to implement P3 for transportation facilities.
Michigan	Broad		Mich. Comp. Laws Ann. §§ 125.1871 to 125. 1883	The Private Investment Infrastructure Funding Act authorises the department of transportation, county road commission, drain commissioner, city, village or township with jurisdiction of a public facility to establish a negotiating partnership to develop and finance public facilities. While not explicitly recognising P3 in the traditional sense, this Act has enabled agencies to negotiate with private entities for the development and financing of public facilities.
Minnesota	Limited	Yes	Minn. Stat. Ann. §§ 160. 84 to 98	This statute generally authorises State and local road authorities to solicit or accept proposals from and enter into development agreements with private entities to develop, finance, design, construct, improve, rehabilitate, own, and/or

(continued)

Table A1 (continued)

State	Category	Allows for unsolicited proposals?	Statute(s)	Short summary
				operate toll facilities. It also authorises the operation of user fees for high-occupancy vehicle lanes or dynamic shoulder lanes. The extent to which a private entity can operate and maintain a road is significantly limited. Section 160.845 prohibits a road authority or a private operator from converting, transferring, or utilising any portion of a highway to impose tolls or for use as a toll facility (excepting dynamic shoulder lanes or HOV/HOT lanes). Section 160.98 prohibits a road authority from selling, leasing, or executing a development agreement for a build-operate-transfer or build-transfer-operate facility that transfers an existing highway lane, or otherwise relinquishing management of a highway.
Mississippi	Limited	Yes	Miss. Code Ann. §§ 65-43-1 to 85	Authorises the Mississippi Transportation Commission county boards of supervisorsand/ or the governing authorities of municipalities to contract with other governmental agencies or private entities for the purpose of designing, financing, constructing, operating, and maintaining one or more new toll roads or toll bridges in the State. Prohibits non-compete clauses by only authorising toll roads or

(continued)

Table A1 (continued)

State	Category	Allows for unsolicited proposals?	Statute(s)	Short summary
				bridges at and alongside those locations where an alternate un-tolled route exists. Limits contract terms to 50 years, which cannot be extended or renewed. Allows for solicited and unsolicited proposals.
Missouri	Broad	Yes	Mo. Rev. Stat. §§ 227.600 to 669	The Missouri Public-Private Partnerships Transportation Act authorises the Highways and Transportation Commission to enter into agreements with private partners to finance, develop, and/or operate any pipeline, ferry, river port, airport, railroad, light rail, or other mass transit facility. Any project which has to been mentioned previously cannot be financed, developed, or operated by a private partner until it is approved by a people's vote. Allows for solicited and unsolicited projects.
Missouri			Mo. Rev. Stat. §§ 238.300 to 367	Authorises the creation of special purpose, non-profit "transportation corporations" by private parties, which can enter into agreements with the Highways and Transportation Commission to fund, promote, plan, design, construct, maintain, and operate one or more transportation projects. Authorises such corporations to issue bonds and to establish and charge user fees for projects. No part of the earnings or assets of a

(continued)

Table A1 (continued)

State	Category	Allows for unsolicited proposals?	Statute(s)	Short summary
				transportation corporation can represent a benefit for any private interests, person, or entity.
New Jersey	Limited	Yes	TBD; SB 865	This law authorises local government entities to enter into P3 agreements for the "development, construction, reconstruction, repair, alteration, improvement, extension, operation, and maintenance of any building, road, structure, infrastructure, or facility constructed or acquired by a local government unit to house local government functions, including any infrastructure or facility used or to be used by the public or in support of a public purpose or activity; provided that, with respect to a roadway or highway project, a qualifying project shall include an expenditure of at least US$ten million in public funds, or any expenditure in solely private funds." P3 lease terms are limited to 30 years. Qualifying projects have to be submitted to the New Jersey Economic Development Authority for its review and approval. The law allows for unsolicited proposals.
Nevada	Limited		Nev. Rev. Stat. §§ 338.161 to 167	This law authorises counties with a population exceeding 700,000 to enter into P3s for transportation projects,

(continued)

Table A1 (continued)

State	Category	Allows for unsolicited proposals?	Statute(s)	Short summary
				including mass transit facilities.
Nevada	Limited	Yes	Nev. Rev. Stat. §§ 338. 161 to 168	Allows private entities to submit a request to a public body to develop, construct, improve, maintain, or operate, or any combination thereof, a transportation facility. Excludes toll roads and toll bridges.
Nevada	Limited		Nev. Rev. Stat. Chapter 277A	This statute defines powers for regional transportation commissions and Section. 280 allows for the use of turnkey procurement and competitive negotiation procurement processes.
New Hampshire	Broad		NH Rev. Stat. Ann. 228:107 to 228:115	Establishes a P3 oversight commission to recommend projects to the Transportation Commissioner, using DBFOM or DBOM delivery models. The commission functions as an advisory board during P3 project implementation, by helping to develop the RFP and preparation of agreements.
North Carolina	Limited	No	NC Gen. Stat. § 136-18	Allows the State DOT to enter into a contract with a private developer to accomplish the engineering, design, or construction of improvements for any transportation infrastructure under its jurisdiction. Sets restrictions on such projects, including that DOT participation is limited to the lesser of either 10% of the engineering contract and any construction contract,

(continued)

Table A1 (continued)

State	Category	Allows for unsolicited proposals?	Statute(s)	Short summary
				or US$250,000, and that, in any case, DOT costs cannot exceed normal practices. Requires projects to be constructed in accordance with DOT-approved plans and specifications. Terms must be less than 50 years. Solicited proposals only are acceptable.
North Carolina	Limited	No	NC Gen. Stat. §§ 136-89.180 to 198	Authorises the North Carolina Turnpike Authority to enter into agreements with the State DOT, political subdivisions and private entities, and to expend such funds as it deems necessary pursuant to such agreements, and also to finance the acquisition, construction, equipping, operation, or maintenance of any turnpike project. Authorises the Authority to set and collect tolls and fees for the use of a turnpike project. Prohibits non-compete clauses by requiring the DOT to maintain an existing, alternate, comparable non-toll route which correspond to each turnpike project which is constructed pursuant to this article. Enables the authority to study, plan, and conduct preliminary design work on up to nine projects and then to design, establish, purchase, construct, operate, and maintain five identified projects only. Any additional projects require legislative approval.

(continued)

Table A1 (continued)

State	Category	Allows for unsolicited proposals?	Statute(s)	Short summary
Ohio	Broad	Yes	Ohio Rev. Code Ann. § 5501.71 to 5501.75	This statute defines the authority of the State DOT to enter into public-private initiatives, including guidelines for solicitation and selection. The State DOT can use P3 for public or private highway, road, street, parkway, public transit, aviation, or rail project, and any related rights-of-way, bridges, or tunnels. The DOT may use sealed bidding for tenders and the selection of proposals using qualifications or best value (or both).
Oklahoma	Limited		Okla. Code Ann. Tit. 74 § 5151 to 5158	The Oklahoma Public and Private Facilities and Infrastructure Act establishes a Partnership Committee to determine potential P3 projects. The statute requires that the Committee provide a public sector comparator for each project. The OK Office of P3 is responsible for procurement practices. The State DOT and Turnpike Authority are exempt from the law.
Oregon			Or. Rev. Stat. § 184.631	OR DOT's Research and Development Program can use P3 for State highways.
Oregon	Broad	Yes	Or. Rev. Stat. §§ 367.800 to 826	Establishes the Oregon Innovative Partnerships Program within the State DOT, which is authorised to enter into agreements with private entities to plan, acquire, finance, develop, design, construct, reconstruct, replace, improve, maintain, manage, repair,

(continued)

Table A1 (continued)

State	Category	Allows for unsolicited proposals?	Statute(s)	Short summary
				lease, and/or operate transportation projects. Lists specific goals for the programme, including to speed up project delivery, maximise innovation, and develop partnerships with private entities. Lists specific requirements for P3 agreements, including financing, risk management, penalties for non-performance, and incentives for performance. Allows for solicited and unsolicited proposals.
Oregon	Broad	Yes	Or. Rev. Stat. §§ 383. 001 to 075	Authorises the State DOT to enter into agreements with private entities and/or units of government to acquire, design, construct, reconstruct, operate, or maintain and repair tollway projects. Includes lease agreements. Allows the DOT or the private entity that operates a tollway project pursuant to an agreement with the DOT to impose and collect tolls. Allows for solicited and unsolicited proposals.
Pennsylvania	Broad	Yes	Penn. Conso. Stat.74 §§ 9101 to 9124	The law allows State or local public entities to enter into P3s for the design, construction, operation, maintenance, financing, or lease of transportation facilities. All partnerships must be approved by a Public-Private Transportation Partnerships Board. The bill also allows the legislature to block P3s for State-owned facilities and

(continued)

Table A1 (continued)

State	Category	Allows for unsolicited proposals?	Statute(s)	Short summary
				requires legislative approval for P3s on the Pennsylvania Turnpike.
Puerto Rico	Broad	No	PR Laws Ann. Tit. 9, §§ 2001 to 2021	Creates the Puerto Rico Highway and Transportation Authority. Empowers the Authority or the Department of Transportation and Public Works to contract with private parties to design, construct, operate, and maintain new highways, bridges, avenues, expressways, and ancillary transit facilities, and informative electronic signboards or billboards. Limits contract terms for the operation, administration, and maintenance phases to 50 years. Requires the Secretary of Transportation and Public Works or an official designated by him/her to be the representative of the public interest and to ensure that the private entity fulfils its contractual obligations, among other duties. Creates a negotiated competitive bidding process. In cases when an existing road is converted into a toll road, an alternate road that is not tolled has to be provided.
Puerto Rico	Broad	No	PR Laws Ann. Tit. 9, §§ 2001 to 2021P.R. Laws Ann. tit. 27, §§ 2601 to 2623	A comprehensive statute which authorises P3s, which was passed in 2009 (Senate Bill 469). States the Commonwealth's motives and goals for authorising P3s. Establishes the Public-Private Partnership Authority as

(continued)

Table A1 (continued)

State	Category	Allows for unsolicited proposals?	Statute(s)	Short summary
				an entity of the Government Development Bank. Empowers the Authority to establish P3s for infrastructure projects, and makes the Authority the sole government entity responsible for implementing public policy regarding P3s, as set forth in this act. Limits term lengths to 50 years, with extensions being subject to legislative approval. Creates guidelines for evaluating, approving, contracting, and overseeing P3 projects. The authority nominates a separate committee for each proposed project and the Authority members and the Project Committee assess the credentials of each project, with the Committee being able to issue RFQs and to negotiate contracts. Final approval of P3 contracts rests with the Governor.
South Carolina	Broad		SC Code Ann. §§57-5-1310 to 1495	Allows the State DOT to construct and operate turnpike facilities. Section 57-5-1330(1)(4) provides for the use of P3s for these facilities by allowing the DOT to exercise such authorisations as are granted by the provisions in other statute law to designate, establish, plan, abandon, improve, construct, maintain, and regulate turnpike facilities.

(continued)

Table A1 (continued)

State	Category	Allows for unsolicited proposals?	Statute(s)	Short summary
South Carolina	Broad		SC Code § 57-3-200	Authorises the State DOT to expend such funds as it deems necessary to enter into partnership agreements with private entities to finance, by tolls and other methods, the cost of acquiring, constructing, equipping, maintaining, and operating highways, roads, streets, and bridges in the State.
Tennessee	Limited		Tenn. Code §§ 54-3-101 to 54-3-113	Authorises the use of tolls as an additional and alternative method for funding or financing transportation facilities. Authorises the State DOT to enter into agreements with private parties to develop or operate a tollway, toll facility, or any part thereof. Limits authorisation to levy tolls initially to a pilot programme of two projects. Provides that existing highways cannot be converted into toll roads, but that additional lane capacity constructed on or along an existing highway or bridge can be developed and operated the same way as a tollway. Requires legislative approval.
Tennessee	Limited	Yes	Tenn. Code §§ 54-6-101 to 54-6-121	This law enables the DOT to use P3 delivery for a tollway or toll facility. The law outlines procedures for project procurement and determines the metrics that the DOT can consider when evaluating a proposal. Allows for unsolicited proposals.

(continued)

Table A1 (continued)

State	Category	Allows for unsolicited proposals?	Statute(s)	Short summary
Texas			Tex. Transportation Code Ann. §§222.001 to 107	Relates generally to funding and federal aid, with provisions pertaining to P3s. Prohibits the State DOT from using state highway funds to guarantee loans or insure bonds for costs associated with a toll facility of a public or private entity. Authorises the DOT to otherwise participate in the cost of acquiring, constructing, maintaining, or operating a toll facility of a public or private entity. Allows the DOT to enter into an agreement with a public or private entity to pay pass-through tolls (also known as shadow tolls) to the respective entity as reimbursement for the design, development, financing, construction, maintenance, or operation of a toll or non-toll facility in the State highway system.
Texas	Limited	Yes	Tex. Transportation Code Ann. §§ 366.401 to 409	Authorises regional tollway authorities to use comprehensive development agreements with private entities to design, develop, finance, construct, maintain, repair, operate, extend, or expand turnpike projects.
Utah	Limited	Yes	Utah Code Ann. § 63G-6-503; § 63G6a-103; § 6 3G-6a702; § 63G6a-703; § 63G-6a-707	Authorises the State DOT to accept proposals for, and to enter into tollway development agreements with public or private entities to study, predevelop, design, finance, acquire, construct, reconstruct,

(continued)

Table A1 (continued)

State	Category	Allows for unsolicited proposals?	Statute(s)	Short summary
				maintain, repair, operate, extend, or expand tollway facilities. Defines the terms that must be included in such agreements. Tollway development agreements must be approved by the Utah Transportation Commission. Allows for solicited and unsolicited proposals.
Utah	Limited		Utah Code Ann. §72-6-118; Utah Code Ann. 72-2-120	Authorises the State DOT to establish, expand, and operate tollways and related facilities. Authorises the DOT to enter into contracts, agreements, licences, franchises, tollway development agreements, or other arrangements for tollway projects. Prohibits the DOT or any other entity from establishing or operating a tollway in an existing State highway, unless approved by the Transportation Commission and the Legislature, except for high occupancy toll lanes or additional capacity lanes. Requires revenue generated from tollway development agreement projects to be deposited into the Tollway Special Revenue Fund created in Section. 72-2-120, which is to be used for transportation facilities within the corridor served by the tollway, unless the revenue is to the private entity or identified for a different purpose under the agreement.

(continued)

Table A1 (continued)

State	Category	Allows for unsolicited proposals?	Statute(s)	Short summary
Vermont	Limited	Yes	19 V.S.A. § 26	This statute established, in 2019, a pilot programme for P3s. This programme accepts unsolicited proposals as well as solicited proposals to undertake a P3 project. The statute describes the factors used to evaluate proposals and requires the total estimated State funding over the lifetime of the project to be less than US $2000,000.00. Eligible projects requiring legislative approval are defined as projects which have not been approved in the most recently adopted Transportation Program, or projects with an estimated State funding greater than US $2000,000.00 over the project's lifetime. The statute also describes legislative oversight requirements and the report to be made regarding the pilot programme's impact.
Virginia	Broad	Yes	Va. Code §§ 33.2-1800	The Public-Private Transportation Act of 1995 (subsequently modified) is a comprehensive P3 statute which is intended to encourage private investment in transportation facilities. Authorises a private entity to develop and/or operate a qualifying transportation facility, subject to approval from and a comprehensive agreement with the responsible public entity. Contains detailed

(continued)

Table A1 (continued)

State	Category	Allows for unsolicited proposals?	Statute(s)	Short summary
				implementation guidelines, including specific requirements for comprehensive agreements. Stipulates the powers and duties of a private entity in a P3 and provides financing mechanisms. Allows for solicited and unsolicited proposals.
Washington	Broad	Yes	Wash. Rev. Code §§ 47.29.010 to 900	Authorises the State DOT to enter into P3s for transportation projects, whether capital or operating, where the State's primary purpose for the project is to facilitate the safe transportation of people or goods via any mode of travel. Defines the terms which must be included in agreements. Requires a review by and the approval of the Transportation Commission for P3 contracts or agreements. Requires an advisory committee for any project that costs US $300 million or more. Authorises the DOT to solicit or accept unsolicited proposals after 1 January, 2007, for eligible transportation projects.
Washington, D.C.	Broad	Yes	D.C. Code §§ 2-271.01 to 2-275.01	Establishes an Office of Public-Private Partnerships within the City Administrator's office and specifies its duties, including the established of a fund to pay for the Office's activities. The statute details the procurement process, including that of the receipt of unsolicited proposals.

(continued)

Table A1 (continued)

State	Category	Allows for unsolicited proposals?	Statute(s)	Short summary
				Section § 2–273.09 describes the transparency measures and the Office's relationship with the City Council.
Washington, D.C.	Broad		D.C. Code § 2-356.01	This statute provides general authority for construction projects and related management services. Authorised delivery models include architectural and engineering services, construction management, construction management at risk, design-bid-build, design-build, design-build-finance-operate-maintain, design-build-operate-maintain, and, operations and maintenance.
West Virginia	Broad	No	WVa. Code §§ 17-28-1 to 12	Authorises the Highways Division to enter into comprehensive agreements with private entities to acquire, construct, or improve transportation facilities. Sets guidelines for soliciting proposals. Specifies the content of comprehensive agreements. Allows a private developer to charge user fees, as long as they are consistent with the rate of return specified in the agreement; requires the schedule and amount of initial user fees and any fee increase to be approved by the Commissioner of the Highways Division. The original bill expired in 2011 and was re-installed in 2013.

(continued)

Table A1 (continued)

State	Category	Allows for unsolicited proposals?	Statute(s)	Short summary
Wisconsin	Limited	No	Wis. Stat. Ann. § 84.01 (30)	Authorises the State DOT to enter into build-operate-lease or transfer agreements with private entities for the construction of transportation projects and for the maintenance or operation of projects which are not purchased by the State upon their completion. Lists specific provisions which must be included in every agreement. An agreement may not be entered into unless the DOT determines that it advances the public interest and that the private entity fulfils certain pre-established criteria.

Source: Adapted from FHWA 2018

References

Albalate, D., Bel, G., & Fageda, X. (2015). When supply travels far beyond demand: Causes of oversupply in Spain's transport infrastructure. *Transport Policy, 41*, 80–89.

Albalate, D., & Bel-Piñana, P. (2019). The effects of public private partnerships on road safety outcomes. *Accident Analysis & Prevention, 128*, 53–64.

Allard, G., & Trabant, A. (2008). Public-private partnerships in Spain: Lessons and opportunities. *International Business & Economics Research Journal (IBER)*, 7(2).

Andrade, J. S., & Duarte, A. P. (2016). Crowding-in and crowding-out effects of public investments in the Portuguese economy. *International Review of Applied Economics, 30*(4), 488–506.

Araújo, J. F. F. E., & Silvestre, H. C. (2014). As parcerias público-privadas para o desenvolvimento de infraestrutura rodoviária: experiência recente em Portugal. *Revista de Administração Pública, 48*(3), 571–593.

Armijo, L. E., & Rhodes, S. D. (2017). Explaining infrastructure underperformance in Brazil: Cash, political institutions, corruption, and policy Gestalts. *Policy Studies, 38*(3), 231–247.

ASCE. (2017). *Infrastructure report card: 2017*. American Society of Civil Engineers, Technical Report.

Baer, W. (2001). Brazilian economy: Growth and development. ABC-CLIO.

Bitran, E., Nieto-Parra, S., & Robledo, J. S. (2013). *Opening the black box of contract renegotiations: An analysis of road concessions in Chile, Colombia and Peru* (No. 317). OECD Publishing.

Carpintero, S., & Ole, H. P. (2014). PPP projects in transport: Evidence in Spain. *Public Money and Management, 34*(1), 43–50.

Carranza, L., Daude, C., & Melguizo, Á. (2014). Public infrastructure investment and fiscal sustainability in Latin America: Incompatible goals? *Journal of Economic Studies, 41*.

Casady, C. B., & Geddes, R. R. (2016). *Private participation in US infrastructure: The role of PPP Units*. American Enterprise Institute.

Catalão, F., Cruz, C. O., & Miranda Sarmento, J. (2019). Exogenous determinants of cost deviations and overruns in local infrastructure projects. *Construction Management and Economics, 37*(12), 697–711.

Corral, A. M. L., Soliño, A. S., & López, S. C. (2006). Las conceciones de infraestructuras y equipamientos públicos en España. *Boletín económico de ICE, 2890*.

Cruz, C. O., & Marques, R. C. (2011). Revisiting the Portuguese experience with public-private partnerships. *African Journal of Business Management, 5*(11), 4023–4032.

Cruz, C. O., & Marques, R. C. (2013a). Risk-sharing in highway concessions: Contractual diversity in Portugal. *Journal of Professional Issues in Engineering Education and Practice, 139*(2), 99–108.

Cruz, C. O., & Marques, R. C. (2013b). Endogenous determinants for renegotiating concessions: Evidence from local infrastructure. *Local Government Studies, 39*(3), 352–374.

Cruz, C. O., & Marques, R. C. (2013c). Exogenous determinants for renegotiating public infrastructure concessions: Evidence from Portugal. *Journal of Construction Engineering and Management, 139*(9), 1082–1090.

Cruz, C. O., & Marques, R. C. (2014). Theoretical considerations on quantitative PPP viability analysis. *Journal of Management in Engineering, 30*(1), 122–126.

Cruz, C. O., & Sarmento, J. M. (2019). Traffic forecast inaccuracy in transportation: A literature review of roads and railways projects. *Transportation*, 1–36.

Curristine, T., Lonti, Z., & Jourmard, I. (2008). Improving public sector efficiency: Challenges and opportunities. *Presupuesto y gasto público, 51*, 161–198.

Da Cruz, N., & Marques, R. C. (2012). Mixed companies and local governance: No man can serve two masters. *Public Administration, 90*(3), 737–758.

Deloitte. (2016). *Point of view: Infrastructure industry and concessions in Chile*.

Deloitte. (2017). *Closing the infrastructure gap: The role of public-private partnerships*. Research Study.

Deloitte, Uría Menéndez and Seopan (2017). *Hacia un modelo eficiente de colaboración público-privada*. Technical Report, Febrero 2017.

Deye, A. (2015). *U.S. infrastructure PPPs: Ready for takeoff?* Opinion, World Bank PPP Blog. Washington, DC.

Engel, E., Fischer, R., & Galetovic, A. (2011). *Public-private partnerships to revamp us infrastructure*. Hamilton Policy Brief, Brookings Institution.

Engel, E., Fischer, R. D., & Galetovic, A. (2014a). *The economics of public-private partnerships: A basic guide*. Cambridge: Cambridge University Press.

Engel, E., Fischer, R., & Galetovic, A. (2014b). *Renegotiations in public-private partnerships: Theory and evidence*. International Transport Forum Discussion Paper.

Engel, E., Fischer, R., & Galetovic, A. (2015). *Soft budgets and renegotiations in public-private partnerships: Theory and evidence*. Univ. de Chile, Department de Economía.

Engel, E., Fischer, R. D., & Galetovic, A. (2019). International experience with public-private partnerships in infrastructure. In *Economics of Infrastructure Investment*. University of Chicago Press.

EPEC. (2014). *Portugal: PPP units and related institutional framework*. Technical Report.

Evans, P. B. (2018). *Dependent development: The alliance of multinational, state, and local capital in Brazil*. Princeton University Press.

Federal Highway Administration. (2019). *Public-private partnerships (P3 procurement: a guide for public owners)*. FHWA-HIN-18-004.

Fernandes, E., & Pacheco, R. R. (2018). Managerial performance of airports in Brazil before and after concessions. *Transportation Research Part A: Policy and Practice, 118*, 245–257.

Fraga, M.V., & Ortiz, A.M.S. (2019). *The public-private partnerships Law Review* – Edition 5: Spain. Available from https://thelawreviews.co.uk/edition/the-public-private-partnership-law-review-edition-5/1189717/spain

FHWA. (2018). *State P3 legislation*. Available at https://www.fhwa.dot.gov/ipd/p3/legislation/

Froud, J. (2003). The Private Finance Initiative: Risk, uncertainty and the state. *Accounting, Organizations and Society, 28*(6), 567–589.

Garrido, L., Range, T., Baeza, M. D. L. A., & Vassallo, J. M. (2019). Does EU support contribute to economically successful public-private partnerships? A panel data analysis of road PPP projects in Spain. *Journal of Public Policy, 39*(1), 65–87.

Guasch, J. L., Laffont, J. J., & Straub, S. (2003). *Renegotiation of concessions contracts in Latin America*. Policy research working paper 3011, The World Bank.

Guasch, J. L., Laffont, J. J., & Straub, S. (2006). Renegotiation of concession contracts: A theoretical approach. *Review of Industrial Organization, 29*(1–2), 55–73. https://doi.org/10.1007/s11151-006-9109-5.

Guasch, J. L., & Straub, S. (2009). Corruption and concession renegotiations. Evidence from the water and transport sectors in Latin America. *Utilities Policy, 17*(2), 185–190. https://doi.org/10.1016/j.jup.2008.07.003.

H.M. Treasury. (2010). *Managing complex capital investment programmes utilising private finance – A current best practice model for departments*. National Audit Office & Infrastructure UK, London.

H.M. Treasury. (2012). *A new approach to public private partnerships*. Technical Report, ISBN 978-1-909096-14-1.

Heald, D. (2003). *Value for money tests and accounting treatment in PFI schemes*. Accounting, Auditing & Accountability Journal.

Hodge, G. A., & Greve, C. (2007). Public–private partnerships: an international performance review. *Public Administration Review, 67*(3), 545–558.

Kearney, A.T. (2015). *Priority areas for sustainable investment in infrastructure in Spain*. Technical Report.

Kurihara. (2016). Spanish construction companies leading the global PPP market. Mitsui Global Strategic Studies Institute Monthly Report.

Li, B., Akintoye, A., Edwards, P. J., & Hardcastle, C. (2005). Critical success factors for PPP/PFI projects in the UK construction industry. *Construction Management and Economics, 23*(5), 459–471.

Lorenzen, C. C., Barrientos, M. E., & Babbar, S. (2001). To*ll road concessions: The Chilean experience*. PFG Discussion paper series, Number 124.

Macário, R., Ribeiro, J., & Costa, J. D. (2015). Understanding pitfalls in the application of PPPs in transport infrastructure in Portugal. *Transport Policy, 41*, 90–99.

Martinez, A. L., & Queiroz, C. (2017). PPP challenges: The case of Spain. *Advances in Public-Private Partnerships* (pp. 541–548).

Martín-Oliver, A., Ruano, S., & Salas-Fumás, V. (2017). The fall of Spanish cajas: Lessons of ownership and governance for banks. *Journal of Financial Stability, 33*, 244–260.

Ministry of the Economy. (2019). www.planejamento.gov.br. Accessed from December 16, 2019.

Mirchandani, D., & Jacobo, A. R. (2020). *United States*. The public-private partnership law review – edition 6.

Neto, D. D. C. E. S., Cruz, C. O., & Sarmento, J. M. (2017). Understanding the patterns of PPP renegotiations for infrastructure projects in Latin America: The case of Brazil. *Competition and Regulation in Network Industries, 18*(3–4), 271–296.

e Neto, D. D. C. S., Cruz, C. O., & Sarmento, J. M. (2019). Renegotiation of transport public private partnerships: Policy implications of the Brazilian experience in the Latin American context. *Case Studies on Transport Policy, 7*(3), 554–561.

Neto, D., Cruz, C. O., Rodrigues, F., & Silva, P. (2020). PPP development and governance in Latin America: An analysis of Brazilian state PPP units. *Journal of Infrastructure Systems*.

Opara, M., & Rouse, P. (2019). The perceived efficacy of public-private partnerships: A study from Canada. *Critical Perspectives on Accounting, 58*, 77–99.

Osborne, S. (2000). *Public-private partnerships: Theory and practice in international perspective*. Routledge.

Pereira, A. M., & Andraz, J. M. (2005). Public investment in transportation infrastructure and economic performance in Portugal. *Review of Development Economics, 9*(2), 177–196.

Pereira, A. M., & de Fátima Pinho, M. (2008). Public investment and budgetary consolidation in Portugal. *Portuguese Economic Journal, 7*(3), 183–203.

Pereira, A. M., & Roca-Sagalés, O. (2003). Spillover effects of public capital formation: Evidence from the Spanish regions. *Journal of Urban Economics, 53*(2), 238–256.

PWC. (2016). *Public-private partnerships in the US: The state of the market and the road ahead*. November, 2016.

Richards, M., Calder, K., & Hadrill, A. (2019). *The Law Reviews: The public-private partnerships law review*, Edition 5. Accessible at https://thelawreviews.co.uk/edition/the-public-private-partnership-law-review-edition-5/1189721/united-kingdom

Roumboutsos, A., & Anagnostopoulos, K. P. (2008). Public–private partnership projects in Greece: Risk ranking and preferred risk allocation. *Construction Management and Economics, 26*(7), 751–763.

Sarmento, J. M. (2010). Do public-private partnerships create value for money for the public sector? The Portuguese experience. *OECD Journal on Budgeting, 10*(1), 1–27.

Sarmento, J. M. (2018). *Public finance and national accounts in the European context*. Berlin: Springer International Publishing.

Sarmento, J. M., & Renneboog, L. (2015). 16 Portugal's experience with public private partnerships. *Public Private Partnerships: A Global Review*, 266.

Sarmento, J., & Renneboog, L. (2016a). *Renegotiating public-private partnerships*. European Corporate Governance Institute (ECGI)-finance working paper (416).

Sarmento, J. M., & Renneboog, L. (2016b). Anatomy of public-private partnerships: Their creation, financing and renegotiations. *International Journal of Managing Projects in Business*.

Sener and Seopan. (2017). *Análisis de la inversion en infraestructuras prioritarias em España*. Techincal Report, Febrero, 2017.

Shadrina, E., & Vinogradov, D. (2013). PPP Legislation: An economic justification and international experience. *Public Administration Issues, 4*, 164–188.

Shaoul, J. (2005). A critical financial analysis of the Private Finance Initiative: Selecting a financing method or allocating economic wealth? *Critical Perspectives on Accounting, 16*(4), 441–471.

Siemiatycki, M. (2015). Public private partnerships in Canada. In *Public Private Partnerships* (pp. 79–93). Routledge.

Silvestre, H. C., & de Araújo, J. F. F. E. (2012). Public-private partnerships/private finance initiatives in Portugal: Theory, practice, and results. *Public Performance & Management Review, 36*(2), 316–339.

UTAP. (2019). *Annual report on PPP expenditure*. Technical Report, Lisbon.

Van Den Hurk, M., & Verhoest, K. (2016). The challenge of using standard contracts in public–private partnerships. *Public Management Review, 18*(2), 278–299.

Wanke, P. F. (2013). Physical infrastructure and shipment consolidation efficiency drivers in Brazilian ports: A two-stage network-DEA approach. *Transport Policy, 29*, 145–153.

Wanke, P., & Barros, C. P. (2016). New evidence on the determinants of efficiency at Brazilian ports: A bootstrapped DEA analysis. *International Journal of Shipping and Transport Logistics, 8*(3), 250–272.

Yescombe, E. R., & Farquharson, E. (2018). *Public-Private Partnerships for Infrastructure: Principles of Policy and Finance*. Butterworth-Heinemann.

Zymler, B., & Almeida, G. H. D. L. R. (2008). O controle externo das concessões de serviços públicos e das parcerias público-privadas 2a edição. Editora Forum.

Chapter 6
Renegotiation Case Studies

6.1 Methodology Framework

This Subsection provides a brief overview of the methodology used by the authors in the case-studies of Public-Private Partnerships (PPPs)[1] renegotiations presented in the next chapter.

As we have seen in the previous chapters, the literature on PPP renegotiations has mainly been focussed on the macro aspects of the process. As described above, the literature is particularly centred on the determinants of renegotiations (see for instance, Guasch 2004; Guasch et al. 2003, 2007, 2008; De Brux 2010; Cruz and Marques 2013a; Domingues and Zlatkovic 2015; Domingues and Sarmento 2016; Reis and Sarmento 2017; Sarmento and Renneboog 2015, 2016a, b; Neto et al. 2017, 2019). Studies have been carried out to understand what drives and influences renegotiations, what are the causes and principle outcomes of the renegotiation process, and what contractual, political, institutional, and governance aspects of a PPP increases or reduce the likelihood of a renegotiation event. Furthermore, the literature has been focussed on the determinants of a renegotiation lead by one of the parties (either a private or public-led renegotiation) (Guasch and Straub 2006, 2009). In addition, studies have analysed the fiscal impacts of renegotiations (Bitran et al. 2013) and others have been focussed more on conceptual models to determine the likelihood and impacts of renegotiations (Estache et al. 2003, 2009; Engel et al. 2006a, 2009; Roumboutsos 2015; Pantelias and Roumboutsos 2015). However, few studies have used case-studies to analyse the why and how of PPP renegotiations (e.g., Macário et al. 2015a, b; Sarmento and Renneboog 2016a).

In this section, we analyse six case-studies of PPP contracts in the transport sector, which focus on the renegotiation of these contracts. The PPPs in question

[1]For a definition of PPPs please see Chap. 2, or Grimsey and Lewis (2005); OECD (2008) or Sarmento (2010).

C. Oliveira Cruz, J. Miranda Sarmento, *The Renegotiations of Public Private Partnerships in Transportation*, Competitive Government: Public Private Partnerships, https://doi.org/10.1007/978-3-030-61258-0_6

[Indiana toll road (US); A1 (UK); MG-50 (Brazil); Transantiago (Chile); Fertagus (Portugal), and; AP-7 highway (Spain)] cover various countries and analyse the roads and rail transportation sectors.

Case studies are frequently used in management as a research tool (Yin 2008). This author emphasises that these case studies should not be confused with the case-studies that are used for teaching purposes, as the criteria differ substantially. However, relatively few cases have been developed in this area. Despite the fact that the stereotype of this method is considered to be a weak research method, we consider that this method is extremely valuable for this particular field of knowledge, partly due to the intrinsic characteristics of case-studies.

The first of these characteristic of case-studies is that they are appropriated for new areas of research (Eisenhardt 1989). To new areas, with recent and scarce knowledge, carrying out a study through the analysis of selected examples can be a useful tool to understand the concepts and decisions involved in PPP contracts. This type of research can be used to achieve various research aims, for example: to provide a description of phenomena, to develop or test a theory, and to explore areas where the existing knowledge is limited. Therefore, case-studies are useful when "research and theory are at the early formative stages" (Benbasat et al. 1987). This context is particularly suitable for the study of PPPs, which are a new and recent subject, particularly in this area, where academic research is still in its advent and many issues still need to be addressed. The six case-studies analysed in the next section of this book enable an understanding of the specific characteristics and idiosyncrasies of PPPs and the complex process of renegotiations and its outcomes.

According to Yin (2008), case-studies can be used to explore, describe, or explain. The two questions are "how" and "why". In the next chapter, we aim to answer following questions for each case-study:

1. Why was the PPP renegotiated? (i.e., what were the main motives that trigger the renegotiation and which party was more interested in the process);
2. How did the renegotiation occur? (i.e., what main steps and tools were used in the renegotiation process);
3. How was the renegotiation concluded? (which of the main objectives were achieved and how, and what can be learned from the case study).

In this way, we attempt to identify a set of decisions which govern renegotiation and also to determine why specific decisions were taken, how they were taken, and what results each decision produces. Our focus will be on the in-depth understanding of a phenomenon and its context.

The reasons for choosing these case-studies were the following: (1) multiple case-studies are considered to be a more robust approach; (2) the choice of case studies enables a comparison of the different outcomes from renegotiation which are motivated by different conditions and decisions, and; (3) contrasting results due to predictable reasons can be compared.

However, the limits of case-studies first needs to be understood. Even though case studies present a variety of evidence, they do not provide a base for scientific generalisation, as they tend to generalise theoretical propositions, rather than populations or universes. The goal is to expand and generalise theories and not to enumerate frequencies (Yin 2008). According to this author, the advantage of case studies is that they provide a wealth of detail, give credibility to situations, and provide real outcomes. The result theory is often novel, testable, and empirically valid (Eisenhardt 1989).

Based on this, each case-study presented in the next section has the following structure:

1. Introduction (describing the main features and objectives of the project and also the public partner);
2. The PPP process (describing the tendering and the winning bid—the private partner);
3. The financial structure of the PPP;
4. The risk allocation matrix;
5. The renegotiation case;
6. The main findings from the case study.

6.2 Case Study: The Indiana Toll Road in the US

6.2.1 Introduction

The Indiana toll road open in 1956, comprising 157 miles (251 km), crossing Northern Indiana, from the Ohio border to the Illinois State line, connecting Chicago Skyway with the Eastern seaboard of the United States. In 2006, not only did the State of Indiana require funding for new infrastructures, as the highway was losing money as tolls had not been increased for over 20 years, but also most of the revenues originated from non-Indiana drivers (particularly from commercial trucks) (Samuel 2006). The highway was a concession awarded to a firm called the Indiana Toll Road Concession Company (ITRCC). In addition to a fee payment to the State of US$3.8 billion, this company invested US$200 million in improving the highway and in the maintenance, repair, and operation of the infrastructure. As compensation, the company collects the tolls from the highway users [under a lease agreement, which Gilmour (2012), compares to a bond revenue, but with the added advantage that revenue risk was allocated to the private sector, and therefore, this was not recognised in the state's public debt]. The private consortium filed for bankruptcy in September of 2014 (Chap. 11[2]) and started a renegotiation process which is analysed below in this case-study.

[2]Chapter 11: Typically filed by businesses who intend to continue operations and repay creditors at the same time, through the implementation of a court-approved reorganisation plan. This reorganisation can involve restructuring debt and also the rescaling of operations for profitability (Adarkwa et al. 2017).

6.2.2 The PPP Process

The election of a new governor in 2005 led to a change in the state policy regarding infrastructures and transportation (Wensits 2006). The Indiana Finance Authority was authorised to enter into a concession agreement with a private partner to upgrade and operate the Indiana toll road. The state requested bids for a 75 years lease of the Toll Road, in exchange for the right to maintain, operate, and collect tolls (a long-term lease of the toll road was an innovator process in the US at the time, Zhang et al. 2013). The state stipulated the operational and legal requirements, together with the minimum standards. Bidding companies calculated the level of investment required to maintain these requirements and standards (Bel and Foote 2009) and by October of 2005, the state had received proposals and had selected the qualified bidders and had issued invitations to tender. The state announced the winner at the end of January, 2006.

The tender was won by a consortium comprised of the construction firm Cintra of Spain and Macquarie Atlas Roads (MQA) of Australia (each company owning 50%—which were the same firms that had won the tender for the Chicago Skyway in 2004), with a bid of US$3.8 billion, which exceeded the 2nd highest bid by US$1 billion (a total of four bidders[3] competed for this tender, which were all invited after a pre-qualification process, with price being the only bid criterion). As Bel and Foote (2009), mentioned, both the city of Chicago (in the case of the Chicago skyway) and the State of Indiana maximised the concession prices by the way that they organised the tender process and the concession structure).

The private partner was responsible for four expansions of the Indiana toll road: (1) the implementation of an electronic toll system; (2) the expansion from two to three lanes from Milepost 14 to Milepost 15.5; (3) the expansion from three to four lanes from Milepost 10.6 to Milepost 14, and; (4) the expansion from two to three lanes from Milepost 18.5 to Milepost 20.27. The concession agreement was signed on June 29, 2006, and the two companies formed the Indiana Toll Road Concession Company to operate the highway, starting in July, 2006. Several court cases were instigated by the non-winning bids, however a decision was made a few years later ruling in favour of the State of Indiana.

6.2.3 The Financial Structure of the PPP

The concession revenues were exclusively commercial, mainly originating from tolls, together rents from commercial activities. The operator forecast that 95% of total revenues would come from tolls, with the other 5% originating from commercial activities (Zhang et al. 2013). Tolls were allowed to be increased by a set amount

[3]The other three bidders were: *Itenere; Babcock & Brown/Challenger-Transfield; Morgan Stanley/ Autostrade.*

for the first few years [although up until 2010, they were not increased (Gilmour 2012)]. They were then permitted at the rate of the greater of one of the following three factors: 2% a year, the rate of inflation (the CPI), or the growth in GDP per capita (Checherita and Gifford 2007). The initial investment amounted to US€4 billion (US€3.8 billion for the fee payed, as well as US€200 million of capex).

The project finance was mainly raised through debt (US$3.25 billion—81%), with equity amounting to US$750 million (19%). According to Healey (2014) and Garvin (2019), the debt was arranged in three tranches: Series A was a US$3.25 billion term loan, Series B was a US$150 million liquidity facility to fund certain interest payments during the early period, and; Series C was a US$665 billion liquidity facility to fund capital improvements through to 2014; all the tranches were due in 2015. The private firm expected an IRR of 13%, with a payback of 15 years. However, according to Bel and Foote (2009), when comparing the value of US$3.8 billion for the EBITDA of 2005 (which represents the year before the concession was awarded) with the EBITDA of US$64 million in 2015 (from revenues of $98 million), the multiple factor of the transaction was 68×. The authors compare this value of 68× with the similar value for the multiple factor of the Chicago Skyway concession (2004) of 63×, and also with that of concessions in France, which had multiple factors of approximately 12×. The authors conclude that the high value of the US concession was related with the forecast for the increase in toll prices and the increase in efficiency—which would both lead to gains for the private sector.

When analysing efficiency gains, it is important to refer that the EBITDA/ revenues for the Indiana Toll Road was close to 65%, which represents a value which is close to that of the other highways in both the US and France (Bel and Foote 2009). This could show that the potential efficiency gains were not as high as those expected by the private partner. Furthermore, as mentioned by the authors, this highway has a strong monopolistic characteristic, which the private sector expected to exploit by setting high tolls, in order to maximise profits. In addition, a study carried out at the time of the concession by Crowe-Chizek (2006) shows that the NPV of the forecast future revenues should tolls increase by as much as that of the previous decades was US$1.9 billion. This implies that in the US, the additional increase of tolls, together with the increase of traffic and the higher efficiency of the private sector amounted to US$2 billion, in NPV terms. However, Enright (2006), using more optimistic forecasts, estimated a NPV of forecast future revenues of US $1 billion greater than the winning bid.

6.2.4 *The Risk Allocation Matrix*

The private partner was responsible for the upgrade and improvement of the highway, with an investment of US€200 million. In addition, all operation and maintenance risks, together with the financial risks, were allocated to the private partner. There was also a "non-compete" clause, which was designed to assure that if the State of Indiana decided to build a new "comparable highway" in direct competition to the Indiana toll road, then the private partner would be financially compensated. All revenue risk are borne by the concessionaire.

6.2.5 The Motives for the Renegotiation

Several renegotiations took place until the private firm filed for bankruptcy in 2014, as traffic was less than 35% of the forecast (Mallett 2014). The first renegotiation occurred in 2006, when the private partner accepted to not increase tolls prices until the electronic tolling system was fully implemented. As compensation, the public sector paid the ITRCC consortium US$60 million. The second renegotiation also took place in 2006, with the public sector accepting a reduction in the investment contracted. The third renegotiation event occurred in 2007, with some investment being delayed until 2010. The fourth renegotiation was in 2010, with the public sector agreeing with certain investments being postponed until 2011.

The last renegotiation was that of 2014, following the bankruptcy of the private firm (Berke et al. 2012). The motives were mainly the following two: first, revenues from tolls during the first years of operation were substantially below those forecast, particularly after the 2008 financial crisis (Schnitzler 2009); second, the project's interest rate swaps—which was a condition imposed by the lenders—worked against the consortium's financial position by increasing its debt by US$2.15 billion (Gifford et al. 2014). It is important to mention that traffic forecast was characterised by great uncertainty—due to major construction projects of other highways of the Indiana network and also to changes in the toll system (Zhang et al. 2013). Additionally, the 2008 financial crisis led to a substantial decrease in traffic, particularly of commercial trucks, which represents the main component of tolls revenues in this project (which is more sensitive to economic cycles). In effect, the ITRCC consortium's bid in 2006 was excessively high, as it was submitted at the peak of a "bubble" in the financial markets with high levels of leverage and asset prices. In 2013, ITRCC was liable to US$193 million in debt service, whereas its revenue was only US$158 million (Randazzo and Fitzgerald 2014).

ITRCC used a financing structure with an interest rate swap, which fixed its interest rates with a counterpart with a variable interest rate. When this swap was negotiated at the timer of the celebration of the contract in 2006, it was likely that the forecast value of each party's position would be equal, however interest rates reached historic lows in 2008 on account of the financial crisis, which led to almost US$2 billion of losses for the company, triggering its bankruptcy.

6.2.6 The Renegotiation Case

When the private consortium filed for bankruptcy[4, 5] its shareholders sold the company to a new investor (Australia's IFM Investors),[6] which conducted the bankruptcy process without discharge the duty to continue the provision of the service.[7]

6.2.7 Main Findings from the Case-Study

The case of the Indiana toll road renegotiation originated from an overestimation of forecasted traffic and an underestimation of financing costs. As in other projects (e.g., the AP7 highway in Spain, which is also discussed in this book), it was impossible to recover from the financial distress caused by the 2008 financial crisis,

---

[4]The company had about $6.3 billion in obligations to secured lenders (Bathon 2014).

[5]The proposal sought an early exit from Chap. 11 requesting that the court allow a post-bankruptcy approval of an asset sale by August 2015 with proceeds distributed among its creditors, OR if the asset sale was unsuccessful its creditors could buy a 95.75% stake in the restructured company, using proceeds from a $2.75 billion additional borrowing to restructure its debt (Randazzo and Fitzgerald 2014). The plan had support from more than 87% of senior secured debtholders and 100% support from equity owners (Schnitzler 2009).

[6]Roumeliotis and Stone (2014) as follows:

1. A consortium of Canada Pension Plan Investment Board (CPPIB) with Ferrovial SA's toll road operator Cintra and Canadian investment manager Brookfield Asset Management;
2. Australia's Hastings Funds Management who partnered with the California Public Employees' Retirement System (Calpers) and Italian toll road operator Autostrade Meridionali SpA;
3. Spanish infrastructure operator Abertis Infraestructuras SA with Borealis, which is the infrastructure investment arm of the Ontario Municipal Employees Retirement System;
4. Alberta Investment Management Corporation (AIMCo) and Abu Dhabi Investment Authority (ADIA); and
5. Australian infrastructure fund manager IFM Investors, which is owned by 30 Australian pension funds.

[7]Australia's IFM Investors reached a $5.73 billion agreement to purchase ITRCC's lease of ITR for 66 years until 2081. IFM contributed $3.2 billion in equity, expecting yields ranging from 8 to 9%; the balance of the funds came from $2.5 billion in senior debt financing from nine banks and three institutional investors (Reinhardt 2015a). ITRCC, indicated that current traffic levels will generate revenues sufficient to repay the new senior debt, so IFM's large equity contribution was critical (Reinhardt 2015a). By July 2015, IFM had refinanced a portion of the bank debt through the issue of over $1 billion of senior secured revenue bonds by ITRCC; the notes were rated BBB and applied to a $551 million bridge loan and a portion of a $1.27 billion term loan (Reinhardt 2015b). Deal between the state and ITRCC where the state would receive $1 billion over three years from ITRCC in exchange for a one-time 35% toll increase on commercial trucks; the Indiana Finance Authority (IFA) subsequently approved the arrangement (Carden 2018). The deal, however, caught legislators by surprise, and several voiced concerns about the transparency of the arrangement and their lack of involvement (Kelly 2018a, b).

Table 6.1 Main features of A1 PFI

PFI contract	Year	N° Km	Scope	Private consortium (DBFO)
A1 (M) Alconbury–Peterborough	1996	21	Road management and motorway widening	Peterborough Services (Peterborough) Ltd. (Shareholders: Barclays Integrated Infrastructure Fund 41.66%; Kellogg Brown & Root 25%, and; Abertis Motorways UK Ltd. 33.33%)
M1–A1 Motorway Link	1996	30	New motorway, motorway widening and new interchange	Yorkshire Link Ltd. (Shareholders: Balfour Beatty 50% and Barclays Infrastructure Investors 50%)
A1 Darrington–Dishforth	2002	22	Construct two new sections of motorway and communications	Road Management Services (Darrington) Ltd. (Shareholders: Barclays Infrastructure Investors Ltd. 25%, Semperian 50% and Kellogg Brown & Root Ltd. 25%)

Own table
DBFO Design, Built, Finance, and Operate (with the main risks being allocated to the private sector in these PFI)
Source of information: "DBFO Information" (Highways Agencies); ACCA (2004), "evaluating the operation of PFI in roads and hospitals"

which led to the bankruptcy of the project. In the case of ITRCC, the bankruptcy process provided an orderly process for reorganising the operation and the assets. Although the investors suffered considerable losses, the service remained interrupted and the Indiana state government did not have to renegotiate the contract. This case provides a model for how to handle unexpected events which impact PPPs and concessions, as, in reality, the risk was allocated to the private sector—which bore the losses of low levels of traffic and revenues.

6.3 Case Study: The A1(M) Highway in the UK

6.3.1 Introduction

The A1(M) is the designation of four separate highways in England (United Kingdom—UK). The A1(M) is the result of an upgrade of a former highway crossing north-south of England, which connects London with Edinburg (Scotland), which was formerly designated the A1. The first section of the highway was opened in 1961 and was developed under traditional public procurement, being operated by public authority. In the 1990s, several parts of this highway were built and operated using a PFI (Private Finance Initiative—the UK equivalent to PPP, as seen in the UK experience subchapter) (Table 6.1).

Table 6.2 Financial structure of A1 PFI

PFI contract	Capex (£ million)	PSC	Contract (N° years)	Revenues
A1(M) Alconbury–Peterborough	128	22	30	Traffic (shadow tolls)
M1–A1 Motorway Link	214	372	30	Traffic (shadow tolls)
A1 Darrington–Dishforth	210	xx	33	Traffic (congestion management)

Own table
Capex capital expenditure, *PSC* Public Sector Comparator (6% discount rate)
Source of information: DBFO Information (Highways Agencies); ACCA (2004), "evaluating the operation of PFI in roads and hospitals"

6.3.2 The PPP Process

In the case of the A1 Darrington–Dishforth PFI project, the ministerial decision was made in December, 1998, with the submission of expression of interest occurring in September, 2000, and the sending out of tender invitations taking place by March, 2001 (four consortia were invited to tender), with a deadline for bids by September of that year. The preferred bidder selection (BAFO—Best And Final Offer—with two tenders) was closed in September, 2002, with the contract being awarded in February, 2003. Construction work started in May, 2003 and was finished by November, 2006 (Highways Agency), which represented the anticipation of the opening of the highway several months ahead of schedule, with a good construction quality and safety record (despite problems with the surfacing—which were included in the private sector risk).

6.3.3 The Financial Structure of the PPP

The A1 Darrington–Dishforth PFI project involved the investment of £210 million, with the finance structure employed mainly being debt (as is common in Project Finance—see, for instance, Sarmento and Renneboog 2016a, or Cruz and Sarmento 2018). Equity finance was 20% and debt was 80% (half of the debt in the form of a loan from the EIB, and the other half was raised from issuing a bond—with a Triple A rating). The DSCR[8] was of 1.25 (with a minimum of 1.19) which obligated (by comparing with the initial proposal) the winning consortium to increase equity at the BAFO stage, and to extend the contract from 30 to 33 years (Stafford et al. 2010; Acerete et al. 2019) (Table 6.2).

[8]Debt Service Cover Ratio—Calculated as: (Free Cash flow to the Firm/Debt service) (Yescombe 2011).

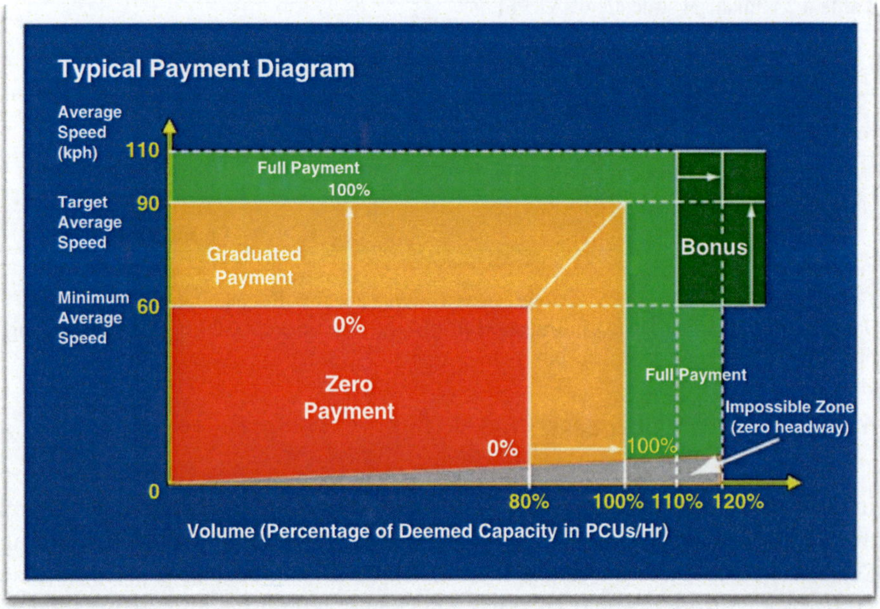

Fig. 6.1 Mechanism payment for the A1 Darrington–Dishforth PFI. Source: Highways Agency

6.3.4 *The Risk Allocation Matrix*

In the case of the A1 Darrington–Dishforth project, the allocation of risks for the private sector included the following main risks[9]: construction, operation and maintenance, finance, and demand risk. In this project, the payment mechanism consists of a congestion management system (measuring the traffic and the average speed of traffic within contractually-defined payment targets), rather than being based on shadow tolls (which is a more commonly-used for PFI highways in the UK) (Fig. 6.1). Additionally, a safety performance adjustment bonus was established for the project, based on the measurement of the level of safety of the road, resulting the payment of either a bonus or penalties, according to the number of accidents and how many users were seriously injured and also the response levels of the concessionaire to critical incidences. The public sector allocation of risks mainly included the Acts of God, and archaeological findings, as well as unilateral and contractual changes.

[9]This contract included active traffic management, inspection and maintenance of bridges, pavements, earthworks, motorway communications and a range of other highway assets, a comprehensive winter maintenance programme and provision of 24-h emergency response teams, cyclical highway maintenance and a range of environmental works, including grass cutting of highway verges, landscaping and horticultural improvements (source: contract).

6.3.5 The Motives for the Renegotiation

The motives for the first renegotiation, which occurred during the financial close of the contract (in 2003), were related with changes to the standard of road assets and construction works (such as materials, assets, and the workforce). According to Fatokun (2018), this renegotiation was associated with roads and bridging work standards, including the supervised notes issued by Highways England (with the aim to keep the construction and operation of the highway aligned with the best practices in the field). The author also refers that it was the contracting authority which initiated the renegotiation process for this project: "*It was due to the experience they have had on other PFI projects, where standards were frozen, and the projects have a 30 years duration date*". These implies that the public sector partner let the renegotiations of the contract take place, due to its previous experience with other DBFO-managed roads. We can therefore summarise the main motives for this first renegotiation as being: (1) changes to the standards of the project, and; (2) additional construction works.

Changes in the standards of the project are often see to be simply a readjustment which represents a cost overrun to the project. However, some authors argue that scope changes do not necessarily implicate a cost overrun per se (e.g., Invernizzi et al. 2018; Love and Ahiaga-Dagbui 2018). The client (or grantor) can require a scope change, with an associated cost overrun, although this does not necessarily correspond to the poor performance of the project. This is generally related with one of two motives: either a poor planning process, or a justified change in circumstances. Nevertheless, it is very difficult to identify, for a set of projects, whether a scope change is due to a justified modification of the project by the client, or due to poor planning and/or the poor overall performance of the project. In the case of the A1(M) contract, it is necessary to scrutinise the motives behind the scope changes.

Irrespective of the motives, in this case one aspect is clear. Changes in the standards of the project and/or additional works, are most likely to increase the government spending with the project, and originate the economic and financial reequilibrium.

6.3.6 The Renegotiation Case

The main impacts of this renegotiation were on the construction costs (as the contract cost remained the same, with no increase in the returns to the private sector partner), neither on the duration of the concession nor the service quality. Although changes were made to the payment mechanism, this renegotiation did not impact the deliverer of the highway—which opened on time, in accordance with the terms of the contract. Furthermore, no changes to the risk allocation matrix occurred.

6.3.7 Main Findings from the Case-Study

Roads are long-term assets which are subject to several changes. Some of these changes are related with the inevitable technical improvement of road components and construction/management processes. In this case of the A1(M), the grantor decided to renegotiate the contract to incorporate changes which were motivated by new and updated technical standards. This is an interesting example of how renegotiations can be beneficial, given that there was no increase in projects costs and neither was there a decrease in service quality.

6.4 Case Study: MG50, Brazil

6.4.1 Introduction

Highway MG-50 in Brazil is located in the states of Minas Gerais and São Paulo (it connects the capital of Minas Gerais, Belo Horizonte, with the region of São Paulo) and is approximately 400 km long. The concession contract was signed in 2007 for a brownfield project. The objective of the project was to repair and expand the existing road, upgrading it to a highway-level service. This was the first PPP in highways to be awarded in Brazil since the launch of a new PPP law in 2004 (Neto et al. 2017) and it is frequently cited has a case study of the Brazilian experience with PPPs. Since then, Brazil has launched several PPP projects in the transport sector (Neto et al. 2019), as well as also in other sectors (Neto et al. 2017; Izar 2019). Minas Gerais state has been a major actor in developing PPP in Brazil and in 2003, the government of Minas Gerais passed the first law and created the first unit in PPPs in Brazil.

6.4.2 The PPP Process

The PPP contract for this brownfield project was signed on 21 July, 2007 between the Minas Gerais State transport department and the private partner, after a tender process which commenced in 2006. The contract was awarded to a consortium comprising a joint-venture between an international highway operator (the Italian group, Atlantia) and a local group (Grupo Bertin) designated "Holding Atlantia Bertin Concessões" (owned equally by each entity). This company currently detains four highway concessions in Brazil, including the MG-50 (the others being Tiete highways, Colinas Highways, and Triangulo do Sol highways, all of which are located in the São Paulo region).

6.4.3 The Financial Structure of the PPP

A 25-year contract was signed for this brownfield project (2007–2032), with the 750 million Reais of capex being entirely financed by the private partner (the equivalent to approximately US$250 million at the time) of which was mainly destined for duplicating the lanes and improving the quality of the highway. The contract forecast public payments (besides the collection of tolls by the private operator, in the range of 50 million Reais in the first year (the equivalent to approximately US$18 million), with an annual growth rate of 2% of 10 million Reais each year (the equivalent to approximately to US$3.5 million in the first year), with an increase linked to inflation.

6.4.4 The Risk Allocation Matrix

The risk allocation matrix followed the basic assumptions that the private sector assumes the construction (in this case the upgrade and improvement of the existing infrastructure), operation and maintenance, and finance risks. In addition, in this case, the private sector also assumed the expropriation risk. The public sector grantor (i.e., the government) assumed the risks of "acts of God", unilateral changes, and specific legislation changes.

However, demand risk was not totally allocated to the private sector. First, as already mentioned, the private company collects the revenues from the tolls, but it is also paid a yearly fee by the public partner. In addition, and more importantly, the contract previewed a minimum revenue guarantee mechanism (MGR), designed to reduce the impact of traffic variation in revenues, which therefore reduces the overall risk of the concession (which reduces the cost of capital). This MGR was basically a shared allocation of the demand risk. Any variation higher or lower than 10% from the forecast demand (and therefore of the expected revenue) would result in the sharing of the upside or downsize (above or below that threshold) 50:50 between the private operator and the state government. For instance, if demand is only 60% of that forecast, then the state government should pay 50% of the shortfall to the private operator (paying 20% of the revenues: 50% × 40%). However, public loss was limited to 25 million Reais a year. As another example, if demand is 20% above that expected, then public payments would be reduced by 10% of the expected revenues (50% × 20%) (Table 6.3).

6.4.5 The Motives for the Renegotiation

All information regarding these renegotiations was collected from the original contracts, as were the renegotiation terms (which are called "*Termos Aditivos*").

Table 6.3 Risk matrix for the MG-050 concession

Risk classification	Risk allocation		Observation
	Public	Private	
Political	X		
Financial	X	X	Interest rates for loans are assumed by the concessionaire, however the variation in inflation rates are borne by the public sector
Legal	X		
Force majeure	X	X	The concessionaire assumes those risks that are insurable, whilst the public sector assumes the remaining risks
Expropriation	X	X	The concessionaire assumes the majority of the expropriation risk, however the public sector can be held responsible for any action that can cause delays in expropriation
Design and construction		X	
Operation		X	
Demand	X	X	Variations within a band of ±10% of the initial forecast are assumed by the concessionaire, however if the variations are greater, then both parties split the gain (or loss) 50:50
Environmental		X	

Source: Cruz et al. (2015)

The original contract previewed conditions in several clauses which enable the private sector partner to request a renegotiation in order to obtain the financial re-equilibrium of the concession. These conditions were (as long as they result in a reduction of revenues and/or an increase in costs): (a) unilateral changes; (b) force majeure events; (c) specific legal changes; (d) delays in administrative expropriations due to public services; (e) changes in the project requested by the government, and; (f) changes in the operational costs due to changes in the prices established by government, the creation of new taxes and changes in current taxes, with exception of the corporate tax. The financial rebalance of the concession is based on the NPV of the case base, using a discount rate of 12%. The financial rebalance can be accomplished through various methods, namely: by increasing the concession period; the revision of the capex obligations; the reduction of service levels; an increase in tariffs, or; any combination of these methods.

6.4.6 The Renegotiation Case

From the moment of the signature of the contract up until the beginning of this concession seven renegotiations had already been carried out. The first renegotiation occurred less than a year after the signature of the contract (2008), which was due to the demand from the state government for changes in the project, mainly with regards the highway layout, together with the building of a new bridge. The second

Table 6.4 Renegotiations of the MG-050 concession

Changes in contract	Year of the concession	Civil year	Reason for the renegotiation
1st	2	2008	Changes in the design of the road
2nd	3	2009	Changes in the investment plan
3rd	3	2009	Changes in the legal designation of the grantor
4th	4	2010	Limitation of the concessionaire's responsibility for the occupancy of lateral roadway for the purpose of construction works
5th	4	2010	Changes in the list of key performance indicators
6th	7	2013	Changes in the investment plan
7th	11	2017	Changes in the investment plan

Source: Cruz et al. (2015)

renegotiation occurred in 2009, which introduced new requirements to the project, accelerating the pace of investments. The third renegotiation (also in 2009) was just a formal change in the contract, due to the fact that the public grantor transferred the concession rights to a new public entity. The fourth renegotiation occurred in 2010, which reflected a change in the service level regarding an increase in the number of security strips of the highway. The fifth renegotiation, which also occurred in 2010, had to do with the demand for new requirements by the state government concerning the project, which included changes to the signalling system of the highway, new service requirements, and, additionally, a new chronogram of future major repairs. The sixth renegotiation took place in 2013, when the state government decided to expand the lanes between the local cities of Itauna and Divinopolis (approximately 40 km long) and also requested new highways exits and pedestrian passages in several locations. The 7th renegotiation occurred in 2017, where, once again, the state government requested several expansions and changes to the original (and subsequently-changed) project, with the construction of extra lanes in several locations.

In all these renegotiations the government decided not to increase the concession period, neither the tariffs. Instead, the renegotiation compensation consisted of "lump sum" public payments to cover the increase of the concessionaire's costs. Table 6.4 summarises the main renegotiations of the concession.

6.4.7 The Main Findings from the Case-Study

The MG050 case is a milestone in Brazilian PPPs and it illustrates a typical problem resulting from poorly-prepared projects—project changes. The previous section has shown that the majority of motives for renegotiating which have an economic impact on the project are those related with changes in the investment plan. The MG050 project has suffered from multiple renegotiations, as a result of systematic changes to the projects (e.g., changes in layout, capacity, execution, the chronogram, etc.). This problem can be rooted in the insufficient technical maturity of the project when it is put out to tender, which is probably a consequence of the political pressure to launch the project—which can lead to a lack of preparation and technical maturity, resulting in the request for technical changes very early on in the project.

This project also suffered from negative perceptions by the users, as discussed by Cruz et al. (2015). For there has been public contestation over the years due to increases in tolls and the delay in investments, which have negatively impacted the original high expectations regarding the project. The investment plan has been revised several times and the concessionaire has acknowledged these delays. However, no penalties were applied, which means that users are in effect paying for a service which is not being fully provided, which reflects the poor performance of the grantor in terms of contract monitoring and enforcement. This risk affects many PPP projects in different sectors, in many countries. For the privatisation of public services often implies an increase in prices, and when the concessionaire provides the service at a lower quality level than originally expected, the users tend to be penalised. Furthermore, often when the concessionaire performs poorly, a deduction in the public compensation results, although the price of tolls for the users remains the same.

Problems involving the independent and effective regulation and monitoring of PPP contracts are frequent in many countries.

PPP contracts are monitored at different levels (both public and private). On the public sector side, this follow up is carried out by the PPP Unit, whether this is a centralised unit of the Ministry of Finance, or of the sectoral ministry, as well as by the responsible sectorial entities. Thus, it is necessary to establish contract management institutions ("contract management")—for defining and establishing the responsibilities and communication mechanisms which bring about the realisation of an effective relationship between the public and private sector in a PPP. Establishing this "contract management" entity implies the definition of the responsibilities for contract management in the public sector and how to manage the relationship with the SPV. This includes designating a "PPP contract manager" (or a team) within the PPP Unit. It should be made clear for which areas the contract manager has autonomy where they are able to act with discretion and where also where they need to consult or obtain approval from ministerial tutelage. It may also be useful for the PPP Unit to include a dedicated team which is specifically focused on the renegotiation and financial rebalancing processes, as these processes tend to be very complex and involve responsibilities which are very different from the monitoring of a contract.

The main concern regarding monitoring by the public sector should be whether the quantity and quality of the conditions of the contracted service are being met, and also whether the public payment is being properly calculated and if the concession is financially-sustainable (in an attempt to anticipate situations of financial disruption which could jeopardise the service or lead to financial rebalances). Still within the sphere of the public sector, there should be periodic monitoring of PPPs by the Court of Auditors or a similar oversight body, albeit adopting a logic of the inspection and control of public funds. Such monitoring is largely designed to guarantee performance across the operational environment, rather than just be confined to the carrying out of a bureaucratic exercise in "contract management"—for a good partnership will allow for a certain flexibility which enables the adoption of sensitive approaches for the resolution of unforeseen problems and issues.

6.5 Case Study: TranSantiago, Chile

6.5.1 Introduction

The Transantiago concession (which is now called Red Metropolitana de Movilidad—since 2019) is the urban public transport which serves the metropolitan area of the capital of Chile, Santiago. This concession started in 2007, resulting from the merger of multiple operators. At this time, the metropolitan area had almost six million inhabitants and the annual demand for urban transport (passengers by year) was more than 100 million. Furthermore, 35% of transportation in the city was carried out using public transport (Gómez-Lobo and Briones 2013). Up until 2007, there were multiple operators existed (most of which were informal) accounting for approximately 6000 buses, characterised by the absence of tariff integration and a low quality of service (Estache and Gómes-Lobo 2005). The spatial coverage was very good, with buses representing almost 50% of all vehicle journeys in the metropolitan area of Santiago, which was complemented by a modern and efficient Metro service (Gomez-Lobo 2012). The resultant effect was the need to create a PPP concession for urban public transport with an integrated network of the various public transportation options (connecting buses and the metro) and electronic payment. Soon after the creation of this PPP, several problems arose in terms of the planning and implementation of the system (Ureta 2014), which led to a renegotiation in the first year of the concession.

The merge of the multiple operators and the advent of the concession had several objectives. First, to promote the use of public transportation in the metropolitan area of Santiago. Second, to improve the quality of the service, including the renewal of the fleet of buses and the reduction of travel time (Galetovic and Jordán 2006). An additional objective was to reduce pollution (air and noise) and improve the quality of the air (Paget-Seekins et al. 2015). The bus services were divided into two sub-systems: one for the main lines, which complements the Metro network, and the other with the branch lines (organized into ten units). The latter is used for short journeys and enables many users to then connect to the main network and the Metro.

At the time of the merger and the start of the concession, the conditions of the metropolitan transport system were extremely deficient. For one thing, the existence of multiple operators created a system which was complex, inefficient, full of redundancies, expensive, and beset by a high level of tariff fraud. In several cases, such as that of Santiago, multiple operators resist being brought into the formal economy, which implies the payment of taxes and the obligation to comply with labour and transport regulation (Flores Dewey 2013). Often, governments also tend to avoid the cost (economic, social, and political) of reforming and merging operators, however, in this case, the Chilean government decided to follow a strategy based on "competition in the market" (Paget-Seekins et al. 2015). The status quo was an insufficient infrastructure (which was mostly in poor conditions) together with not enough buses. Furthermore, the fare collection system was not fully operational, the lack of centralisation resulted in multiple overruns and redundancies in some of the lines, and the average speed was low, with frequent delays, leading to unnecessarily long journey times (Hidalgo and Graftieaux 2008). Through the creation of companies limited to operating exclusively in a certain urban area, the aim of the government was to create incentives for these companies to rationalise their services, reduce costs, and optimise the size of their firm, thus increasing mobility and quality of service.

6.5.2 The PPP Process

The bidding process was very competitive, despite the influence of transport trade unions and existing competitors (see Flores Dewey 2013; Muñoz and Gschwender 2008), attracting national and international bidders and featured pre-defined tariffs and fares. No competitor could be awarded the concession for more than four units. Santiago chose to opt for an open bidding tender, which proved successful in promoting competition for the benefit of the system users, although it generated certain barriers when it came to implementation. The business-case stipulated the following requirements (Muñoz and Gschwender 2008): create incentives for companies to transport more passengers; improve the level of service; increase the regularity and reliability of services; generate revenues in line with the operational costs; keep demand risk low, and; include new operators, as well some of the incumbents.

Five years later, Munoz et al. (2014) concluded that the concession, despite the initial chaos (which is described latter in this case-study), was able to overcome difficulties and improved the transport network of Santiago. The authors evaluation that 5 years after its inception, the concession was operating with more than 6000 buses (with the average age of the fleet having been reduced from 8.4 to 5.2 years), had over 370 routes with a substantial increase in the number of trips, and improved environmental standards. Segregated corridors passed from 13 to 90, leading to an increase in bus-only lanes from 68 to 101 (despite some opposition). In addition, the Metro system has been adapting its level of service and increased the length of its network from 66 to 104 km, with the number of stations increasing from 78 to 108 and the number of trains being increased from 636 to 967, leading to virtually the triplication of the annual ridership [all data from Munoz et al. (2014)].

The system has been operated by 14 private companies since 2019 (which do not compete among themselves) and has more than 200 km of new segregated corridors and 4.6 km of new road connections, in addition to the 62.7 km of improvements of the existing roads (Gomez-Lobo 2012). Over the last 10 years, the operators have acquired more than 4000 buses (with different typologies, such as low-floor articulated or feeder buses). A private operator is responsible for the financial management (with all payments being electronic) and the Metro system remained being operated by a State-Owned-Enterprise (SOE). On an average weekday, this system transports more than four million passengers (Hidalgo and Graftieaux 2008), however, the authors mention that the process was very chaotic at the beginning, due to the lack of planning (given rise to street protest at the beginning of the process) and that it took several years to complete. This led to the renegotiation of the incentives for the private firms, as described below in this case study. However, noticeable improvements were achieved after a few years and safety also increased substantially, with a decrease in fatalities and injuries of more than 50% (Gomez-Lobo 2012). Traveling time has also reduced (along with the use of the Metro, which was operating below capacity—Gallegos et al. 2011) and air pollution has diminished, due to the operation of new, more energy-efficient buses. However, it has to be said that the overall cost of travelling for users has substantially increased.

6.5.3 The Financial Structure of the PPP

The total capex of the new private operators was approximately US$190 million, with an average contract duration of 15 years (Paget-Seekins et al. 2015). Revenues are based solely on traffic and other commercial revenues (Muñoz and Gschwender 2008) and no public payments were contemplated in the original concession (Ureta 2014). The increase in the fleet of buses was mitigated by the reduction in the number of seats, resulting in each bus to accommodate more passengers.

6.5.4 The Risk Allocation

The contracts signed in 2007 were mainly designed to attract investors and therefore the risks were minimised (Tamblay et al. 2017). The private companies were responsible for the investment and operation and maintenance risks and they also assume the demand risk [although this was mitigated by the calculation of tariffs, see Monuz and Gshwender (2008) and Gómez-Lobo and Briones (2014) for further details], as revenues were derived from fares and tickets, as well as other commercial income. However, as can be seen below, compensation was introduced to limit this risk (Gómez-Lobo and Briones 2013).

6.5.5 The Motives for the Renegotiation

Several rounds of renegotiation were needed to fine-tune the contractual arrangements so as to allocate demand risk and adequately rewarded service performance. In the case of TranSantiago, all the renegotiations of the contract were initiated by the public authorities, owing to the danger of the imminent collapse of the system which thus provided the grantor with a strong bargaining position to impose new contractual conditions on the private operators (Gómez-Lobo and Briones 2014).

6.5.6 The Renegotiation Case

The renegotiations were intended to respond to the chaos[10] which occurred at the beginning of the concession.[11, 12] The idea of the renegotiation was to respond to the crisis (which was considered by many to be the worst political policy ever implemented in Chile, Munoz et al. 2014) by implementing an increase in the quantity of buses, in order to restore capacity, reduce congestion, and also reduce waiting and journey time. However, the obligation to increase the number of buses led to private operators having to increase their capex and also the operational costs. Contracts were amended to increase the number of buses and also to enable the private firms to use old buses, if necessary (Gomez-Lobo 2012). In addition, an emergency fleet was introduced in 2007, which was later integrated in the private operators.

Modifications to the contracts included an increase in the demand risk assumed by the private operators. According to (Gomez-Lobo 2012), after the renegotiations, the operators assumed the risks of roughly 35% of the deviations of effective demand from the 'reference demand', compared to a percentage 10% before this renegotiation change was implemented. As a compensation, payments to operators was conditional on an index of compliance with the operational plan, which was calculated as the ratio between the buses' operating capacity[13] and the required capacity, which was measured each half-hour. Payment was to be made on a 2-week period—

[10]Chaos in the transport network led to strong protests in the streets at the beginning of the operation. This was due to several causes: changes in government; a lack of preparation, and; a too big an approach to a large network. For more details see Gschwender (2007) and Monuz and Gshwender (2008).

[11]The renegotiation also has led to the termination of one small concession operator, which was unable to provide the service in accordance with the terms of the contract. The concession was subsequently awarded to a new operator.

[12]The expansion of the network created a problem of overlap in some of the systems, which led to a new renegotiation by 2009.

[13]By operating, a bus needed to be in movement 5 min out of each 30 min. This created considerable difficulties for the monitorisation of the index, which resulted in the implementation of changes to the control system in 2008.

which was calculated as being the income of the original contract, multiplied by this index. The index was later changed in 2008, as described by (Gomez-Lobo 2012):

> The Frequency Compliance Index (ICF) and the Regularity Compliance Index (ICR). The first index measured the proportion of buses at the head of a route service compared to the buses required on that route by the operational plan. The ICR measured the regularity (variance in headway) between buses at the head of a route service. Both indices provide a much finer control over compliance with the operational plan.

However, this increase in the size of the fleet was carried out during the first years of the concession without the implementation of any increase in the prices (as the prices had already been substantially increased at the moment of the merger, which contributed to the general lack of satisfaction with the level of service and the cost). This naturally led to an increased in the losses of the operators (as they were obliged to increase their capex and opex without receiving the benefit of an increase in revenues from tariffs). According to Gomez-Lobo (2012), at this time, the operational deficit of most private operators was running at more than 40% of operational costs. Accordingly, various mechanisms were created in 2008 to compensate the private partners. These included a direct grant from the Chilean government and a bank loan from the development bank (which was overruled in court, leading to an increase in the value of the government grant). In 2009, a transport subsidy law was amended, which resulted in establishing a permanent grant (as well as a complementary, transitory grant). The evolution of prices was used to assure that the annual deficit of the private operators did not exceed the yearly value of the grant. Since then, ticket prices have been increasing substantially. According to Munoz et al. (2014), public subsidies for the transportation concession amounted to US$50 million a month, and tariffs increased 11 times over a period of 6 years, leading to a total increase of 58%. The authors also refer that after this major renegotiation, a further 17 renegotiations occurred during the following 6 years. These smaller renegotiations were carried out in reaction to unforeseen events and also with the objective to improve regulatory issues. As mentioned by Paget-Seekins et al. (2015), the Chilean government decided not put these concessions out to tender again (despite a certain concentration of ownership among the operators), its decision being based on the need to ensure stability and reduce uncertainty. This learning process (which is a very relevant, yet little-described topic in the field of renegotiations, see Sarmento and Renneboog 2016b) has enabled the regulatory framework to be strengthened, resulting in a more stable system and an independent regulatory authority.

Another important renegotiation occurred in 2012, which led to a change in the compensation scheme—which was changed from a per-kilometre basis to a per-passenger basis (Beltrán et al. 2013; Tamblay et al. 2017). However, these modifications were subject to adjustments to reflect changes in the cost of inputs, such as labour or fuel. It should be mentioned that regular (every 2 years) and extraordinary revisions had already been implemented before this time, which are subject to revisions based on the occurrence of reductions in demand which are not caused by the direct action of a private operator (Tamblay et al. 2017). However, if demand is higher, private firms are obliged to return part of this additional benefit to the government. Extraordinary revisions can be made if requested by the private operator, in the case of specific events occurring (such as changes in prices, regulation, or the need to open new lines), adjusting the concession to reflect new conditions (which were not foreseeable at the time of the celebration of the initial contract).

The majority of the revenue is now generated from the quantity of passengers (through tariffs and from public compensation—with companies receiving up to 70% of their compensation from payments by passengers—according to Tamblay et al. 2017). However, the above-mentioned compliance indicators have remained mostly unchanged (Tamblay et al. 2017) and, in addition, clauses to reduce the demand risk were added. As a result, contracts become more attractive to investors, providing them with financial stability and sustainability. In return, the government expected the quality of service to be improved.

6.5.7 The Main Findings from the Case-Study

As described above, the main cause for renegotiation of the Transantiago concession contract was the need to rapidly increase the capacity of the system. The levels of demand required an increase in production and overall capacity, which subsequently led to an increase in both the capex and opex of the private operators (as more vehicles had to be acquired to satisfy the new operational plan). It is important to mention that most cases of the renegotiation of PPP contracts are in response to changes in demand originated from the verification of lower levels of demand than those initially forecast—which was not the case for the TransSantiago concession, where the opposite occurred. For in the case of TransSantiago in Chile, the levels of demand were much higher, which created severe problems for the sustainability of the systems. These changes in demand led to an increase in tariffs and government subsidies. This example from Chile illustrates a common problem with PPP contracts—which is rigidity. For PPP contracts often do not have the flexibility to cope with changes in forecast values, especially those concerning demand. This flexibility can be more difficult to implement in road projects, however this case study proves that it can certainly be used for bus or bus-rapid-transit systems.

6.6 Case Study: Fertagus, Portugal

6.6.1 Introduction

The Fertagus concession operates the urban railway over the Tagus Bridge, which connects the two sides (north and south) of Lisbon area, Portugal. The concession opened in 1999, as the bridge (built in the 1960s with the same design as that of the

Golden Gate of San Francisco, in the US) originally only catered for a road service—although the original bridge construction already included the necessary infrastructure to support a railway service. Therefore, the concession contract did not include technical changes to the bridge, but rather the private partner was only to be responsible for the acquisition of the rolling stock and the construction of a few rail stations along the south margin, together with the operation of the rail service—with a total extension of 54 km, 14 stations, and an average of more than 100,000 passengers a day (Macario et al. 2013). The operation of this rail service was supposed to be solely based on tariffs and other commercial revenues, with the demand risk being shared, whereby a lower band limit was established, which contemplated a renegotiation if the demand was proven to be below that minimum threshold. According to Sarmento and Renneboog (2016a), this renegotiation clause represented the government's guarantee to the private sector in response to the possibility of overoptimistic initial government traffic projections, whereby Fertagus could request an extension of the concession period, an increase in tariffs, and/or financial compensation. When it occurred, the Fertagus renegotiation was a success, which rendered the concession financially viable, as both parties were committed to achieving a more sustainable concession. This renegotiation was a success for two reasons: firstly because Fertagus belonged to a group which already had experience operating in transportation in the Lisbon area, and secondly due to the fact that the renegotiation was requested by the private sector, in the face of imminent bankruptcy.

6.6.2 The PPP Process

The concession was awarded after the launch of a public tender, which was won by a Portuguese group called Barraqueiro. This group was already operating several bus service concessions in the metropolitan area of Lisbon, as well as the light rail service on the south bank. The Fertagus concession represented the award of a 30-year contract, with the possibility of an extension for a further 15 years. The concessionaire is responsible for the acquisition of the rolling stock and the operation of the rail service.

6.6.3 The Financial Structure of the PPP

The total capex of the acquisition of the rolling stock and the new rail stations amounted to approximately €112 million. Almost 70% of this investment was originally financed by a syndicated loan (Sarmento and Renneboog 2015). The revenues of the operator were fully provided for by the tariffs paid by users, together with other commercial revenues (e.g., the rental of commercial spaces in the stations, publicity, etc.), with the tariff revenues being designed on a band system. The

Fertagus contract comprised a band traffic system composed of three bands (an upper band, a reference band, and a lower band), in order to share the traffic risk between the government and the private company. On the one hand, should the traffic estimations be understated, with real traffic levels exceeding the upper band, then Fertagus would be liable for a reduction in tariffs and would be responsible for improving the service. On the other hand, if the traffic projections were too optimistic, with real traffic levels falling below the lower band, then Fertagus could demand a financial rescue package.

6.6.4 The Risk Allocation Matrix

The private partner was allocated several risks, such as the operational, financial (interest rate risk), and maintenance risk. However, the demand risk was shared in the original contract, as discussed above. On the one hand, the private sector operator assumed some of the demand risk, however this was capped by a minimum threshold, which was designed to trigger renegotiation. On the other hand, as is normal in PPP contracts, the public sector assumed the risks of force majeure, unilateral changes, and specific legislation changes, as well as the risk of the construction of new competitive rail crossing of the river.

6.6.5 The Motives for the Renegotiation

During the first 4 years of operation (from 1999 to 2003), demand was substantially below that forecast, and was also significantly below the minimum threshold. This led to the private partner claiming for a renegotiation. In 1999, the negative deviation in traffic from the minimum limit was 68%, moving to 40–50% below over the next years. This reduced level of traffic had a substantial impact on the concession revenues. For the original financial case had forecast annual base revenues of €20–25 million and this deviation amounted to more than €10 million each year. The concession had an expectation of annual profits of approximately €1.5 million, but and instead the losses were €4–6 million annually (Fig. 6.2).

6.6.6 The Renegotiation Case

Renegotiation occurred between 2002 and 2004, leading to a substantial change in the original concession conditions. Several of these conditions were to the benefit of the private operator: first, Fertagus received a lump-sum payment to financially rebalance the concession to the tune off approximately €45 million in 2005, whereby the government acquired the rolling stock and leased it back to Fertagus—which

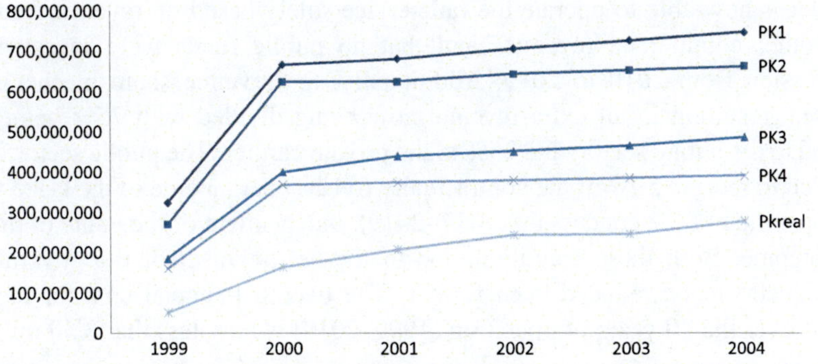

Fig. 6.2 Traffic bands and real traffic. Note: Pk1 stands for the upper limit, and Pk4 for the lower limit. PKreal stands for the real demand. Source: the Authors

consequently amortised this part of the private partner's asset costs. In addition, Barraqueiro was paid an annual compensation for each year from 2006 to 2010 which totalled approximately €50 million, which led to an increase in the public funding of close to €95 million. Fertagus was allowed to increase the price of tariffs and was also permitted to manage tariffs prices more flexibly. Furthermore, Fertagus was allowed to reduce the service level at certain times of the day, and this change in the demand risk enabled Fertagus to be more flexible in commercial issues (especially those related to traffic, such as prices, discount policies, and timetables) and to focus more on operations.

Nevertheless, these conditions came with several other conditions which were to the benefit of the public sector and/or the users, namely: first, the concession duration was reduced from 30 years to 10 years, which meant that the concession was to end in in 2010, with the possibility of a 9 year prorogation (which came to pass, as the concession had become financially sustainable by 2010). In addition, the IRR required from the private partner was reduced from 10.9 to 7.8%. Furthermore, the private partner agreed to assumed more risk, as, in effect, the demand risk was now fully transferred to Fertagus. This new conditions led to the establishment of a new forecast of the level of demand, although, however, the threshold limit was abandoned. The new level of forecast demand were substantially more realistic than the original one and, additionally, a new clause was introduced, which, in effect, shares above-forecast additional revenue between the private and the public sector. The first 5% of above-forecast revenues are divided by apportioning 75% the private partner, and 25% to the public partner. Should revenues be greater by 5%, then this extra amount is divided with 25% going to the private partner, and 75% to the public sector. In practice, this led to almost €15 million of extra revenues for the public sector between 2006 and 2010 and as the private sector became responsible for some of the costs of the infrastructure, the overall net payment by the government to Fertagus was reduced to a value of approximately €70 million.

In 2010 the contract was extended by an additional 9 years. This new contract was subject to some additional changes in the concession conditions. First, and foremost, the concession is currently (2019) financially sustainable. This means that the private partner is now able to operate the rail service solely based on revenue from tariffs and other commercial revenues and that no public funds were invested in the concession from 2010 to 2019. Additionally, the revenue share mechanism was revised, resulting in all extra revenue now being divided with 75% being apportioned to the public sector, and 25% to the private partner. The public sector was also entitled to receive 50% of the contractually forecast net income of the last 3 years of the operation of the concession (2017–2019), independent of the value of the actual net income. Both these conditions led to the net payment of the government to Barraqueiro to be reduced even further. The overall financial cost for the public sector over the 20 years of operation (1999–2019) is now less than €50 million.

6.6.7 *The Main Findings from the Case Study*

The renegotiation of the Fertagus PPP contract resulted in a more sustainable and robust concession, which ended up with Fertagus becoming financially independent, once it solely relied on commercial revenues (after 2010). This renegotiation was initiated by the private company, as it was facing imminent bankruptcy, and thus gave more bargaining power to government. The fact that Fertagus belongs to a group whose sole business is the operation of several public transportation firms in the Lisbon region could have had an impact on the private partner's negotiating position, for according to Sarmento and Renneboog (2016a), the private group wanted to avoid the potential reputational cost arising from the collapse of the project, or from the PPP being perceived by the public as inefficient and a waste of public money. The public sector also benefitted from the renegotiation, as the mechanisms for sharing above-forecast revenue enabled the government to be compensated for part of the original public financial effort, due to the fact that demand increased to levels greater than the new projections for traffic. In addition, the reduction in the project risk for the government resulted in a reduction in the profitability of the private company. This renegotiation established a new equilibrium between the private partner's profit and the public sector's interests.

The Fertagus' renegotiation is proof that when both parties are committed to sustain a current and future relationship, then they are prone to negotiate a better agreement for each party, which ensures long-term sustainability and value for both of them. From 1999 to 2004 (the renegotiation year), Fertagus recorded an accumulated loss of €32 million (representing a deviation of—600%) in relation to the initial base case. However, from 2005 to 2010, the concession company generated a total profit after tax of €56 million (which represents an increase in net profit of 42% in comparison to the renegotiated base case). The main causes of this turnaround were improved concession conditions, better management, and greater demand.

As mentioned by Macario et al. (2015a), Fertagus is often considered to be a PPP success story, as it proves that through renegotiation, this concession was progressively rebalanced up to a point where the private partner was able to operate the concession without the need for public subsidies to sustain the desired level of service.

6.7 Case Study: The AP7 Highway, Spain

6.7.1 Introduction

The AP-7 highway in Spain (called "La autopista del Mediterráneo") is a route that crosses all the Mediterranean coast until France (totalising 980 km). Parts of the highway is tolled, and other parts are toll-free. A toll-free national road (N-340) runs parallel with this highway. The highway is divided into five concessions, all of which are operated by different operators, namely: (1) Abertis (France-Alicante); (2) SEITT (a former Ciralsa concessionaire, which is now a SOE—State Owned Enterprise after the renegotiation of this concession, known as the Alicante Circulation-Bypass); (3) Ausur (Crevillente-Cartagena); (4) SEITT (Cartagena-Vera, formerly operated by the Aucosta concessionaire), and; (5) Ausol (Fuengirola-Guadiaro).

The case-study analyses the two former highway concessions operated by Ciralsa and Aucosta, as well as the process of renegotiations which led to the Spanish government taking into hand these two concessions in 2018 (starting on 1 April).[14] The bankruptcy of these two companies led the government to assume the management of each concession in order to assure the maintenance of the operation and guaranteed the integrity of the assets (otherwise the bankruptcy of the private operator could have forced the highways in question to be closed to traffic, which would have led to severe consequences from a public interest point of view). Spain's public procurement law determines if a concessionaire goes bankrupt, the Governments must assume the concession. Over the last years, on several highway concessions in Spain have been declared bankrupt—mainly due to the economic and financial crisis—with the government taking on the management of these concessions. This has resulted in the loss of capital for the shareholders and losses for debtors, as well as a decrease in forecast public sector financial compensations. Table 6.5 presents the main features of the AP7 highway.

6.7.2 The PPP Process

At the beginning of the century the Spanish government launched a new wave of PPPs, this time not in greenfield projects (this is to say, not in the construction and

[14] During the life of the concession several renegotiations were carried out, as described in Albalate and Bel-Piñana (2016), which are not detailed in this case-study.

Table 6.5 Main features of the AP7 highway

PPP concession	Year	N° Km	Scope	Private consortium (DBFO)
Ciralsa (Alicante bypass)	2004	33	The building of a new highway	ACS (50%); Abertis and Globalvia (25% each)
Aucosta (Cartagena-Vera)	2004	115	The building of a new highway	

Source: The Authors' own table

operation of new highways), but rather in brownfield projects (through a programme designed to upgrade, rehabilitate, maintain, and operate existent infrastructure). The goal was to upgrade the design standards and the overall quality/performance of the first free expressways which were built in Spain (during the 1970s and 1980s), upgrading the maintenance and operation to modern standards (Ortega et al. 2016).

6.7.3 The Financial Structure of the PPP

The duration of the Ciralsa contract was for 33 years, ending in 2037, with an extension clauses for a further 3 years. In the case of Aucosta, the duration of the contract was fixed for 36 years, ending in 2040. In the case of both concessions, the private sector assumed the demand risk, as concession revenues were solely based on traffic.

6.7.4 The Risk Allocation

In both highway concession contracts, the private sector was allocated the following main risks: construction; finance; operation; maintenance, and; traffic. To the public sector it was allocated mainly the risks of "acts of God", unilateral changes and specific legislation. Expropriations was the responsibility of the private partner. However, each concession was underwritten with a State guarantee in the value of €520 million for both the construction and expropriations (RPA—"*Responsabilidad Patrimonial de Estado*") (Bel-Piñana 2018).

6.7.5 The Motives for the Renegotiation

Both companies had faced financial problems since 2008/2009, with revenues from the concessions being insufficient to cover the debt service. This was due to two main reasons:

First, traffic and revenues were substantially below those forecast, even before the 2008 financial crisis [according to Bel-Piñana (2018), during the first years of operation, traffic was more than 50% below forecast—see the detailed data in Ortega et al. (2016)]. Usually, there is a "ramp-up" effect in highways, whereby the first 3–5 years tend to be the period when the highway experiences an increase in traffic volume, which is then consolidated. After these years of traffic growth a stabilisation of traffic volume occurs, unless economic conditions or oil prices substantially change. This was not the case for the AP7, as the problem with this concession was a substantial inaccuracy in the original forecasts [which is a common problem—see, for instance, the literature review on traffic forecast in Cruz and Sarmento (2019)]. However, in the case of the AP7, the problem was mainly due to an optimism bias in the cases of forecasts for the private partner.

The 2008 financial crisis led to a downturn in the Spanish economy (which hit the economy much harder than in most other European countries, Ortega et al. 2016). GDP fell 9% from 2008 to 2013, and unemployment rose to 26% (source: AMECO database). There was a reduction in traffic of over 40%. This reduction (as the highway was already operating during the years before the crisis, albeit with a volume of traffic substantially below that forecast) increased the financial distress of the concessionaires (Baeza and Vassallo 2010, 2012). This reduction in traffic was even higher than in other highway concessions in Spain, due to the bursting of the housing bubble. For as the highway was built in a highly touristic area, the impact on the real estate crisis was particularly strong in the cases of this concession (Sierra et al. 2014).

Second, additional costs were incurred in expropriations and in carrying out the additional construction works of the infrastructure [which represents a classic problem in large infrastructures, see, for instance, Flyvbjerg et al. 2004; Love and Ahiaga-Dagbui 2018; and particularly for transportation, as showed by Love et al. (2016) and Catalão et al. (2019)]. These extra costs required higher levels of investment, which consequently affected the concessionaires' financial position and profitability (Vassallo et al. 2011).

With revenues being substantially below those forecast, and with higher costs, the concessionaires suffered financial distress, which resulted in losses during most of the years, and negative returns for the shareholders (Baeza and Vassallo 2014). However, of most concern was the fact that revenues were unable to cover the debt service[15] (with a DSCR[16] of below 1).

On 18 February, 2011, the concessionaire submitted a request to the Spanish Government for the restoration of the economic and financial feasibility of the AP7/AP4 concession which it managed. Apart from the shortfalls in revenue and financial distress, this claim was also due to the economic impact of the construction of competing roads running in parallel with the AP7/AP4, whereby no waiver with

[15]Debt service is the sum of interests and yearly debt repayments maid in accordance with the initial financial case-base and the contract signed with lenders (Cruz and Sarmento 2018).

[16]DSCR- Debt Service Cover Ratio: Free cash-flow to the firm/Debt Service (Yescombe 2011).

compensation had been included in the original agreement approved by Royal Decree No. 457/2006. The shareholders claimed financial compensation of €3 billion from the government for loss of traffic revenues and the costs of additional works.

The company requested the adoption of the necessary measures to restore the economic and financial feasibility that had been lost, in order to offset in full the losses it had suffered as a result of the loss of traffic and revenue; and, secondarily, should these requested measures not be adopted, then the company demanded the acknowledgement of its right to compensation for damages resulting from a breach of the related contractual terms and conditions. The aforementioned damages were to include the total amount of the loss of revenue from 2002 up until to the forecast end of the concession in 2019. In fact, both the failure of traffic and revenues forecasts and the increase costs of additional works led this concessionaire to file for bankruptcy.

6.7.6 The Renegotiation Case

The financial break-down of this concession led the government to intervene. First, it paid for the servicing of the debt in order to avoid the liquidation of the company. Since 2009, this concession (along with others experiencing financial problems) has been receiving government aid to cover its debt service (Bel-Piñana 2018). Part of this aid was funded the provision of State guarantees to the private partner, while the other part was in form of loans (subordinated public participation loans—SPPLs, see Vassallo and Sanchez 2007). In practice, the concessionaire was able to take out loans from the government each year to pay the debt service. As a guarantee that the loan would be repaid, the government permitted both an extension of the loan term (together with an extension of the concession period—Villalba-Romero and Liyanage 2014) and a planned increase in toll rates, with this additional revenue being allocated to the debt repayment. At the end of 2010, the Spanish Parliament approved a law to guarantee under-performing concessionaires the difference between 80% of the revenues originally forecast and the revenues actually collected—for a period of 3 years. The revenues of most of the toll concessions vary between 50 and 70% of the original forecast values. It should be added that the funds provided by the government are supposed to be paid back to the government with an interest rate equivalent to the SPPLs (Ortega et al. 2016). This intervention by the government was in reaction to the fear that the bankruptcy of the concessionaire could lead to a disruption in the service of the highway.

However, all these measures failed to solve the financial problems of the concessionaire, and they filed for bankruptcy and a court decision determined the closing of the firm.[17] Due to this court decision, the Spanish government decided to trigger the call-back of this concession in 2018, as otherwise the private firm would no longer be able to operate the highway after 1 of October of that year, owing to the legal decision (which obliged the termination of all contracts with employees, for instance) and the highway would have been closed to traffic as from that moment. Concession contracts usually allow for this type of action from the government, although it is important to mention that the tangible asset (in this case, the highway structure) always remain a government asset (as it is considered legally to be a public domain asset). Accordingly, the only asset recognised in the private partner's balance sheet is an intangible asset—the concession contract. It is this contract that the government is allowed to call-back in specific circumstances—which are mainly cases when the concessionaire fails to provide the service (or goes bankrupt during the construction stage) or when serious malfunctions of the infrastructure are verified. In these cases of call-back, the government assumes both the benefits of the concession (as well as the management of the asset and the underlying revenues) and also the costs. The government assumes the construction costs if the call back is put into effect during the construction phase and also the future maintenance and operation costs and in addition in some causes it can also assume the financial debt of the concessionaire. In effect, in this specific case the court decision leads to the trigger of the State guarantees in order to enable the repayment of debt to lenders by the private partner.

Initially, the government plan was to put out a new tender for the concession, in order to mitigate losses. However, those plans were shelved in 2018, when the government decided to reduce tolls tariffs and to make the highway toll-free at night, as a way of recuperating levels of traffic volume.

6.7.7 *The Main Findings from the Case-Study*

The case of the AP7 provides some interesting insights in to how excessive optimism in traffic forecasts and underestimations of costs (in this case, expropriation costs and additional works) can jeopardise the economic and financial equilibrium of a PPP project. The AP7 is an example of an extreme case, due to the fact that the initial financial distress of the project eventually led to the bankruptcy of a concessionaire as a result of the deteriorating macroeconomic environment. Considering that public infrastructures have a crucial economic and social role, their operation cannot simply

[17]During 2018 and 2019, at least eight highway concessions were closed on decision of the courts, nasmely: [R-2 (Madrid-Guadalajara), R-3 (Madrid-Arganda), R-4 (Madrid-Arganda), R-5 (Madrid-Navalcarnero), AP-41 (Toledo), AP-7 (Cartagena-Vera y la Circunvalación de Alicante), AP-3 (Ocaña-La Roda), and M-12 (Eje Aeropuerto)]. This could represent a total cost to the government of €5 billion, although at this moment the Spanish government has only recognized €1.6 billion of liabilities.

be stopped. In this case, the mechanism used by the government to maintain the public interest was the call-back of the concession.

6.8 Comparative Analysis and Policy Implications

The previous subsections have provided an overview of several renegotiation processes. This subsection provides a final comparative analysis of the case studies. Table 6.6 presents a summary of the case studies.

These case studies illustrate some of the main findings of the literature which were reviewed in Chaps. 3 and 4. As mentioned in these chapters, the main motives for renegotiations are related with overoptimistic traffic forecasts, increase in costs (financing, construction, expropriations, etc.), and also changes in projects (technical standards, an increase in service levels, overall changes in layout, an increase in capacity, etc.). These motives generally represent an increase in costs and a decrease in revenues, which leads to the deterioration of the economic equilibrium of the concession. Such impacts can led to the concessionaires being obliged to request financial compensation—often in accordance with the terms of the risk-sharing agreement. The concessionaire cannot be compensated if it is entirely responsible for the demand risk, and in such cases, the company can be forced into liquidation (as was the case of Indiana and the AP7). Overoptimistic forecasting of traffic and revenues was also the main motive for renegotiation for the Fertagus case in Portugal, where the private partner accepted the government forecast of traffic volume, although it did not accepted a full transfer of demand risk. In fact, in the Fertagus case, the demand risk was shared, as the low level of traffic contractually enabled the company to be financially compensated.

The case studies demonstrate that most adverse events result in financial distress for the concessions, and, in some cases, even bankruptcy (Indiana and the AP7). Ultimately, the Government is obliged to provide additional funding for the projects and/or actions the call-back of the concession. For projects cannot simply be stopped or closed, as most PPP projects provide a public service.

In the case of TransSantiago in Chile, there was an increase in revenues, however this was clearly insufficient to cover the significant increase in costs and investments, which also led to the financial distress of the concessionaires. In this case, protests and riots led the government to renegotiate the concession in order to prevent prices from escalating.

The lessons learnt from these cases studies can be transferred to a policy making perspective, identifying critical improvements areas that can increase the resilience of the projects to renegotiations. This will be discussed next.

Policy Implications

The empirical evidence discussed in the previous chapters and the case studies has shown that renegotiations are inevitable, bearing in mind the level of uncertainty that surrounds such projects. This uncertainty can be of different types, as follows:

Table 6.6 Comparative analysis

	A1	TransSantiago	MG050	Indiana	AP7	Fertagus
Country	UK	Chile	Brazil	US	Spain	Portugal
Economic/political context	Neutral	Political crisis	Neutral	Economic crisis	Economic crisis	Neutral
Motives	– Change in technical standards	– Increase in service levels	– Changes in projects – Increase in capacity	– Optimistic forecasts – Increased financing costs	– Optimistic forecasts – Increased construction and expropriation costs	– Optimistic forecasts
Impact on costs	Neutral	Increase	Increase	Increase	Increase	Neutral
Impact on revenues	Neutral	Increase	Neutral	Decrease	Decrease	Decrease
Overall impact on the economic equilibrium	Neutral	Financial distress	Financial distress	Bankruptcy	Bankruptcy	Financial distress
Results	No change	Government payments; changes in risk-sharing matrix	Government payments (lumpsum)	N.A.	Call-back by the government	Reduction of the contract duration and a shift of investment responsibilities to the government

- Technical: changing technical standards, innovation in materials and processes, outdated technologies, construction overruns, etc.;
- Economic and financial: economic context, financing conditions, etc.;
- Social and demographic: changing demographic patterns;
- Legal: changing rules and regulations and laws;
- Political: political instability;

The impact of uncertainty is higher in PPPs, because typically these projects involve large amounts of investment and long payback periods. Bearing in mind that besides project-related uncertainties, PPPs are also vulnerable to exogenous sources of uncertainty, there is an exponential increase in the overall level of uncertainty and subsequence risk that these projects have to face.

PPP contracts are designed with a base scenario which is prepared with pre-defined forecasts and assumptions regarding socio-economic variables, such as growth in demand, inflation, tariffs, and operational costs (including fuel, which has a significant level of uncertainty, etc.), all of which are used to generate overall demand/revenue and cost forecasts. Each one of these estimates accounts for significant risk (Shen et al. 2006).

However, the uncertainty factors surrounding PPPs are not just exogenous, for uncertainty can also result from opportunistic behaviours and strategies, as discussed by Williamson (1976), Hong and Shum (2002), and Ubbels and Verhoed (2008). Aggressive bidding and/opportunistic behaviours can increase the level of risk of the projects and, as such, render a PPP more vulnerable to potential situations of financial distress and/or even bankruptcy (as in the case of the Indiana and the AP7 road concessions). It is also important to mention that these opportunistic behaviours can also occur on the public sector, as suggested by Engel et al. (2006b) and Guasch and Straub (2009), but with much less frequency. Such opportunistic behaviour occurs primarily on account of the incomplete nature of contracts, as extensively discussed in Chap. 2.

In addition, the case studies also illustrate how excessive risk transfer can be harmful. For instance, the full risk transfer in the case of Indiana and the AP7 led to an overestimation of traffic volume (with potentially even aggressive bidding), which ultimately resulted in the bankruptcy of concessionaires.

Some research as suggested the need to develop flexible contracts, as flexible contracts would provide the necessary flexibility to cope with changing circumstances, as discussed by Chiara and Garvin (2008), Cruz and Marques (2012, 2013b), and Athias and Saussier (2018). Such flexibility mechanisms could be imbedded in the PPP contract (e.g., variable durations for contracts), or they could be applied to the infrastructure itself (e.g., by establishing an expansion plan based on level of demand) (Martins et al. 2014, 2015). This would enable the mitigation of both the probability and impact of the occurrence of renegotiations.

References

Acerete, B., Gasca, M., & Stafford, A. (2019). Two decades of DBFO roads in the UK and Spain: An evaluation of the financial performance. *Annals of Public and Cooperative Economics, 90* (2), 269–289.

Adarkwa, O., Smadi, O., & Alhasan, A. (2017). Lessons to be learned from bankruptcy filings in public-private partnership (PPP) projects in the United States. *MOJ Civil Engineering, 2*(2), 66–70. https://doi.org/10.15406/mojce.2017.02.00030.

Albalate, D., & Bel-Piñana, P. (2016). Winners and losers in tolled motorway renegotiations: An empirical evaluation of the Spanish pioneers. *Public Money and Management, 36*(5), 365–372.

Athias, L., & Saussier, S. (2018). Are public private partnerships that rigid? And why? Evidence from price provisions in French toll road concession contracts. *Transportation Research Part A: Policy and Practice, 111*, 174–186.

Baeza Muñoz, M., & Vassallo Magro, J. M. (2012). Traffic uncertainty in toll motorway concessions in Spain. *Proceedings of the Institution of Civil Engineers-Transport, 165*(2), 97–105.

Baeza, M. D. L. Á., & Vassallo, J. M. (2010). Private concession contracts for toll roads in Spain: Analysis and recommendations. *Public Money and Management, 30*(5), 299–304.

Baeza, M. A., & Vassallo, J. M. (2014). *Es una empresa pú blica la solución al problema de las autopistas de peaje en Espana?* Paper presented at XVII Congreso Panamericano de Ingeniería de Transporte. Santander: Transito y Logistica.

Bathon, M. (2014). *Indiana Toll Road seeks bankruptcy as traffic declines*. Bloomberg. Retrieved from www.bloomberg.com

Bel, G., & Foote, J. (2009). Tolls, terms and public interest in road concessions privatization: A comparative analysis of recent transactions in the USA and France. *Transport Reviews, 29*(3), 397–413.

Bel-Piñana, P. (2018). *Public-private partnerships in roads: Economic and policy analyses* (Doctoral dissertation, Universitat de Barcelona).

Beltrán, P., Gschwender, A., & Palma, C. (2013). The impact of compliance measures on the operation of a bus system: The case of Transantiago. *Research in Transportation Economics, 39* (1), 79–89.

Benbasat, I., Goldstein, D. K., & Mead, M. (1987). The case research strategy in studies of information systems. *MIS Quarterly, 11*(3), 369–386.

Berke, J., Brumby, S., & Gilligan, E. (2012, November 7). Indiana Toll Road paves the way for restructuring with advisors. *Debtwire*.

Bitran, E., Nieto-Parra, S., & Robledo, J. S. (2013). *Opening the black box of contract renegotiations*. Paris: OECD Library.

Carden, D. (2018, September 20). State board approves deal hiking toll road truck rates in exchange for Indiana getting $1 billion. *NWI Times*. Retrieved from www.nwitimes.com

Catalão, F. P., Cruz, C. O., & Sarmento, J. M. (2019). The determinants of cost deviations and overruns in transport projects, an endogenous models approach. *Transport Policy, 74*, 224–238.

Checherita, C., & Gifford, J. (2007). *Risk sharing in public-private partnerships: General considerations and an evaluation of the US Practice in road transportation* (No. 1428-2016-118601).

Chiara, N., & Garvin, M. J. (2008). Variance models for project financial risk analysis with applications to greenfield BOT highway projects. *Construction Management and Economics, 26*(9), 925–939.

Crowe-Chizek. (2006). *Indiana East-West toll road financial analysis*. Report prepared for the Indiana Finance Authority.

Cruz, C. O., & Marques, R. C. (2012). Using the economic and financial reequilibrium model to decrease infrastructure contract incompleteness. *Journal of Infrastructure Systems, 19*(1), 58–66.

Cruz, C., & Marques, R. (2013a). Exogenous determinants for renegotiating public infrastructure concessions: Evidence from Portugal. *Journal of Construction Engineering and Management, 139*(9), 1082–1090.

Cruz, C., & Marques, R. (2013b). Flexible contracts to cope with uncertainty in public private partnerships. *International Journal of Project Management, 31*(3), 473–483.

Cruz, C. O., & Sarmento, J. M. (2018). The price of project finance loans for highways. *Research in Transportation Economics, 70*, 161–172.

Cruz, C. O., & Sarmento, J. M. (2019). Traffic forecast inaccuracy in transportation: A literature review of roads and railways projects. *Transportation, 47*, 1–36.

Cruz, C. O., Marques, R. C., & Franco, D. (2015). Road-network development in quickly growing economies: Brazilian case study MG-050. *Journal of Infrastructure Systems, 21*(4), 05015002.

De Brux, J. (2010). The dark and bright sides of renegotiation: An application to transport concession contracts. *Utilities Policy, 18*(2), 77–85.

Domingues, S., & Sarmento, J. M. (2016). Critical renegotiation triggers of European transport concessions. *Transport Policy, 48*, 82–91.

Domingues, S., & Zlatkovic, D. (2015). Renegotiating PPP contracts: Reinforcing the 'P' in partnership. *Transport Reviews, 35*(2), 204–225.

Eisenhardt, K. M. (1989). Building theories from case study research. *The Academy of Management Review, 14*, 532–550.

Engel, E., Fischer, R., & Galetovic, A. (2006a). *Renegotiation without holdup: Anticipating spending and infrastructure concessions* (National Bureau of Economic Research Working Paper Series (Vol. no. 12399)). https://doi.org/10.3386/w12399

Engel, E., Fischer, R., & Galetovic, A. (2006b). *Renegotiation without holdup: Anticipating spending and infrastructure concessions* (NBER working paper no. 12339).

Engel, E., Fischer, R., & Galetovic, A. (2009). *Soft budgets and renegotiations in public-private partnerships* (National Bureau of Economic Research Working Paper Series (Vol. no. 15300)). https://doi.org/10.2139/ssrn.1460688

Enright, D. (2006). *Then there were two ... Indiana Toll Road vs. Chicago Skyway: An analytical review of two public/private partnerships*. Jersey City, NJ: Northwest Financial Group.

Estache, A., & Gómez-Lobo, A. (2005). The limits to competition in urban bus services in developing countries. *Transport Reviews, 25*(2), 139–158.

Estache, A., Guasch, J.-L., & Trujillo, L. (2003). *Price caps, efficiency payoffs and infrastructure contract renegotiation in Latin America* (World Bank Policy Research working paper 3129). https://doi.org/10.1596/1813-9450-3129

Estache, A., Guasch, J. L., Iimi, A., & Trujillo, L. (2009). Multidimensionality and renegotiation: Evidence from transport-sector public-private-partnership transactions in Latin America. *Review of Industrial Organization, 35*, 41. https://doi.org/10.1007/s11151-009-9225-0.

Fatokun, A. O. (2018). *Value for money integration in the renegotiation of public private partnership road projects* (Doctoral dissertation, University of Central Lancashire).

Flores Dewey, O. (2013). *Expanding transportation planning capacity in cities of the global south: Public-private conflict and collaboration in Chile and Mexico* (Unpublished PhD dissertation). Cambridge, MA: Massachusetts Institute of Technology.

Flyvbjerg, B., Skamris Holm, M. K., & Buhl, S. L. (2004). What causes cost overrun in transport infrastructure projects? *Transport Reviews, 24*(1), 3–18. https://doi.org/10.1080/0144164032000080494a.

Galetovic, A., & Jordán, P. (2006). *Santiago: dónde estamos y hacia dónde vamos*. Santiago: Centro de Estudios Públicos.

Gallegos, F., Montero, J. P., & C. Salas (2011, October). *The effect of transport policies on car use: Theory and evidence from Latin American cities*. Department of Economics, draft, Pontificia Universidad Catolica de Chile.

Garvin, M. J. (2019). Case studies of financially distressed highway public–private partnerships in the United States. In *Public Private Partnerships* (pp. 65–88). Cham: Springer.

Gifford, J., Bolaños, L., & Daito, N. (2014). Renegotiation of transportation public-private partnerships: The US experience. In *International transport forum discussion papers, no. 2014/16*. Paris: OECD Publishing. https://doi.org/10.1787/5jrw2xz9xhs1-en.

Gilmour, J. B. (2012). The Indiana toll road lease as an intergenerational cash transfer. *Public Administration Review, 72*(6), 856–864.

Gómez-Lobo, A. (2012). *The ups and downs of a public transport reform: The case of Transantiago*. Serie documentos de trabajo SDT354. Santiago: Universidad de Chile, Departamento de Economía.

Gómez-Lobo, A., & Briones, J. (2013). *Incentive structure in transit concession contracts: The case of Santiago, Chile, and London, England*. Washington, DC: Clean Air Institute.

Gómez-Lobo, A., & Briones, J. (2014). Incentives in bus concession contracts: A review of several experiences in Latin America. *Transport Reviews, 34*(2), 246–265.

Grimsey, D., & Lewis, M. (2005). Are Public Private Partnerships value for money? Evaluating alternative approaches and comparing academic and practitioner views. *Accounting Forum, 29* (4), 345–378.

Gschwender, A. (2007). *A comparative analysis of the public transport systems of Santiago de Chile, London, Berlin and Madrid: What can Santiago learn from the European Experiences?* (Doctoral dissertation, Universität Wuppertal, Fakultät für Architektur und Bauingenieurwesen» Bauingenieurwesen» Dissertationen).

Guasch, J. (2004). *Granting and renegotiating infrastructure concessions: Doing it right*. Washington, DC: World Bank.

Guasch, J., & Straub, S. (2006). Renegotiation of infrastructure concessions: An overview. *Annals of Public and Cooperative Economics, 77*(4), 479–493.

Guasch, J., & Straub, S. (2009). Corruption and concession renegotiations: Evidence from the water and transport sectors in Latin America. *Utilities Policy, 17*(2), 185–190.

Guasch, J., Laffont, J., & Straub, S. (2003). *Renegotiation of concession contracts in Latin America* (Vol. 3011). Washington, DC: World Bank.

Guasch, J., Laffont, J., & Straub, S. (2007). Concessions of infrastructure in Latin America: Government-led renegotiation. *Journal of Applied Econometrics, 22*(7), 1267–1294.

Guasch, J., Laffont, J., & Straub, S. (2008). Renegotiation of concession contracts in Latin America: Evidence from the water and transport sectors. *International Journal of Industrial Organization, 26*(2), 421–442.

Healey, A. (2014, October 8). ITR expected to ignite interest. *Project Finance International*.

Hidalgo, D., & Graftieaux, P. (2008). Bus rapid transit systems in Latin America and Asia: Results and difficulties in 11 cities. *Transportation Research Record, 2072*(1), 77–88.

Hong, H., & Shum, M. (2002). Increasing competition and the winner's curse: Evidence from procurement. *Review of Economic Studies, 69*(4), 871–898.

Invernizzi, D. C., Locatelli, G., & Brookes, N. (2018, March 15). *Cost overruns—Helping to define what they really mean*. Retrieved from https://ssrn.com/abstract=3141044 or https://doi.org/10.2139/ssrn.3141044

Izar, P. (2019). Can public–private partnerships help achieve the right to the city in Brazil? The case of Casa Paulista program in São Paulo. *Journal of Urban Affairs*, 1–16. https://doi.org/10.1080/07352166.2019.1654895

Kelly, N. (2018a, September 4). Indiana toll road rates going up. *The Journal Gazette*. Retrieved from www.journalgazette.net

Kelly, N. (2018b, September 16). Toll road move surprises: Holcomb's $1 billion deal skipped legislators. *The Journal Gazette*. Retrieved from www.journalgazette.net

Love, P. E. D., & Ahiaga-Dagbui, D. D. (2018). De-bunking 'Fake News' in a Post-Truth Era: The Plausible Untruths of Cost Underestimation in Transport Infrastructure Projects. *Transportation Research Part A Policy and Practice, 113*, 357–368.

Love, P. E. D., Ahiaga-Dagbui, D. D., & Irani, Z. (2016). Cost overruns in transportation infrastructure projects: Sowing the seeds for a probabilistic theory of causation. *Transportation Research Part A: Policy and Practice, 92*, 184–194. https://doi.org/10.1016/j.tra.2016.08.007.

Macário, R., Ribeiro, J., & Couchinho, R. (2013). *Fertagus train, Portugal. COST action TU1001 public private partnerships in transport: Trends & theory*, pp. 108–115.

Macário, M., Costa, J., & Ribeiro, J. (2015a). Cross-sector analysis of four renegotiated transport PPPs in Portugal. *Transport Reviews, 35*(2), 226–244.

Macário, R., Ribeiro, J., & Costa, J. (2015b). Understanding pitfalls in the application of PPPs in transport infrastructure in Portugal. *Transport Policy, 41*, 90–99.

Mallett, W. J. (2014, September 29). *Indiana Toll Road bankruptcy chills climate for public-private.*

Martins, J., Marques, R. C., & Cruz, C. O. (2014). Maximizing the value for money of PPP arrangements through flexibility: An application to airports. *Journal of Air Transport Management, 39*, 72–80.

Martins, J., Marques, R. C., & Cruz, C. O. (2015). Real options in infrastructure: Revisiting the literature. *Journal of Infrastructure Systems, 21*(1), 04014026.

Muñoz, J. C., & Gschwender, A. (2008). Transantiago: A tale of two cities. *Research in Transportation Economics, 22*(1), 45–53.

Muñoz, J. C., Batarce, M., & Hidalgo, D. (2014). Transantiago, five years after its launch. *Research in Transportation Economics, 48*, 184–193.

Neto, D., Cruz, C. O., & Sarmento, J. M. (2017). Understanding the patterns of PPP renegotiations for infrastructure projects in Latin America: The case of Brazil. *Competition and Regulation in Network Industries, 18*(3–4), 271–296.

Neto, D., Cruz, C. O., & Sarmento, J. M. (2019). Renegotiation of transport public private partnerships: Policy implications of the Brazilian experience in the Latin American context. *Case Studies on Transport Policy, 7*(3), 554–561.

OECD. (2008). *Public-private partnerships: In pursuit of risk sharing and value for money*. Paris: OECD.

Ortega, A., de los Angeles Baeza, M., & Vassallo, J. M. (2016). Contractual PPPs for transport infrastructure in Spain: Lessons from the economic recession. *Transport Reviews, 36*(2), 187–206.

Paget-Seekins, L., Flores Dewey, O., & Muñoz, J. C. (2015). Examining regulatory reform for bus operations in Latin America. *Urban Geography, 36*(3), 424–438.

Pantelias, A., & Roumboutsos, A. (2015). A conceptual framework for transport infrastructure PPP project credit assessments. *Journal of Finance and Economics, 3*(6), 105e111.

Randazzo, S., & Fitzgerald, P. (2014, September 22). Indiana toll road operator files for bankruptcy. *Wall Street Journal.* Retrieved from www.wsj.com

Reinhardt, W. (2015a). Indiana Toll Road lease now worth $5.7 billion to pension fund investors. *Public Works Financing, 304*.

Reinhardt, W. (2015b). IFM refinances ITR bank loans with toll revenue bonds. *Public Works Financing, 306*.

Reis, R. F., & Sarmento, J. M. (2017). "Cutting costs to the bone": The Portuguese experience in renegotiating public private partnerships highways during the financial crisis. *Transportation, 46*, 1–18.

Roumboutsos, A. (2015). Public private partnerships in transport infrastructure: An international review. *Transport Reviews, 35*(2), 111–117.

Roumeliotis, G., & Stone, M. (2014). Exclusive: Infrastructure investors line up for Indiana toll road. *Reuters.* Retrieved from www.reuters.com

Samuel, P. (2006, January 23). Cintra-Macquarie bid of $3.85b for Indiana TR accepted. *TollRoads News*. Retrieved from tollroadsnews.com

Sarmento, J. M. (2010). Do public-private partnerships create value for money for the public sector? The Portuguese experience. *OECD Journal on Budgeting, 2010*(1), 93–119.

Sarmento, J. M., & Renneboog, L. (2015). 16 Portugal's experience with Public Private Partnerships. *Public Private Partnerships: A Global Review*, 266.

Sarmento, J. M., & Renneboog, L. (2016a). Anatomy of public-private partnerships: Their creation, financing and renegotiations. *International Journal of Managing Projects in Business, 9*(1), 94–122.

Sarmento, J. M., & Renneboog, L. (2016b). *Renegotiating public-private partnerships* (European Corporate Governance Institute (ECGI)-Finance Working Paper 416).

Schnitzler, P. (2009, August 3). Toll-road lease tumbles in value. *Indianapolis Business Journal*. Retrieved from www.ibj.com

Shen, L. Y., Platten, A., & Deng, X. P. (2006). Role of public private partnerships to manage risks in public sector projects in Hong Kong. *International Journal of Project Management, 24*(7), 587–594.

Sierra, J., Vassallo, J. M., & Baeza, M. A. (2014). Unbundling tolls from contracts: A new road PPP model. *Public Money and Management, 34*(6), 447–451. https://doi.org/10.1080/09540962.2014.962373.

Stafford, A., Acerete, B., & Stapleton, P. (2010). Making concessions: Political, commercial and regulatory tensions in accounting for European roads PPPs. *Accounting and Business Research, 40*(5), 473–493.

Tamblay, S., Gschwender, A., Dragicevic, M., & Muñoz, J. C. (2017). Risks involved in transit provision of bus contracts: Case study of Transantiago, Chile. *Transportation Research Record, 2649*(1), 89–96.

Ubbels, B., & Verhoed, E. T. (2008). Auctioning concessions for private roads. *Transportation Research Part A, 42*(1), 155–172.

Ureta, S. (2014). Normalizing Transantiago: On the challenges (and limits) of repairing infrastructures. *Social Studies of Science, 44*(3), 368–392.

Vassallo, J. M., & Sanchez Solino, A. (2007). Subordinated public participation loans for financing toll highway concessions in Spain. *Transportation Research Record: Journal of the Transportation Research Board, 1996*, 1–8. https://doi.org/10.3141/1996-01.

Vassallo, J. M., Ortega, A., & Baeza, M. D. L. Á. (2011). Impact of the economic recession on toll highway concessions in Spain. *Journal of Management in Engineering, 28*(4), 398–406.

Villalba-Romero, F. J., & Liyanage, C. (2014). Radial 2 (R-2) toll motorway. *COST Action TU1001 Public Private Partnerships in Transport: Trends & Theory P3T3*, 191.

Wensits, J. (2006, January 22). Indiana's Toll Road seen as link in a chain. *South Bend Tribune*. Retrieved from www.southbendtribune.com

Williamson, O. E. (1976). Franchise bidding for natural monopolies—In general and with respect to CATV. *The Bell Journal of Economics, 7*(1), 73–104.

Yescombe, E. R. (2011). *Public-private partnerships: Principles of policy and finance*. Oxford: Elsevier.

Yin, R. K. (2008). *Case study research: Design and methods*. London: Sage.

Zhang, Z., Bai, Q., Labi, S., & Sinha, K. C. (2013). General framework for evaluating long-term leasing of toll roads: Case study of Indiana I-90 Highway. *Transportation Research Record, 2345*(1), 83–91.

Chapter 7
Conclusions

The global experience with PPP arrangements has been largely trial-and-error, with expensive lessons for governments and citizens/users alike, and much more rarely, for private partners. The underlying economic principle of PPPs is to achieve greater value for money—i.e., the delivery of better services at lower costs. However, the complexity and liabilities inherent to the PPP model have often eroded any of the advantages from applying competitive market pressure to public infrastructure sectors. The PPP model simultaneously has fierce advocates and fierce critics, although the latter group has not been able to provide feasible alternatives to finance public infrastructure without either private involvement, or realistic alternatives to the use of private financing with entirely different arrangements. The trend therefore has been to incrementally build upon and improve existing PPP models.

It is unlikely that the recourse to private financing will decrease in the near future. For while infrastructure assets continue to deteriorate and maintenance deficits persist in developed economies, there is a growing desire to maximise efficiency and productivity in public services and infrastructures. The assumption still prevails that private management is better suited to accomplish these objectives. Furthermore, a crucial driver for the growth of PPPs has been the fact that the principal financiers tend to promote the use of this procurement model. For example, development banks, multilateral agencies, sovereign funds, and bilateral governmental financing agreements have all promoted the use of PPPs for infrastructure development, and in most cases, the financing is even conditional on demanding a large private sector involvement in the project. Development banks actively support reinforcing the government's capacity to create a fertile basis for private sector growth and participation in public infrastructure delivery. This behaviour occurs not only in emerging countries, but also in advanced economies. The bailouts of Greece, Ireland, and Portugal are recent examples of financial aid which is conditioned to a reform programme which is based on an overall strategy of opening infrastructure services to a greater degree of private sector participation in the form of PPPs, or full privatisations.

C. Oliveira Cruz, J. Miranda Sarmento, *The Renegotiations of Public Private Partnerships in Transportation*, Competitive Government: Public Private Partnerships, https://doi.org/10.1007/978-3-030-61258-0_7

Nevertheless, the use of the PPP model is at a crossroads. For the documented failures of the past use of PPPs—particularly with regards renegotiations, as well as their harmful results and excessive capital costs, have led policy-makers to seek new models for partnerships. One example which is currently gaining momentum is the non-profit distribution (NPD) scheme, which was developed in Scotland. Derived from the well-known private finance initiative (PFI) model, the NPD scheme represented an innovative relationship model between the public and the private sectors. The main innovation of the NPD model is that it caps the level of returns and re-invests any surplus arising from the development of a project in non-profit activities. The search for these more collaborative models is designed to combat the assumption that during the development of a contract, private partners are prone to engage in opportunistic rent-seeking strategies and can gain large profits. The NPD model also tries to prevent detrimental strategic behaviour, such as lowball bidding in the expectation of achieving post-award gains after renegotiation. However, other, more conservative alternatives are being considered to decrease capital costs, an example being debt funding competition, where it is possible to achieve a lower capital cost, whereby both the private and public sector jointly search for the most favourable sources of financing after signing the contract.

The profile of projects is also changing. The literature suggests that projects are evolving towards high value transactions, which in some cases bundle smaller-scale dispersed projects into a single large transaction, similar to the Pennsylvania Rapid Bridge Replacement Project in the US, or the Secondary School Building Modernisation Programme in Portugal. Governments are becoming more and more creative in extracting potential benefits from private sector expertise. For instance, in order to improve the selection mechanism of projects, countries such as Brazil are promoting market-led, unsolicited proposals. This model places the responsibility or the initiative for analysing and selecting those projects which guarantee higher returns on the private sector. However, although it allows for a preliminary screening of financially viable projects, this model does not ensure a comprehensive analysis of infrastructure needs, neither the maximisation of social welfare.

In conclusion, the market for PPP development is growing and so is the appetite of private financiers and governments for this solution. In 2014, the G20 launched the G20 Global Infrastructure Initiative, which is a multi-year programme to support public and private investment in quality infrastructure, acknowledging the need to structure knowledge and know-how and to help governments successfully deliver much-needed infrastructures, while engaging the use of private financing. Success in the design and implementation of PPP projects depends on a myriad of factors, although one emerges as being the most relevant for the years to come—the building up of trust between the public and private sectors. The pitfalls in the use of PPPs—particularly costly renegotiations, rent-seeking strategies by private sector bidders, and unilateral changes by governments, have all converged to create an environment where a lack of trust inevitably leads to higher risk premiums, more expensive projects, and ultimately the inability to deliver projects successfully.

There is a need to build trust at different levels. At the strategic level, political commitment assumes a fundamental role in the good governance of infrastructure projects. For infrastructure projects are often used by the opposition as a political battleground against incumbent governments, transforming the process of infrastructure delivery into a long-lasting stop-and-go exercise. At a tactical level, trust should be built by setting up proper institutional regulatory bodies in order to assure the steady and reputable governance of infrastructure delivery programmes which particularly aim at attracting relevant private sector interest and participation. At the operational level, trust is promoted through transparent, clear, and competitive tenders—which facilitate well-informed decisions based on cost benefit analysis, value for money tests, and robust forecasts, among other tools, as well as a flexible contract design which is able to respond to rapidly-changing environments. It is unrealistic to expect that such long-term contracts can be complete. However, the contractual framework can be equipped to deal with this inherent incompleteness—providing the proper mechanisms to regulate and manage contractual changes. The existence of a mature economic, political, and regulatory environment is a requisite for engaging the private sector in infrastructure delivery and infrastructure governance at a fair cost, which provides value for money for both the user and the government.

7.1 Renegotiations

Renegotiations will always be an important feature of PPP management, particularly when dealing with large public infrastructure which are subject to a high level of uncertainty. The potential inevitability of renegotiations does not mean that areas exist where it is possible to innovate and develop mechanisms to improve the performance of renegotiation processes.

The empirical evidence suggests that exogenous determinants play a fundamental role in PPPs renegotiations, and that consequently all institutional and governance improvements at a country-wide level that lead to an increase in the efficiency of the government, regulators, and the rule-of-law can all reduce the likelihood of renegotiations and/or improve a contract's performance. Nevertheless, these are changes that can take a generation to occur, and thus the influence of a project manager is practically null. Does this mean that little can be done to reduce the probability of renegotiations in the short term? Quite to the contrary.

The literature review detailed in the first chapters provides evidence that endogenous determinants also play a fundamental role. For example, construction delays, or the risk-sharing or financing structure can all be used to reduce the likelihood of renegotiation.

At the level of contract design, research is evolving towards the concept of "flexible contracts", as discussed, for example, by Cruz and Marques (2013f), Xiong and Zhang (2014), and Athias and Saussier (2018). In this case, the rationale is that if the future cannot be entirely predicted, then the contract should be as flexible as possible. This flexibility can be in the form of contractual flexibility, whereby, for example, a flexible payment mechanism can be implemented which can be adjusted to changing demand conditions. However, the potential impact of such contractual flexibility is more limited than the possibility of embedding options in the infrastructure design which can be exercised under new circumstances.

In the future, we expect that research in PPP renegotiation will evolve into two directions. First, to increase knowledge of the patterns of renegotiations outcomes—which are still relatively unknown. Examples include knowing what determines opting for government payments, rather than contract extensions or an increase in users' tariffs, and also what are the dynamics of the renegotiation process from a project management perspective. Second, to explore the concept of "flexible contracts" and to see how the recent trend towards digitalisation in construction and infrastructure can be used to reduce uncertainty, or to enable a better adaptation to uncertainty in the long-term, which would thus minimise the need to renegotiate in an asymmetric environment.

Finally, it is important to mention the profound role that digitalisation will have in procurement in the future. In this field, several topics of relevance have emerged, namely: the development of web-based solutions for monitoring contracts, real-time measurement of quality provided by the internet-of-things, and the development of smart-contracts based on blockchain technology, among others. Although these emerging trends are still at a very early stage of development, they will be inevitable for the carrying out of any research or work on the procurement of construction projects.

This book provided a mix of theoretical analysis and practical "hands-on" empirical evidence, to provide a unique manual that can help academics, practitioners and policy makers to understand and improve the way PPP renegotiations can occur.

References

Athias, L., & Saussier, S. (2018). Are public private partnerships that rigid? And why? Evidence from price provisions in French toll road concession contracts. *Transportation Research Part A: Policy and Practice, 111*, 174–186.

Cruz, C. O., & Marques, R. C. (2013f). Flexible contracts to cope with uncertainty in public–private partnerships. *International Journal of Project Management, 31*(3), 473–483.

Xiong, W., & Zhang, X. (2014). The real option value of renegotiation in public–private partnerships. *Journal of Construction Engineering and Management, 142*(8), 4016021.